1. Table of Contents

MW00452175

Table of Contents

2. Welcome

Introduction

The purpose of this chapter is to introduce the purpose of this book and acknowledge those people who have made this book possible. This chapter also contains a disclaimer and revision history, along with information on how to get to the source code for the examples.

Acknowledgements

First and foremost, thanks to my wife Jill and her patience. I hope she is enjoying herself doing her favorite things like Paddle boarding, Kayaking and being at one with nature. I hope she never reads this book because it would bore her.

I would also like to acknowledge the amazing work done by the Google engineers. When I ran the profiler and saw just how fast the UI was redrawing, I was blown-away. Google has some amazing talent, what a team of engineers.

Purpose

I wrote this book to broaden my own knowledge of this technology and I still have a way to go. However, I learnt a lot in writing this book and I hope it helps others.

Work

I have to be honest; I also wrote this book for some self-promotion. After this book is published, I intend to continue working on apps for my wife's business and find some part-time Flutter work. If you are interested, shoot me an email at markclow@hotmail.com or communicate with me via my LinkedIn page here: https://www.linkedin.com/in/mark-clow-9a61362/.

Disclaimer

Let's get this over with as quickly as possible. Some of this information in this book may be incorrect (I am a human being that makes mistakes) and that this publication is somewhat opinionated. I am trying my best to be as technically accurate as possible, but I am still learning a lot and have much to learn about Flutter and Dart. I have opinions but please don't take them too seriously. I do not intend to harm anything or anyone, I am not smart enough for that.

Revisions

This book has taken a long time to write and I will continue to improve it whenever I have time, adding more content when possible. So, if you get an earlier version of the book it may be slightly less complete than later on. If this is the case, email me a proof of purchase at markclow@hotmail.com and I will send you a PDF version, which will be watermarked with your name (sorry but its prevent copying). I welcome (constructive) criticism and input so if you have any, please email me at markclow@hotmail.com.

Date	Description
3/31/2019	Initial version.
4/7/2019	Added chapter name to footer. Applied corrections from printed proof notes – many!. Simplified chapters re setup. Added Animations Chapter. Added Dismissible Widget.

Source Code

Location

This book has many examples & exercises. The source code is available here:
https://github.com/markclow/flutter_book_examples

Example & Exercise Names

Each example or exercise should have a name in quotes (see the example below in the box). The name in quotes is the directory in which the source code is located.
This is the format:

> ## Example – 'gesture_app'
> The source code for this example is located in 'gesture_app'.

One File

Another thing to bear in mind is that the exercises have all been written to use a single file. This was so that there could be one single continuous listing in the book. In reality, you would obviously split your project up into many smaller files.

3. The Big Picture

Introduction

The purpose of this chapter is to give the reader a quick introduction to the world of Mobile Application development, and to introduce him or her the problem of cross-platform development, and how it was approached by different companies.

Mobile Applications

A mobile application (shortened to 'mobile app') is a computer program or software application designed to run on a mobile device such as a phone/tablet or watch. Writing mobile apps sounds easy but is complicated by the number of platforms that are available. Your app could run on an iPhone, it could run on an iPad, it could run on an Android Phone etc. Also remember that these platforms could change quickly as new devices appear on the market.

Before Cross-Platform Mobile Application Development

In the past, in order to produce performant applications, developers had to write the application code specifically for each platform, writing what is called native apps. There would often be one codebase (and developers) for iOS (iPhone) and another codebase (and developers) for Android. For native iOS, Objective-C and Swift are the preferred programming languages. For native Android, Java and Kotlin are the preferred languages.

This complicated matters:

- You had to keep two sets of code in sync.
  - If you change the iPhone code, you should change the Android code to match.
- You had to have developers with multiple skillsets.
  - Expensive.
- Sometimes the app for one platform would look very different from the other platforms.

Early Cross-Platform Development Tools

Anyway, Silicon Valley soon realized what a problem this was and set to work on developing tools for cross-platform mobile application development. They quickly split into two groups of development tools: those that used native libraries and those that didn't.

Development Tools That Used Native Libraries

These tools created a 'Unified' API on top of the native SDK supplied by Apple and Google. The problem with these types of applications is that the 'Unified API' does not cover 100% and leaves the developers with many burdens, such as having to still write a large chunk of platform-specific code. Many of these development tools, for example Xamarin, Appcelerator, Nativescript are still around.

Development Tools That Didn't Use Native Libraries

These tools took a different approach. Most of these attempted to bypass the SDK approach and write code that runs on the platform's browser. This had the advantage of being able to use many of the HTML5 and JavaScript capabilities already built-in. The app would run in a 'web view'. A "webview" is a browser bundled inside of a mobile application producing what is called a hybrid app. Using a webview allows mobile apps to be built using Web technologies (HTML, JavaScript, CSS, etc.) but still package it as a native app and put it in the app store.
The problem with these types of applications is speed. They are not running natively in compiled machine code, they are running on a hidden web browser.
Many of these development tools, for example Cordova, PhoneGap are still around.

Modern Cross-Platform Development Tools

More recently, two main rivals have emerged and look to be leading the field of mobile app development tools: Facebook React Native and Google Flutter.

React Native

React.JS is an excellent JavaScript framework that has been popular for years and works with both mobile and non-mobile websites equally well. Developers write user interfaces with Component objects, like lego blocks. These Components can contain code so that they can react to the user's input and produce an interactive user interface. React Native is like React, but it uses native components instead of web components as building blocks.

How Does It Work?

React Native runs in two parts.
1. The UI.
    o It displays the ui and receives user input.

2. The JavaScript engine.
   o It interprets and executes the JavaScript application code.

The two parts communicate with a bridge.

Conclusion

React Native is an excellent framework. It has the great advantage of being the more established player because it has been out since 2015. There are also a lot of React developers out there who can quickly cross-train to use React Native rather than React JS. React Native is also a very productive tool because it has many ready-to-use components. It runs an efficient, native UI with interpreted JavaScript, communicating through a bridge. This is not the optimum solution for performance.

Google Flutter

Google Flutter has only been available since 2017 but it is making waves because it takes a different approach to cross-platform mobile app development. Google is currently working on the successor to its Android operating system called Fuchsia and it is writing it using Flutter. So, Flutter is very important to Google.

You write user interfaces using Google Flutter user interface widgets, not the native iOS or Android ui widgets shipped with their retrospective SDKs. A Flutter app made using Flutter widgets will look exactly the same on iOS as it does on Android. Flutter comes with many widgets, including those that mimic Google's Material look & feel and those that mimic Apples iOS look & feel.

The Flutter Default App Running on IPhone on Left, Android on Right

Google Flutter uses its own high-performance rendering engine to draw these widgets and they have been designed to work on all mobile platforms. Also, these widgets are extendable.

You write the application code in Google's Dart language and it is compiled ahead-of-time into machine-code for native-like performance, thus offering a performance advantage over React Native.

There is no bridge between the user interface and the application code.

The only downside that is currently obvious is that developers will have to learn Dart, rather than reuse their existing JavaScript expertise.

Conclusion

If you want to write cross-platform mobile web apps that are performant then Google Flutter appears to be the best choice at the moment. However, things move quickly and that may not be for long!

4. Introduction to Dart

Introduction

The purpose of this chapter is to give the reader a quick introduction to Dart before installing it and starting to use it.

Dart is a general-purpose programming language which was created by Google in 2011. Like Java and C#, it has a similar syntax to 'C'.

Platforms

Unlike conventional languages, Dart has been optimized to be deployed to run on a variety of platforms:

1. Within a web browser as JavaScript
2. As an interpreted application
3. As a native application

1. Within a Web Browser

Dart provides an SDK, which provides command-line tools to transpile Dart source code into JavaScript. This has been developed so efficiently that the resulting transpiled JavaScript is more efficient than its hand-coded equivalent!

You can try out Dart in your web browser by Navigating to https://dartpad.dartlang.org/. You can write your own code or run the sample code. See the 'Sunflower' sample below.

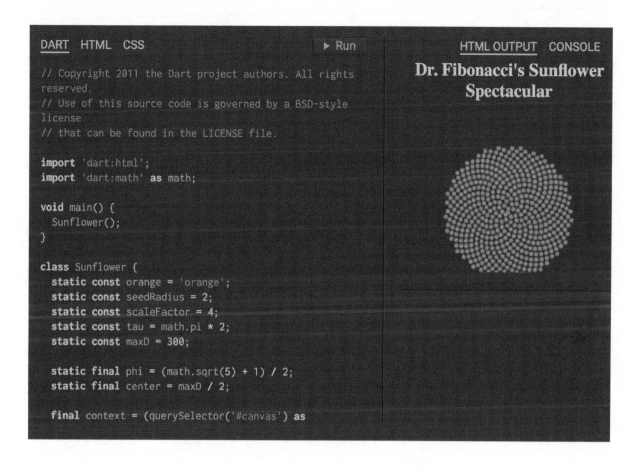

```
DART  HTML  CSS                            ▶ Run        HTML OUTPUT  CONSOLE
                                                        Dr. Fibonacci's Sunflower
// Copyright 2011 the Dart project authors. All rights          Spectacular
reserved.
// Use of this source code is governed by a BSD-style
license
// that can be found in the LICENSE file.

import 'dart:html';
import 'dart:math' as math;

void main() {
  Sunflower();
}

class Sunflower {
  static const orange = 'orange';
  static const seedRadius = 2;
  static const scaleFactor = 4;
  static const tau = math.pi * 2;
  static const maxD = 300;

  static final phi = (math.sqrt(5) + 1) / 2;
  static final center = maxD / 2;

  final context = (querySelector('#canvas') as
```

Just remember that not everything will always be the same.

For example, you cannot read from stdin when running from a browser. I tried to develop a Dart program on dartpad.dartlang.org that would accept user input and it would never work.

2. As Interpreted Application

The Dart SDK includes a Virtual Machine. A virtual machine is a sandbox in which code may run without directly communicating with the underlying operating system. This enables Dart code to be invoked from the command-line, using the 'dart' command-line tool in the SDK. This code is compiled on demand just-in-time as it runs.
Using Dart in this way is a great way to write server-side applications and it performs at a similar level to Java / .Net.

Hot Reloading / Hot Replacing

If the developer is running the Dart application in the Dart virtual machine from the command-line (interpreted), the JIT compiler can reload the code when the underlying source code changes, often while preserving the application state (variables) whenever possible. So, the developer can write and run the code at almost the same time. This makes application development very fast indeed. Yet at the end of the development process, the code can be compiled using the ahead-of-time compiler and deployed as a native application.

Flutter Development (Debug Mode)

When you are developing a Flutter Application, most of the time you run it in Debug Mode and the code is JIT compiled & interpreted. This mode is known as 'check' or 'slow' mode. Under this mode, the assertion functions, including all debugging information, service extensions, and debugging aids such as "observatory," are enabled. This mode is optimized for rapid development and operation, but not for execution speed, package size, or deployment.

Once your app is written you can build it to run in Release Mode as a native application and it will perform much better.

3. As Native Application

Dart code can be compiled ahead-of-time so that the code may be deployed as machine-code. Flutter was mostly written using Dart and runs natively. This makes Flutter fast, as well as customizable (as the Flutter widgets were written in Dart).

Dart SDK

The Dart SDK is available to download here: https://www.dartlang.org/tools/sdk
The Dart SDK comprises of three main elements:

1. Command-line tools.
2. Command-line compilers.
3. Libraries.

1. Command-Line Tools

The Dart SDK contains the following command line tools:

Name	Description
dart	Enables you to execute a .dart file within the Dart Virtual Machine.
dart2js	Compiles dart source code to JavaScript.
dartanalyser	Analyses dart source code. This is used by many of the code editors to provide error and warning highlighting.
dartdevc	Compiles dart source code to JavaScript. Similar to dart2js except that it supports incremental compilation, which lends itself to developers.
dartdoc	Generates Dart documentation from source code. As the seminal book 'Domain-Driven Design' by Eric Evans states: 'the code is the model and the model is the code'.

dartfmt	Formats Dart source code. This is used by many of the code editors to provide Dart formatting.
pub	This is Google's Package Manager. This is important and we will cover this in a later chapter.

2. Command-Line Compilers

Dartium, WebDev and Build_Runner

You can run Dart in a browser called Dartium without compiling it to JavaScript. Dartium is basically Chrome with a Dart VM. However, the mainstream Dart web development route is now writing the code with Dart but compiling and running as JavaScript using the dart2js and dartdevc JavaScript compilers in combination with the webdev and build_runner utilities. More Reading: https://webdev.dartlang.org/tools/webdev.

Dart2js and DartDevC

These two JavaScript compilers have different use cases. Normally these are used with the tool webddev and you don't usually have to worry about which compiler you're using, because it chooses the right compiler for your use case. When you're developing your app, webdev chooses dartdevc, which supports incremental compilation so you can quickly see the results of your edits. When you're building your app for deployment, webdev chooses dart2js, which uses techniques such as tree shaking to produce optimized code.

3. Libraries

Name	Description
dart:core	Built-in types, collections, and other core functionality. This library is automatically imported into every Dart program.
dart:async	Support for asynchronous programming, with classes such as Future and Stream.
dart:math	Mathematical constants and functions, plus a random number generator.
dart:convert	Encoders and decoders for converting between different data representations, including JSON and UTF-8.

5. Basic Dart

Introduction

The purpose of this chapter is to introduce some of the more basic Dart concepts and syntaxes.

Example Code

All the example code for this chapter should be executed on the following website: dartpad.dartlang.org

Entry Point

Dart is a bit like Java, every Dart app must start with a main function.

Example Code

```
void main(){
  print("App started");
  new App();
  print("App finished");
}

class App{
  App(){
    print("Constructing a class.");
  }
}
```

Output

```
App started
Constructing a class.
App finished
```

Introduction to Typing

Typically, computer languages have fallen into two camps:

1. Statically-typed languages.
2. Dynamically-typed languages.

1. Statically-typed languages.

These languages have specific variable types and the developer compiles the code using an 'ahead-of-time' compiler. The compiler type checking is performed before the code is run. This is an excellent way to develop software as the compiler performs static-analysis of the code as part of the compilation, alerting the developer when issues arise. Software typically takes longer to develop in this method, but the software developed in this manner typically works better in complex scenarios.

2. Dynamically-typed languages.

These languages don't have specific variable types and no ahead-of-time compilation is performed. Dynamically-typed languages make the development process very quick as the developer does not typically need to recompile the code. However, code developed in this manner tends to lend itself to simpler scenarios as it can be more error-prone.

Dart Typing

Dart is different because Dart code can be run with both static types and dynamic type variables. The type system in Dart 1 had some issues and they introduced a 'strong mode' for stronger type checking. This mode has become the typing system in Dart 2.0 and it offers strong guarantees that an expression of one type cannot produce a value of another type. Dart performs type checking at two different times:

- When the code is compiled (code is reloaded / or compiled ahead-of-time).
- When the code is run (runtime).

Static Types

These are the most-commonly used and built-in Dart types:

Type	Description
int	Integers (no decimals).
double	Decimal number (double precision).
bool	Boolean true or false.
String	Immutable string.
StringBuffer	Mutable string.
RegExp	Regular expressions.
List, Map, Set	Dart provides Collection classes.
DateTime	A point in time.
Duration	A span of time.
Uri	Uniform Resource Identifier

Error	Error information

Dynamic Types (aka Untyped)

You can define untyped variables by declaring them using the 'var' or 'dynamic' keywords.
- The 'var' keyword declares a variable without specifying its type, leaving the variable as a dynamic.
- The 'dynamic' keyword declares a variable of the type 'dynamic' with optional typing.

There is a difference, but it is subtle.

```
void main() {
  print (multiplyMethod1(2,4));
  print (multiplyMethod2(2,4));
}

dynamic multiplyMethod1(int a, int b){
  return a * b;
}

var multiplyMethod2(int a, int b){
  return a * b;
}
```

This code wont compile. Dartpad displays the following error:

```
Error compiling to JavaScript: main.dart:10:1: Error: The return type can't be 'var'. var
multiplyMethod2(int a, int b){ ^^^ Error: Compilation failed.
```

This is because methods need to return a type and a 'var' does not specify a type.

Type Inference

Often, the variable types are 'inferred' when the program runs. In other words, when the program runs, the runtime figures out what the variable types are based on the values they are set to. This usually works well – see ('Example of Inference #1') but can cause problems if a variable type is inferred at one point in the code then another type is inferred later on – see 'Example of Inference #2' below.

Example of Inference #1:

```
void main() {
  dynamic x = 1;
  if (x is int){
    print('integer');
```

```
  }
}
```

Output

```
integer
```

Example of Inference #2:

```
void main() {
  dynamic x = 'test';
  if (x is String){
    print('String');
  }
  x += 1;
}
```

Output

```
String Uncaught exception: TypeError: 1: type 'JSInt' is not a subtype of type 'String'
```

Type Matching

Dart allows users to check for types using the 'is' keyword.

Example Code

```
main(){
  printType(23);
  printType('mark');
}

printType(dynamic d){
  if (d is int){
    print ('Its an Integer');
  }
  if (d is String){
    print ('Its a String');
  }
}
```

Output

```
Its an Integer
Its a String
```

Type Information

Dart gives the developer a way to get information about an Object's type at runtime. You can use Object's runtimeType property, which returns a Type object.

Example Code

```
void main() {
 var v1 = 10;
 print(v1.runtimeType);

 var v2 = 'hello';
 print(v2.runtimeType);
}
```

Output

```
int
String
```

Strings

Interpolation

One very useful feature of Dart is its string interpolation. You can put the value of an expression inside a string by using ${expression}.

Example Code

```
class Person{
 String firstName;
 String lastName;
 int age;
 Person(this.firstName, this.lastName, this.age);
}

main(){
 Person p = new Person('mark','smith', 22);
 print('The persons name is ${p.firstName} ${p.lastName} and he is ${p.age}');
}
```

Output

```
The persons name is mark smith and he is 22
```

Raw Strings

In Dart, normally you can add escape characters to format your string. For example: '\n' means 'new line'. However, you can prefix the string with an 'r' to indicate to tell Dart to treat the string differently, to ignore escape characters.

Example Code – 'New Lines':

```
main(){
  print('this\nstring\nhas\nescape\ncharacters');
  print('');
  print(r'this\nstring\nhas\nescape\ncharacters');
}
```

Output

```
this
string
has
escape
characters

this\nstring\nhas\nescape\ncharacters
```

Example Code – 'Dollar Sign':

```
void main() {
  double price = 100.75;
  print('Price is: \$$ {price}');
}
```

Output

```
Price is: $100.75
```

Runes

Runes are also special characters encoded into a string.
Here is a link with a lot of the run codes:
https://www.compart.com/en/unicode/block/U+1F300

Example Code

```
main() {
  var clapping = '\u{1f44f}';
  print(clapping);
}
```

Output

Object-Orientated Language Features

Modules

Unlike Java and C#, Dart allows you to declare multiple objects within a single file.
This has made our example code a single cut-n-paste!

Constructors

Default Constructor

If you do not specify a constructor, a default constructor will be created for you without arguments. If you do specify a constructor, the default constructor won't be created for you.

Constructor Syntax Shortcut

If you want to set the value of an instance variable in a constructor, you can use the 'this.[instance variable name]' to set it in the constructor signature.

Example Code

```
class Name{
  String firstName;
  String lastName;

  Name(this.firstName, this.lastName);
}

main(){
  Name name = new Name('mark','smith');
  print(name.firstName);
  print(name.lastName);
}
```

Output

```
mark
smith
```

New Keyword

Dart doesn't need you to use the 'new' keyword when invoking constructors. However, you can keep it if you want.

Example Code

```
void main() {
  Car car = Car("BMW","M3");
  print(car.getBadge());

  Car car2 = new Car("BMW","M3");
```

```
  print(car2.getBadge());
}

class Car{
  String _make;
  String _model;

  Car(this._make, this._model){}

  String getBadge(){
    return _make + " - " + _model;
  }
}
```

Output

```
BMW - M3
BMW - M3
```

Named Constructors

Dart allows named constructors and I have found them very useful indeed if you want to instantiate the same class in different ways. Named constructors (if named correctly) can also improve code readability & intent.

Example Code

```
class ProcessingResult{
  bool _error;
  String _errorMessage;

  ProcessingResult.success(){
    _error = false;
    _errorMessage = '';
  }

  ProcessingResult.failure(this._errorMessage){ //shortcut
    this._error = true;
  }

  String toString(){
    return 'Error: ' + _error.toString() + ' Message: ' + _errorMessage;
  }
}

void main() {
  print(ProcessingResult.success().toString());
  print(ProcessingResult.failure('it broke').toString());
}
```

Output

```
Error: false Message:
Error: true Message: it broke
```

Required Constructor Parameters

If you are creating an object, you can add the '@required'

Constructor Parameters

Constructors can accept different kinds of parameters, similar to methods.

Factory Constructors

You can use the factory keyword when implementing a constructor that doesn't always create a new instance of its class. The factory keyword allows you to return a variable at the end of the constructor. This is useful when you want the constructor to return an instance from a variable or a cache.

Example Code

```
class Printer{
  static final Printer _singleton = Printer._construct();

  factory Printer(){
    return _singleton;
  }

  Printer._construct(){
    print('private constructor');
  }

  printSomething(String text){
    print(text);
  }

}

void main() {
  Printer().printSomething("this");
  Printer().printSomething("and");
  Printer().printSomething("that");
}
```

Output

Note how the constructor was only invoked once.

```
private constructor
this
and
that
```

Instance Variables

Unspecified Visibility

You don't have to specify the visibility of instance variables and if you don't then they are made public.

```
class Name {
  String firstName;
  String lastName;
}
```

Specified Visibility

Unlike Java, Dart doesn't have the keywords public, protected, and private to specify the visibilities of fields or properties. If an identifier starts with an underscore, it's private.

You should replace:

```
class ContactInfo {
  private String name;
  private String phone;
}
```

with

```
class ContactInfo {
  String _name;
  String _phone;
}
```

Default Values

The default values of instance variables are null.

Constructor and Method Parameters

Flutter is very flexible in regard to constructor & method parameters. There are several different kinds:

1. Positional Required
2. Positional Optional
3. Named

1. Parameters - Positional Required

These are declared first.
These are required.

Constructor with required parameters:

```
class Car{
  String _make;
  String _model;
  Car(this._make,this._model){}
}
```

2. Parameters - Positional Optional

These are declared second.
You can make parameters optional, by using the square brackets.
If an optional parameter is not supplied, it has a null value.

Example Code

```
void main() {
  Car car1 = Car("Nissan","350Z");
  Car car2 = Car("Nissan");
}

class Car{
  String _make;
  String _model;
  Car(this._make,[this._model]){
    print('${_make} ${_model}');
  }
}
```

Output

```
Nissan 350Z
Nissan null
```

3. Parameters - Named

All named parameters are optional.
These are declared last.
You can make parameters named, by using the curly brackets.
If a named parameter is not supplied, it has a null value.

Example Code

```
void main() {
  Car car1 = Car("Nissan", model:"350Z", color: "yellow");
  Car car2 = Car("Nissan", color:"red");
  Car car3 = Car("Nissan");
}

class Car{
  String make;
  String model;
  String color;
```

Basic Dart

```
Car(this.make,{this.model,this.color}){
  print('${make}${getOptional(model)}${getOptional(color)}');
}

String getOptional(String str) {
  return str == null ? "" : " " + str;
}
}
```

Output

```
Nissan 350Z yellow
Nissan red
Nissan
```

Interfaces

Dart uses implicit interfaces.

Example Code

```
abstract class IsSilly {
  void makePeopleLaugh();
}

class Clown implements IsSilly {
  void makePeopleLaugh() {
    // Here is where the magic happens
  }
}

class Comedian implements IsSilly {
  void makePeopleLaugh() {
    // Here is where the magic happens
  }
}
```

Further Reading

https://www.dartlang.org/guides/language/language-tour - implicit-interfaces

Other

Method Cascades

Method cascades can help with the brevity of your code.

Example Code

```
class Logger {
  void log(dynamic v){
```

```
    print(DateTime.now().toString() + ' ' + v);
  }
}
main(){

  // Without method cascades
  new Logger().log('program started');
  new Logger().log('doing something');
  new Logger().log('program finished');

  // With method cascades
  new Logger()
    ..log('program started')
    ..log('going something')
    ..log('program finished');
}
```

Output

```
2018-12-30 09:28:39.686 program started
2018-12-30 09:28:39.686 doing something
2018-12-30 09:28:39.686 program finished
2018-12-30 09:28:39.686 program started
2018-12-30 09:28:39.686 going something
2018-12-30 09:28:39.686 program finished
```

6. More Advanced Dart

Introduction

The purpose of this chapter is to introduce some of the more advanced Dart concepts and syntaxes.

Operator Overloading

In Dart, you compare equality using the '==' operator rather than an 'equals' method. Sometimes you need to override it this operator in your class to ensure that instances of the classes are compared correctly.

Example

If you want to be able to compare two Car objects for equality in this way:

```
car1 == car2
```

and your equality test is:

'car make and model should match'

then you would have similar code to that below:

```
class Car {
 String _make;
 String _model;
 String _imageSrc;

 Car(this._make, this._model, this._imageSrc);

 operator ==(other) =>
    (other is Car) && (_make == other._make) && (_model ==    other._model);

int get hashCode => _make.hashCode ^ _model.hashCode ^ _imageSrc.hashCode;

}
```

Warning - hashCode

Note that when you override the '==', you need to override the 'hashCode' method as well. If you don't do that then Flutter will give you a warning.

You should override the two together because the collections framework uses the 'hashCode' method to determine equality, array indexes etc. You don't want equality working in one place and not the other.

Reflection

Reflection allows the inspection of classes, interfaces, fields and methods at runtime without knowing the names of the interfaces, fields, methods at compile time. It enables software to inspect itself. For example, one class can inspect another class (or itself) to see what methods it has available. It also allows instantiation of new objects and invocation of methods.

Dart has a library called 'mirrors' that enables developers to use reflection in Dart code.

Mixins

A Mixin is a class that contains methods for use by other classes without it having to be the parent class of those other classes.

So, a Mixin is a class you can use code from without having to inherit from.

You can refer to the Mixins chapter.

Collections

Introduction

When developing, you often need to keep track of information (objects) in memory. This enables you to search them, sort them, insert them, manipulate them or delete them. That is what the Collection classes are for. Collection classes are used all the time.

Dart offers support for Collections in both its core library and its collection library. The most-commonly used Collection classes are maintained in the core library and the more specific ones are maintained in the collection library.

Lists

A List is an ordered Collection (sometimes called a sequence). Lists may contain duplicate elements.

Unlike other languages, an Array and a List have been combined together and are the same thing. Note how the List in the example below is declared using square brackets, which are normally used for declaring Arrays.

Example Code

This dart code creates a list then sorts it:

```dart
class Person{
  String _firstName;
  String _lastName;
  String _phone;

  Person(this._firstName, this._lastName, this._phone);

  toString(){
    return "${_firstName} ${_lastName} ${_phone}";
  }
}

void main() {
  List<Person> list = [
    Person("Mark", "Clow", "4043124462"),
    Person("Brant", "Sandermine", "4243124462"),
    Person("Phillip", "Perry", "4243124444")
  ];
  print("Not sorted: ${list}");

  list.sort((a, b) => a._firstName.compareTo(b._firstName));
  print("Sorted by first name: ${list}");

  list.sort((a, b) => a._firstName.compareTo(b._lastName));
  print("Sorted by last name: ${list}");
}
```

Output

```
Not sorted: [Mark Clow 4043124462, Brant Sandermine 4243124462, Phillip Perry 4243124444]
Sorted by first name: [Brant Sandermine 4243124462, Mark Clow 4043124462, Phillip Perry 4243124444]
Sorted by last name: [Brant Sandermine 4243124462, Mark Clow 4043124462, Phillip Perry 4243124444]
```

Maps

An object that maps keys to values. Both keys and values in a map may be of any type. A Map is a dynamic collection. In other words, Maps can grow and shrink at runtime.

Example Code

```dart
void main() {
  Map<String, String> stateNamesByStateCode =
  {"AL": "Alamaba",
   "AK": "Alaska",
   "AR": "Arkansas",
   "AZ": "Arizona"
```

```
};

stateNamesByStateCode["GA"] = "Georgia";

for (String key in stateNamesByStateCode.keys){
        print(stateNamesByStateCode[key]);
}

print("\nGet just one: ${stateNamesByStateCode["AK"]}");
}
```

Output

```
Alamaba
Alaska
Arkansas
Arizona
Georgia

Just one: Alaska
```

More-Specific Collection Classes

These classes are contained in the 'dart:collection' library.
To use this library in your code:

```
import 'dart:collection';
```

Assertions

When you are developing code, you will frequently come across bugs, where things aren't going as expected. For example, you have a variable with a value that you never expected.
This is where assertions come in. An assertion is a statement that something is expected to be always true at that point in the code. If not, the assertion will throw an exception.
This is a form of Defensive Programming.

Example Code

```
void main() {
  // .. some good code that calculates age
  int age1 = 50;
  checkAge(age1);
  // .. some good code that calculates age

  // .. some bad code that calculates age incorrectly
  int age2 = 150;
  checkAge(age2);
  // .. some bad code that calculates age incorrectly
}

void checkAge(int age) {
  assert(age < 112, "bad age ${age}");
```

```
}
```

Output

```
Uncaught exception:
Assertion failed: "bad age 150"
```

Assertions & Modes (Flutter)

When you are developing your Dart code, you can add assertions to check that it is working as expected. Later on (once the code is mostly bug-free), you can run the same code without the assertions being executed (without the assertions slowing things down).

You develop your Flutter code in Checked (or Debug) Mode, which checks things like assertions. It also turns on the Dart Observatory. More on that here: Dart Observatory. Later on, you can deploy the compiled code that runs in Release mode, speeding things up.

Further Reading

https://github.com/flutter/flutter/wiki/Flutter's-modes

Errors & Exceptions

Why Have Error & Exception Handling?

Most software systems are complicated and written by a team of people.

Complexity arises from multiple sources:
- The business domain.
- The act of writing software.
- From multiple people working together, each one having different viewpoints.
- etc

The complexity can result in misunderstandings, errors & exceptions.

This is not the end of the world if the code has good error handling.

- If you don't handle your errors & exceptions, your software may act unpredictably, and users may suffer a catastrophic error without knowing it or being able to detect when it happened.

- If you <u>do</u> handle your errors & exceptions, the user may able to continue using the program even with the error / exception and the developers can find the problems over time and improve the software.

Good error & exception handling should not blind the end user with technical jargon, but it should also provide enough information for the developers to trace down the problem.

Dart can throw Errors & Exceptions when problems occur running a Dart program. When an Error or an Exception occurs, normal flow of the program is disrupted, and the program terminates abnormally.

Errors

Errors are <u>serious</u> issues that cannot be caught and 'dealt with'. Non-recoverable.

Examples

- RangeError – programmatic bug where user is attempting to use an invalid index to retrieve a List element.
- OutOfMemoryError

Exceptions

Exceptions are less-serious issues that can be caught and 'dealt with'.
Recoverable.

Examples

- FormatException – could not parse a String.

Handling Errors

Trying to handle non-recoverable errors is impossible. How can you catch and just handle an out of memory error?

The best thing to do is to log what happened and where so that the developers can deal with them. The approach to this is to add a handler to the top level of your application, for example Sentry or Catcher.

Further Reading

https://medium.com/flutter-community/handling-flutter-errors-with-catcher-efce74397862

Handling Exceptions

Try to handle these to prevent the application from terminating abruptly. If you want your code to handle exceptions then you need to place it in a 'try..catch..finally' block. The finally part is optional.

Finally

Dart also provides a finally block that will always be executed no matter if any exception is thrown or not.

```
void main() {
  try {
    // do something here
  } catch (e) {
    // print exception
    print(e);
  } finally {
    // always executed
    print('I will always be executed!');
  }
}
```

Catch Exception

The first argument to the catch is the Exception.

Example Code

This code catches the Exception and prints it out.

```
void main() {
  print('start');
  try {
    int.parse("mark");
```

```
} catch (ex) {
  print(ex);
}
print('finish');
}
```

Output

```
start
FormatException: mark
finish
```

Catch Exception and Stack Trace

The second argument to the catch is the StackTrace.

Example Code

This code catches the Exception and StackTrace. It prints out the StackTrace.

```
void main() {
  print('start');
  try {
    int.parse("mark");
  } catch (ex, stacktrace) {
    print(stacktrace);
  }
  print('finish');
}
```

Output

```
start
FormatException: mark
FormatException: mark
    at Object.wrapException (<anonymous>:370:17)
    at Object.int_parse (<anonymous>:1555:15)
    at main (<anonymous>:1702:11)
    at dartMainRunner (<anonymous>:9:5)
    at <anonymous>:2206:7
    at <anonymous>:2192:7
    at dartProgram (<anonymous>:2203:5)
    at <anonymous>:2210:3
    at replaceJavaScript (https://dartpad.dartlang.org/scripts/frame.html:39:17)
    at https://dartpad.dartlang.org/scripts/frame.html:69:7
finish
```

Catch Specific Exceptions

If you know you want to catch a specific Exception then you can use an 'on' instead of a 'catch'.
Consider leaving a 'catch' at the bottom to catch other Exceptions.
You can optionally add the 'catch(e)' or catch(e, s)' after if you want the Exception and
StackTrace data as arguments.

Example Code

```
void main() {
  print('start');
  try {
    int.parse("mark");
  } on FormatException{
    print('invalid string');
  } catch (ex,stacktrace) {
    print(stacktrace);
  }
  print('finish');
}
```

Output

```
start
invalid string
finish
```

Throw Exception

To throw an Exception simply use the 'throws' keyword and instantiate the Exception.

Example Code

```
throw new TooOldForServiceException ();
```

Rethrow Exception

Once you have caught an Exception, you have the option of rethrowing it so that it bubbles up to the next level. So, you could catch an Exception, log it then rethrow it so it is dealt with at a higher level.

Example Code

```
void misbehave() {
  try {
    dynamic foo = true;
    print(foo++); // Runtime error
  } catch (e) {
    print('misbehave() partially handled ${e.runtimeType}.');
    rethrow; // Allow callers to see the exception.
  }
}

void main() {
  try {
    misbehave();
  } catch (e) {
    print('main() finished handling ${e.runtimeType}.');
  }
}
```

Output

```
misbehave() partially handled JsNoSuchMethodError.
main() finished handling JsNoSuchMethodError.
```

Create Custom Exceptions

It is very simple to create your own custom Exception.
Simply implement the Exception interface.

Example Code

```
class TooOldForServiceException implements Exception {
  Cadet _cadet;

  TooOldForServiceException(this._cadet);

  toString(){
    return "${_cadet.name} is too old to be in military service.";
  }
}

class Cadet {
  String _name;
  int _age;

  Cadet(this._name, this._age);

  get age{
    return _age;
  }

  get name{
    return _name;
  }

}

void main() {
  print('start');

  List<Cadet> cadetList = [
    Cadet("Tom", 21),
    Cadet("Dick", 37),
    Cadet("Harry", 51),
    Cadet("Mark", 52),
  ];

  List<Cadet> validCadetList = [];
  for (Cadet cadet in cadetList){
    try {
      validateCadet(cadet);
      validCadetList.add(cadet);
    } on TooOldForServiceException catch(ex) {
      print(ex);
    } // .. other validation exceptions ...
```

```
  }

  print('finish: ${validCadetList.length} of ${cadetList.length} cadets are valid.');
}

void validateCadet(Cadet cadet){
  if (cadet.age > 50){
    throw new TooOldForServiceException(cadet);
  }
  // .. other validations ...
}
```

Output

```
start
Harry is too old to be in military service.
Mark is too old to be in military service.
finish: 2 of 4 cadets are valid.
```

Console Output

Dart allows you to print to the console using the 'print' command.
Remember the following:

- Printing a variable attempts to call its 'toString()' method go get what to print.
- You can use string interpolation and special characters to format the output.

Example Code

```
void main() {
  int oneVariable = 12;
  String anotherVariable = 'some text';
        print('noneVariable: ${oneVariable} \n\nanotherVariable: \'${anotherVariable}\'');
}
```

Output

```
noneVariable: 12

anotherVariable: 'some text'
```

Asynchronicity

Introduction

Asynchronicity is the ability to do multiple things at the same time.

Example

When a modern web application needs to get data from a server, it sends out a request and waits for the result to come back. However, the application should still be able to do things in the meantime, like respond to user input.

Doing Multiple Things at the Same Time Can Save Time

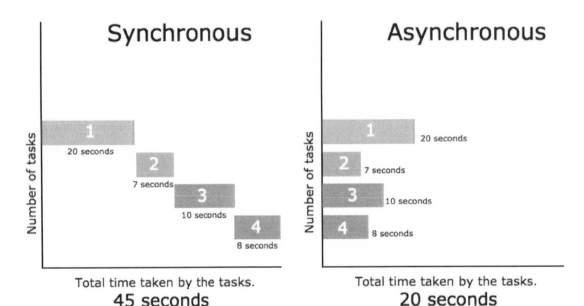

Future

Normally an asynchronous operation results in something, you have a method with asynchronous code that returns something once its finished.
A Future starts off as uncompleted then later ends up being completed (or completed with an error).

Example

The user communicates with a web server to get information and returns the information. Dart uses the Future object to represent the result of an asynchronous operation, starting off as incomplete then later on completed with a value.

Result Type

Futures can complete with result objects. These objects are generics, i.e. they have a specified type.
Example 1: if you are asynchronously getting a Customer object, you would use a Future<Customer>.

Example 2: if your asynchronous operation is not returning any object, you would use a Future<void>.

Exceptions

Futures can fail to complete and can result in exceptions, which you can catch.

Invoking and Handling Asynchronous Operations

Dart offers two ways of handling asynchronous code: using the Future API and using Async-Await. The Future API is the older, more established way of doing things and the Async-Await is the more convenient modern way.

Future API

Before async and await were added in Dart 1.9, you had to use the Future API. You might still see the Future API used in older code and in code that needs more functionality than async-await offers.

As an asynchronous operation can have two possible outcomes (success and failure, otherwise knowns completion and error), the Future API enables a developer to call asynchronous code with callback handlers, one for success and one for failure (optional). The success handler is the 'then' and the failure handler is the 'catchError'.

Exercise

This exercise shows how we can asynchronously run some code that creates a string of numbers using the Future API (callbacks).

Step 1
Open your browser and navigate to https://dartpad.dartlang.org/

Step 2
Paste the following code into the left-side.

```
import 'dart:async';

String countUp(int count){
  print('start count up');
  StringBuffer sb = new StringBuffer();
  for (int i = 0; i < count; i++) {
    sb.write(" ${i}");
  }
  print('finish count up');
  return sb.toString();
}

Future<String> createFutureCounter(int count) {
  return new Future(() { return countUp(count); });
```

```
}
void main() {
  print('start main');
  Future<String> future = createFutureCounter(100);
  print('adding Future API callbacks');
  future.then((value) => handleCompletion(value));
  print('finish main');
}

void handleError(err){
  print('Async operation errored: ${err}');
}

void handleCompletion(value){
  print('Async operation succeeded: ${value}');
}
```

Step 3

Hit the run button and you should see the following output:

```
start main
adding Future API callbacks
finish main
start count up
finish count up
Async operation succeeded:  0 1 2 3 4 5 6 7 8 9 10 11 12 13 14 15 16 17 18 19 20 21 22 23 24 25 26 27 28
29 30 31 32 33 34 35 36 37 38 39 40 41 42 43 44 45 46 47 48 49 50 51 52 53 54 55 56 57 58 59 60 61 62 63
64 65 66 67 68 69 70 71 72 73 74 75 76 77 78 79 80 81 82 83 84 85 86 87 88 89 90 91 92 93 94 95 96 97 98
99
```

Step 4 – Summary So Far

- The 'main' method is short-lived. It calls 'createFutureCounter', is returned a future, adds a callback to the future and finishes. It finishes almost immediately, that means that it was not blocked by invocation of heavy synchronous code.
- The 'createFutureCounter' method is called by the main and returns a new Future object containing a lambda which is executed asynchronously, calling the 'countUp' method.
- The 'countUp' method then does the relatively slow work of counting up the numbers.
- Once the 'count up' completes then the callback (the one that was added in the 'main' method) is fired and we see 'Async operation succeded'.

Step 5 – Add Error Handling

Replace the code in the left side with the following:

```
import 'dart:async';

String countUp(int count){
  print('start count up');
  StringBuffer sb = new StringBuffer();
  for (int i = 0; i < count; i++) {
    if (i > 500){
      throw new Exception("Over 500 not allowed.");
    }
    sb.write(" ${i}");
  }
```

```
  print('finish count up');
  return sb.toString();
}

Future<String> createFutureCounter(int count) {
  return new Future(() { return countUp(count); });
}

void main() {
  print('start main');
  Future<String> future = createFutureCounter(1000);
  print('adding Future API callbacks');
  future.then((value) => handleCompletion(value)).catchError((err) => handleError(err));
  print('finish main');
}

void handleCompletion(value){
  print('Async operation succeeded: ${value}');
}

void handleError(err){
  print('Async operation errored: ${err}');
}
```

Step 6

Hit the run button and you should see the following output:

```
start main
adding Future API callbacks
finish main
start count up
Async operation errored: Exception: Over 500 not allowed.
```

Step 7 – Final Summary

- The 'main' method is short-lived. It calls 'createFutureCounter', is returned a future, adds two callbacks to the future (one for completion, one for error) and finishes. It finishes almost immediately, that means that it was not blocked by invocation of heavy synchronous code.
- As before, the 'createFutureCounter' method is called by the main and returns a new Future object containing a lambda which is executed asynchronously, calling the 'countUp' method.
- The 'countUp' method then does the relatively slow work of counting up the numbers but artificially throws an Exception once it gets to 500.
- The 'count up' never completes but invokes the 'error' callback (the second one that was added in the 'main' method) is fired and we see 'Async operation errored'.

Async & Await Keywords

Async

When an async method is called, a Future is immediately returned, and the body of the method is executed later. Later on, as the body of the async function is executed, the Future returned by the function call will be completed along with its result. At the end of the async method, the value (from the completed Future) can be returned.

Await

Await expressions are used in async methods. They enable you to invoke asynchronous code (that returns a Future). Once the asynchronous code is invoked, the currently running function is suspended until the Future has completed or there is an Error or Exception.

Exercise

This exercise shows how we can asynchronously run some code that creates a string of numbers using the Async & Await keywords.

Step 1
Open your browser and navigate to https://dartpad.dartlang.org/

Step 2
Paste the following code into the left-side.

```
import 'dart:async';

String countUp(int count) {
  print('start count up');
  StringBuffer sb = new StringBuffer();
  for (int i = 0; i < count; i++) {
    sb.write(" ${i}");
  }
  print('finish count up');
  return sb.toString();
}

Future<String> createFutureCounter(int count) {
  return new Future(() {
    return countUp(count);
  });
}

void countUpAsynchronously(int count) async {
  print('Async operation start');
  String value = await createFutureCounter(count);
  print('Async operation succeeded: ${value}');
}

void main() {
  print('start main');
  countUpAsynchronously(100);
```

```
  print('finish main');
}
```

Step 3

Hit the run button and you should see the following output:

```
start main
Async operation start
finish main
start count up
finish count up
Async operation succeeded:  0 1 2 3 4 5 6 7 8 9 10 11 12 13 14 15 16 17 18 19 20 21 22 23 24 25 26 27 28
29 30 31 32 33 34 35 36 37 38 39 40 41 42 43 44 45 46 47 48 49 50 51 52 53 54 55 56 57 58 59 60 61 62 63
64 65 66 67 68 69 70 71 72 73 74 75 76 77 78 79 80 81 82 83 84 85 86 87 88 89 90 91 92 93 94 95 96 97 98
99
```

Step 4 – Summary So Far

- The 'main' method is short-lived. It calls 'countUpAsynchronously' and exits.
- The 'countUpAsynchronously' method is an async method. That means a Future is immediately returned and the body of the method is executed later. The body of the method is executed after the main completes and it invokes the 'createFutureCounter' and waits for it to finish. Once its finished it prints out the counts.
- The 'createFutureCounter' method is called by the main and returns a new Future object containing a lambda which is executed asynchronously, calling the 'countUp' method.

Step 5 – Add Error Handling

Paste the following code into the left-side.

```
import 'dart:async';

String countUp(int count) {
  print('start count up');
  StringBuffer sb = new StringBuffer();
  for (int i = 0; i < count; i++) {
    if (i > 500) {
      throw new Exception("Over 500 not allowed.");
    }
    sb.write(" ${i}");
  }
  print('finish count up');
  return sb.toString();
}

Future<String> createFutureCounter(int count) {
  return new Future(() {
    return countUp(count);
  });
}

void countUpAsynchronously(int count) async {
  print('Async operation start');
  String value;
  try {
    value = await createFutureCounter(count);
    print('Async operation succeeded: ${value}');
```

```
  } catch (ex) {
    print('Async operation errored: ${ex}');
  }
}

void main() {
  print('start main');
  countUpAsynchronously(1000);
  print('finish main');
}
```

Step 6

Hit the run button and you should see the following output:

```
start main
Async operation start
finish main
start count up
Async operation errored: Exception: Over 500 not allowed.
```

Step 7 – Final Summary

- The 'main' method is short-lived. It calls 'countUpAsynchronously' and exits.
- The 'countUpAsynchronously' method is an async method. That means a Future is immediately returned and the body of the method is executed later. Later, the body of the method is executed, and it invokes the 'createFutureCounter' method.
- The 'createFutureCounter' method returns a new Future object containing a lambda which is executed asynchronously, calling the 'countUp' method, which throws the Exception. That exception is then caught by method 'countUpAsynchronously' and the exception is printed out.

Reactive Programming

Reactive programming is a declarative programming paradigm concerned with data streams and the propagation of change. With this paradigm, it is possible to express static (e.g., arrays) or dynamic (e.g., event emitters) data streams and write simple code to process these streams as required.

The Dart language has built-in Stream APIs that are well suited for reactive-like programming.

Nulls

Dart has some unexpected ways of dealing with nulls:

?.

The ?. operator short-circuits to null if the left-hand side is null.

??=

The ?? operator returns the left-hand side if it is not null, and the right-hand side otherwise.

Example

Source Code

```
class Person{
  String _ssn;
  String _name;

  Person(this._ssn, this._name);

  String get ssn {
    return _ssn;
  }

  String get name {
    return _name;
  }

}

void main() {

  Person person1 = null;
  Person person2 = Person("223232323", "Peter Jones");

  String name = person1?.name;
  print("Person 1 Name: ${name}");

  Person person1IfPossibleOtherwisePerson2OtherwiseNull = (person1??=person2);
  name = person1IfPossibleOtherwisePerson2OtherwiseNull?.name;
  print("A Name from Person1 If Possible, Otherwise Person2: ${name}");

}
```

Outputs

```
Person 1 Name: null
A Name from Person1 If Possible, Otherwise Person2: Peter Jones
```

Further Reading

https://medium.com/dartlang/making-dart-a-better-language-for-ui-f1ccaf9f546c

7. Introduction to Flutter

Introduction

The purpose of this chapter is to give the reader a quick introduction to Flutter before installing it and starting to use it.

What is Flutter?

Flutter is not a language (like JavaScript, for example). Flutter uses Dart for its language.

Flutter is Google's mobile SDK / UI framework that enables developers to build native apps that run on Android and iOS devices. Developers write code in a single codebase that works on both platforms.

High Productivity

Flutter was written for high productivity, to get apps out fast.
* You can change your code and hot reload the changes, without any kind of delay.
* Flutter includes the UI Widgets you need.
* Flutter works with most IDEs.

High Quality

The included Flutter UI Widgets work seamlessly and conventionally with the target platform. Scrolling, navigation, icons and fonts match the target system.
* When you write an Android app with the Flutter Widgets it looks like a normal Android app.
* When you write an iOS app with the Flutter Widgets, it looks like a normal iOS app.

High Performance

The code you write in Flutter runs natively so it flies!

It is Free and Open.

Flutter is free and Open Source.

Fuschsia

Fuschsia is Google's next Operating System for mobile devices. All of the apps for Fuschsia are being developed by Google in Flutter.

Flutter Source Code

Google Flutter is open source and it comprises of several repositories hosted on GitHub here:

https://github.com/flutter/flutter

- Flutter
  - Main repository.
- Samples
  - Sample code repository.
- Plugins
  - This repository contains the source code for plugins developed by the core Flutter team to enable access to platform-specific APIs.
- Engine
  - The Flutter runtime, written in C++.
- Flutter Intellij
  - The Flutter plugin for IntelliJ.
- Flutter Website
  - Flutter.io code.

Flutter SDK

The Flutter SDK contains all the elements you need to perform Flutter development:

Dart Platform

We covered the Dart platform in the previous chapter.

Flutter Engine

The Flutter Engine is the runtime for on which Flutter applications run. It provides graphic rendering support, as well as providing an interface (through the Flutter core libraries) to the Android or iOS SDK layer below.

It was written in C++ and is on github here: https://github.com/flutter/engine

Foundation Library

The Foundation library, written in Dart, provides basic classes and functions which are used to construct applications using Flutter, such as APIs to communicate with the engine.

It was written in Dart and is on github here:
https://github.com/flutter/flutter/tree/master/packages/flutter/lib/src/foundation

8. Installing Flutter & Editor

Introduction

The purpose of this chapter is to help the reader install Flutter and an editor.

Note: Developing on a PC for iOS

Introduction

You can develop Flutter applications on a PC, and you will have no problems at all until you want to run your code on an Apple iOS device, like an iPhone or an iPad. Apple has made compiling of iOS applications exclusively available to macOS using their XCode tool.

It's Not as Bad as it Seems

Flutter really works well from a cross-platform point of view and you can do 90% of the development on a PC even if you are planning to deploy to iOS. You really can develop on one platform then run it on another and trust that it will almost completely work on the other.

When you get to testing and deployment you will have some options:
- Buy, borrow or rent a Mac.
- Install a Mac virtual machine on your PC using software like VMWare or Virtual Box.
- Rent a Mac on the cloud for $20 a month using a service like www.macincloud.com.

Install Flutter

Introduction

I am not going to go into every detail about Flutter installation because there are plenty of better sources of information about this:
- Youtube – there are lots of videos on this.
- Official Flutter website: https://flutter.io/docs/get-started/install

It's not a terribly difficult process but I am going to cover the basic process, which is similar on all of the environments.

Step 1: Software Pre-Requisites

Git

One thing I noticed from installing Flutter was that nobody mentioned that Git was a pre-requisite for installing Flutter. So, ensure you have git installed before doing anything else.

Brew

If you are planning on installing Flutter on a Mac, it's a good idea to install Brew first as the Flutter Doctor will ask you to use brew to install additional software when required.

XCode Command-Line Tools

If you are planning on installing Flutter on a Mac, you are definitely going to need these.

Step 2: Download the Flutter SDK

We mentioned the Flutter SDK earlier, how it has all the tools you need to perform basic Flutter development. However, it also has a very useful tool called Flutter Doctor that is used to setup your Flutter Development environment. Download this SDK and copy it into a folder.
Note that the Flutter SDK also contains the Dart SDK.
- Mac: https://flutter.dev/docs/get-started/install/macos
- PC: https://flutter.dev/docs/get-started/install/windows
- Unix: https://flutter.dev/docs/get-started/install/linux

Step 3: Setup Your Path

The Flutter SDK has command-line tools, including Flutter Doctor that need to be run from the command-line. These command-line tools reside in the 'bin' folder of the Flutter SDK. You need to include the bin folder (within the flutter SDK) in your computers path so that you can run the command-line tools from the command-line.

Step 4: Run Flutter Doctor

You will need to run the command below:

```
flutter doctor
```

This will checkout your environment and diagnose (like your doctor) what is good and bad about your flutter development environment. It will provide you with a summary, complete with instructions on what you need to do.

```
C:\Users\venka>flutter doctor

  WARNING: your installation of Flutter is 55 days old.

  To update to the latest version, run "flutter upgrade".




         Welcome to Flutter! - https://flutter.io

  The Flutter tool anonymously reports feature usage statistics and crash
  reports to Google in order to help Google contribute improvements to
  Flutter over time.

  Read about data we send with crash reports:
  https://github.com/flutter/flutter/wiki/Flutter-CLI-crash-reporting

  See Google's privacy policy:
  https://www.google.com/intl/en/policies/privacy/

  Use "flutter config --no-analytics" to disable analytics and crash
  reporting.

Doctor summary (to see all details, run flutter doctor -v):
[√] Flutter (Channel beta, v0.5.1, on Microsoft Windows [Version 10.0.17134.165], locale en-US)
[X] Android toolchain - develop for Android devices
    X Unable to locate Android SDK.
      Install Android Studio from: https://developer.android.com/studio/index.html
      On first launch it will assist you in installing the Android SDK components.
      (or visit https://flutter.io/setup/#android-setup for detailed instructions).
      If Android SDK has been installed to a custom location, set $ANDROID_HOME to that location.
[√] Android Studio (version 3.1)
    X Flutter plugin not installed; this adds Flutter specific functionality.
    X Dart plugin not installed; this adds Dart specific functionality.
[!] IntelliJ IDEA Community Edition (version 2018.1)
    X Flutter plugin not installed; this adds Flutter specific functionality.
    X Dart plugin not installed; this adds Dart specific functionality.
[!] VS Code, 64-bit edition (version 1.21.1)
[!] Connected devices
    ! No devices available
```

Here are my notes from running the install on 3 platforms:
- Just follow the instructions. Some of them are very simple, like saying 'yes' to licenses. Some are more involved.
- You might get a message about installing the missing Android SDK. This can be remedied by installing Android Studio then running it, as the first thing it will do is setup the Android SDK.
  - At this point I usually download Android Studio because:
    - It is free.
    - It sets up the sdk for you.
    - It is great for setting up the Emulators.

- You can still use Visual Studio Code for most of the work and leave Android Studio closed.
- If you are installing Flutter on a Mac (or Unix) rather than on a PC then there are many more dependencies (for iOS compilation, deployment etc.) and it can take much longer.

Install Editor

Once you are done with the Flutter Doctor, you should install your editor.

Editors & UI Builders

None of the Flutter tools currently support a UI builder, where you can just drag and drop to build your UI. You have to code your Flutter UI's 'by hand', which is not difficult anyway. However, these editors help the developers in many ways, offering Code Completion, Error Highlighting, Linting and Debugging.

Flutter Doctor Tells You to Install Android Studio

Flutter Doctor tells you to install Android Studio. This is what the official Flutter website says:

Note: Flutter relies on a full installation of Android Studio to supply its Android platform dependencies.

So, you should already have the Android Studio editor installed by the time you have got past the flutter doctor.

However, this does not stop you from using another editor.

Android Studio

Introduction

Android Studio is the official IDE for android application development as it provides a very comprehensive, well-supported (by Google) solution:

- It is a superb editor.
- It is also free to use.
- It also works (very well) for developing iOS applications in Flutter.

- It was based on IntelliJ IDEA, so it works in a very similar manner.

Thus, the easiest way to get going with an editor is to install the Flutter plugins into Android Studio. Installing the Flutter plugins takes all of five minutes:

1. Start Android Studio.
2. Open plugin preferences (**Preferences > Plugins** on macOS, **File > Settings > Plugins** on Windows & Linux).
3. Select **Browse repositories**, select the Flutter plugin and click **Install**.
4. Click **Yes** when prompted to install the Dart plugin.
5. Click **Restart** when prompted.

Flutter Outline

One of the great things about the Android Studio is the Flutter Outline. When you are editing a file, it shows you the Widgets defined in that file, their variables, their code and their structure. It also lets you select Widgets in your 'build' methods and add Centering, Padding, Rows, Columns etc.

IntelliJ (Android Studio, IntelliJ)

If you are already using Intellij and you don't want to use Android Studio, then you can simply add the Flutter plugin in the same manner as it is installed into Android Studio (see above):

- Installing the plugin takes 5 minutes.
- You can use the free IntelliJ IDEA Community Edition or buy a License to use the 'full-fat' version. I use IntelliJ IDEA all the time and I pay $20 a month, well worth it as I use it for my regular job every day.

Further Reading: https://flutter.io/docs/get-started/editor?tab=androidstudio

Visual Studio Code

Visual Studio code is a great alternative to using Android Studio and it is a little more 'lightweight' (runs faster, uses less memory):

- It is a superb editor.
- It is also free to use.
- Installing the Flutter extension takes 5 minutes.

I had never used Visual Studio code with Flutter before writing this book. I had used Flutter for months using Android Studio. I was really surprised and impressed how well the Flutter Extension works with Visual Studio Code. It is comprehensive, easy to use and fast. I definitely recommend it as an alternative to Android Studio Code.

Further Reading: https://flutter.io/docs/get-started/editor?tab=vscode

9. Create Default Flutter Project

Introduction

The purpose of this chapter is to get the reader generate his or her first Flutter project. However this chapter does not include running it yet! ☺

Default Flutter App

When you create a new Flutter project, it creates a default 'counter' app that displays a counter in the middle of the screen. This app is the same, whether you generate it in Android Studio, Visual Studio Code or the Command-Line. It allows the user to click on a '+' round button on the bottom-right to increment the counter (this is a floating button).

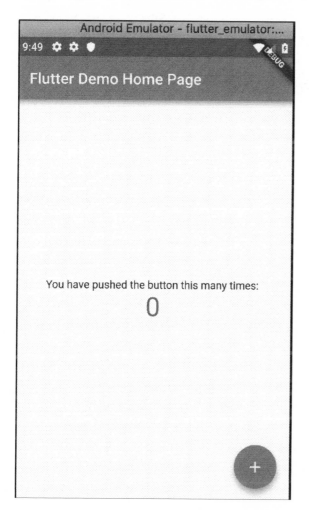

Create Project

You can create a new Flutter Project from your editor or the command-line:
- Android Studio
- Visual Studio Code
- Command Line

Android Studio

1. Select the following menu option: File > New > New Flutter Project. This will open a wizard.

2. Select 'Flutter Application' then hit next.

3. Enter the project name (whatever you want to call it) and hit next.

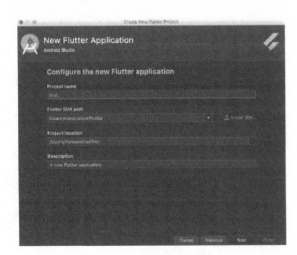

4. Enter the company domain (whatever you want) and hit finish.

5. The editor will take a couple of minutes to setup the files in the project.

6. That's it!

Visual Studio Code

1. Ensure that you have installed the Flutter Extension into Visual Studio Code before doing this.

2. Open the command palette using the keyboard shortcut Ctrl+Shift+P (Command+Shift+P on the Mac) and you will see a list of the available commands. If you start to type 'Flutter' in this box then you will see a list of Flutter commands:

3. Select the command 'Flutter: New Project'.

4. Enter the name of the new project:

5. Select a folder to create the project in.

7. The editor will take a couple of minutes to setup the files in the project.

8. That's it!

Command-Line

-   Ensure that you have installed the Flutter SDK and it is on the path before doing this.
-   Enter the command:

```
flutter create <project name>
```

-   The command will take a couple of minutes to setup the files in the project.
-   That's it!

Project Created

Congratulations - you have created your first Flutter project! Now let's take a look at it.

Project Folders

The default Flutter project is organized into several folders.

Name	Description
[root]	Root folder. This usually contains configuration files. The most important of these configuration files is the 'pubspec.yaml' file, which declares the project dependencies. We will cover this file in detail later.
.idea	Intellij project folder. Feel free to remove this folder if you are using Visual Studio Code.
android	As the name suggests, the folder contains all the Android-related files and code(s) for the application. This is where Android-specific settings and code resides. When building for Android, Flutter uses Gradle as the dependency manager.
build	This folder is created and used by gradle when you build the project.
ios	Similar to the 'android' folder, this folder contains the iOS related files and code(s) for the application. This is where iOS-specific settings and generated code resides. When building for iOS, Flutter uses Cocoapods as the dependency manager.
lib	This is where the application code resides. You should see a file 'main.dart', the entry point for the Flutter application. This is the file you select and run. You will add more files and subfolders into this folder.
test	This is where the unit testing code resides.

> You may add more files and subfolders into this folder.

Project Application Code File

As mentioned earlier, when you create a new Flutter project, it creates a default 'counter' app that displays a counter in the middle of the screen.

The code for this default application resides in a single file: 'main.dart' in the 'lib' folder.

Note

- Dart lets you declare multiple objects within a single file!
- This 'main.dart' acts as the entry point of the application.
  - If you are using an Editor, this is the file you will launch to run your app.

Widgets & Composition

Introduction

Now we are looking at your project, we need to introduce some of the Flutter concepts, like Widgets and Composition.

Widgets are the Building Blocks of your UI.

Whenever we build a user interface in Flutter, it is composed of Widgets.
Putting your widgets together is called Composition.

Think of a user interface as a jigsaw. The jigsaw is composed of pieces (Widgets):

Widget Tree

Widgets can contain other widgets, in a tree structure, a hierarchy. This is often called a Widget Tree.

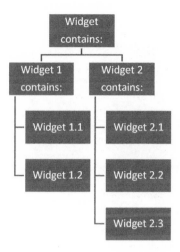

Project Widgets & Composition

If you look at the next diagram, the project's Widget tree is on the left and the project's UI is on the right. Note how the Widget Tree and UI correspond to each other.

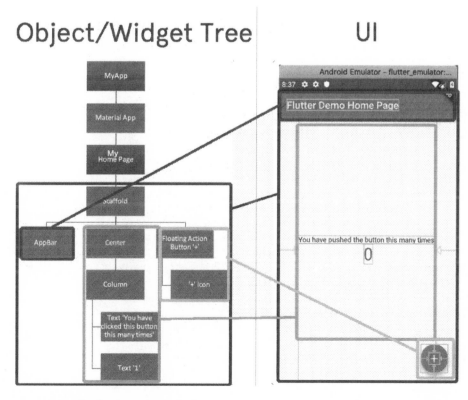

Custom Widgets

Although the default application contains many widgets, only two custom widgets were required to make it work:

MyApp

It is a custom widget for the entire application.

MyHomePage

It is a custom widget that contains the layout for the application, plus the application state (the counter). It covers the main area of the screen.

Example Code

You will see this Widget used in most of the Examples. This Widget is probably the best place to start when examining Example Code

Flutter Widgets

The rest of the widgets were used from the Flutter widget library, already built for us.

Project Code

Now we have some kind of idea of how the Widgets compose the UI in this app, now let's look at the code.

Entry Point

Every Dart app must start with a main function as a starting point. In this case the main function creates an instance of the MyApp object, a StatelessWidget. The method 'runApp' accepts an instance of a widget (in this case an instance of MyApp) and uses it as the root Widget of the App, rendering it to fit the screen, taking up all the available space.

```
void main() => runApp(new MyApp());
```

MyApp Widget

The MyApp object is a StatelessWidget. It sets up a Material App that contains a MyHomePage widget. The MaterialApp widget is a built-in Flutter widget that serves as the container for your whole app and its Widgets. It provides services that child Widgets may use, such as navigation, sizing, themes etc.

```
class MyApp extends StatelessWidget {
  // This widget is the root of your application.
  @override
```

```
Widget build(BuildContext context) {
  return new MaterialApp(
    title: 'Flutter Demo',
    theme: new ThemeData(
      // This is the theme of your application.
      //
      // Try running your application with "flutter run". You'll see the
      // application has a blue toolbar. Then, without quitting the app, try
      // changing the primarySwatch below to Colors.green and then invoke
      // "hot reload" (press "r" in the console where you ran "flutter run",
      // or press Run > Flutter Hot Reload in IntelliJ). Notice that the
      // counter didn't reset back to zero; the application is not restarted.
      primarySwatch: Colors.blue,
    ),
    home: new MyHomePage(title: 'Flutter Demo Home Page'),
  );
}
}
```

MyHomePage Widget

This is a stateful widget, more on these later. This widget holds the count as State (data) and it sets up the child objects in the UI:

- The center widget, which contains a column object, which contains 2 text objects:
  - 'You have pushed the button this many times:'
  - '0'
- The floating action button widget, which contains a '+' icon.
  - When the user clicks on the floating action button, this increments the instance variable '_counter' inside a the 'setState' method.
  - Making a call to the 'setState' method tells Flutter that something has changed and the UI needs to be rebuilt, so it invokes the 'build' method in this widget, which redraws itself with the new counter value.

```
class MyHomePage extends StatefulWidget {
  MyHomePage({Key key, this.title}) : super(key: key);

  // This widget is the home page of your application. It is stateful, meaning
  // that it has a State object (defined below) that contains fields that affect
  // how it looks.

  // This class is the configuration for the state. It holds the values (in this
  // case the title) provided by the parent (in this case the App widget) and
  // used by the build method of the State. Fields in a Widget subclass are
  // always marked "final".

  final String title;

  @override
  _MyHomePageState createState() => new _MyHomePageState();
}

class _MyHomePageState extends State<MyHomePage> {
  int _counter = 0;
```

```
void _incrementCounter() {
  setState(() {
    // This call to setState tells the Flutter framework that something has
    // changed in this State, which causes it to rerun the build method below
    // so that the display can reflect the updated values. If we changed
    // _counter without calling setState(), then the build method would not be
    // called again, and so nothing would appear to happen.
    _counter++;
  });
}

@override
Widget build(BuildContext context) {
  // This method is rerun every time setState is called, for instance as done
  // by the _incrementCounter method above.
  //
  // The Flutter framework has been optimized to make rerunning build methods
  // fast, so that you can just rebuild anything that needs updating rather
  // than having to individually change instances of widgets.
  return new Scaffold(
    appBar: new AppBar(
      // Here we take the value from the MyHomePage object that was created by
      // the App.build method, and use it to set our appbar title.
      title: new Text(widget.title),
    ),
    body: new Center(
      // Center is a layout widget. It takes a single child and positions it
      // in the middle of the parent.
      child: new Column(
        // Column is also layout widget. It takes a list of children and
        // arranges them vertically. By default, it sizes itself to fit its
        // children horizontally, and tries to be as tall as its parent.
        //
        // Invoke "debug paint" (press "p" in the console where you ran
        // "flutter run", or select "Toggle Debug Paint" from the Flutter tool
        // window in IntelliJ) to see the wireframe for each widget.
        //
        // Column has various properties to control how it sizes itself and
        // how it positions its children. Here we use mainAxisAlignment to
        // center the children vertically; the main axis here is the vertical
        // axis because Columns are vertical (the cross axis would be
        // horizontal).
        mainAxisAlignment: MainAxisAlignment.center,
        children: <Widget>[
          new Text(
            'You have pushed the button this many times:',
          ),
          new Text(
            '$_counter',
            style: Theme.of(context).textTheme.display1,
          ),
        ],
      ),
    ),
    floatingActionButton: new FloatingActionButton(
      onPressed: _incrementCounter,
      tooltip: 'Increment',
```

```
      child: new Icon(Icons.add),
    ), // This trailing comma makes auto-formatting nicer for build methods.
  );
  }
}
```

10.Setup Android Emulator & Run Project

Introduction

The purpose of this chapter is to setup an Android emulator, open it from your editor and run the project. Ensure that you have your newly-created project open in your editor before continuing.

Emulators

These are great for developers, enabling them to develop their code to run on multiple devices, see how they look on each device. Later on, you can use the real hardware for final pre-release testing.

You can only run your Flutter code on emulators in Debug Mode. Release Mode is not supported. This is not a big problem because you should be testing release code on the real hardware anyway!

Android Emulator

The Android Emulator simulates Android devices on your computer so that you can test your application on a variety of devices and Android API levels without needing to have each physical device.

The emulator provides almost all of the capabilities of a real Android device and it comes with predefined configurations for various Android phone, tablet, Wear OS, and Android TV devices. An AVD is a virtual device that you setup to run in the Emulator.

Setting Up the Android Emulator

Options

There are multiple ways you can setup the Android emulator:

- Use Android Studio.

- The AVD Manager in Android Studio gives you the most control, it allows you to setup Android Virtual Devices for all kinds of hardware and versions of Android.

- Use Visual Studio Code.
  - If you just want a generic emulator, Visual Studio Code lets you set one up very easily.

- Use Command Line.
  - I would not setup the emulators from the command-line as it is far more difficult.

Mix

You can mix-and-match. You can setup your emulator using one editor but edit your code in another.

Example

You can create your emulators using the AVD Manager in Android Studio (or Visual Studio Code) then control them later from the command line.

Setup Android Emulator in Android Studio

AVD Manager

The AVD Manager in Android Studio is a dialog you can launch from Android Studio that helps you create and manage AVDs.

To open the AVD Manager, do one of the following:
- Select Tools > AVD Manager.
- Click AVD Manager AVD Manager icon in the toolbar.

Using the toolbar is the quickest way to open the AVD Manager:

AVD Manager Dialog

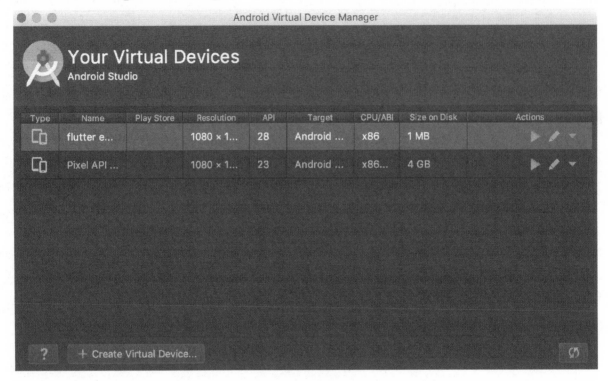

Main Area

The main part of the dialog lists the available AVDs. Note that each AVD has a play button and a pencil button.

Play Button

The play button launches the AVD.

Pencil Button

The pencil button opens a list of commands to do with the AVD to enable the user to perform various tasks:
- Duplicate AVD
- Wipe AVD Data
- Reboot AVD
- Show On Disk
- View Details
- Delete
- Stop (If Launched)

Bottom

The bottom part of the dialog has various buttons, the most important being the button 'Create Virtual Device', which allows the user to download the files for and setup an AVD. Downloading the files can take a while but it is much easier than using the command line!

Setup Android Emulator in Visual Studio Code

Before You Start

Ensure that you have installed the Flutter Extension into Code before doing this.

View Flutter Commands

Open the command palette using the keyboard shortcut Ctrl+Shift+P (Command+Shift+P on the Mac) and you will see a list of the available commands. If you start to type 'Flutter' in this box, then you will see a list of Flutter commands:

Launch Emulator

If you select the 'Flutter: Launch Emulator' command you will list the installed emulators and you can select one to launch it.

Create New Emulator

If you don't have an emulator installed, select the 'Create New' command and Visual Studio Code will create a generic emulator called 'flutter_emulator', which you can then launch.

Setup Android Emulator in Command Line

Introduction

There is a lot of information here: https://developer.android.com/studio/run/emulator-commandline

Android SDK Path

Remember that these command-line tools are part of the Android SDK and need to be setup on your path. Your path should include the following Android SDK folders for these commands to work:

```
/Android/sdk/tools
/Android/sdk/platform-tools
```

To Create a New AVD to Test On:

```
android create avd -n <name> -t <targetID>
```

<name> is the name
<targetID> is the required API level

To List Your Available AVDs:

When you use this option, it displays a list of AVD names from your Android home directory. Note that you can override the default home directory by setting the ANDROID_SDK_HOME environment variable: the root of the user-specific directory where all configuration and AVD content is stored.

```
emulator -list-avds
```

To Launch an Available AVD:

Use the emulator command to start the emulator, as an alternative to running your project or starting it through the AVD Manager.

```
emulator -avd <name>
```

Run Project

Android Studio

Note that on the main toolbar there are two dropdowns then a play button. The first dropdown is used to select the device/emulator to run against. The second dropdown is the run configuration.

Run Configuration

The run configuration is used to provide information about which Dart class is used as the application starting point, as well as run parameters, options. Clicking on the play button invokes the run configuration on the device/emulator.

Visual Studio Code

Steps

1. Go back to the editor and view the file list (explorer) on the left.

2. Click on the 'lib' folder to open it up.

3. Right-mouse click on 'main.dart' and you should see a popup menu containing the commands to run or debug. Select run or debug to install and run the app on the emulator. This will run the project on the emulator.

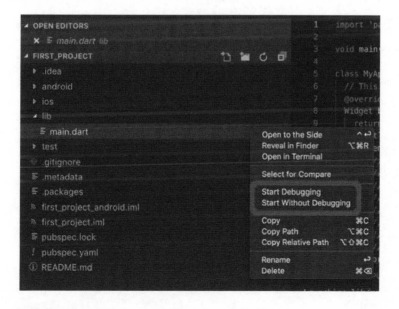

Command-Line

Steps

1. Ensure that you are in the root folder of the project.

2. Enter the 'flutter run' command.

```
flutter run
```

11.Setup iOS Emulator & Run Project

Introduction

The purpose of this chapter is to setup an iOS emulator, open it from your editor and run the project. Ensure that you have your newly-created project open in your editor before continuing.

PCs

Obviously, this is not going to work on a PC. So, get your Mac ready (or virtual Mac ready)! You can use the iOS emulator for most of your development and then find a device to test on when you're nearly done.

XCode

XCode is Apple's integrated development environment (IDE) that you use to build apps for Apple products including the iPad, iPhone, Apple Watch, and Mac. XCode provides tools to manage your entire development workflow—from creating your app, to testing, optimizing, and submitting it to the App Store.
You don't need to have XCode running to use the Emulator, but you can launch the Emulator from XCode.

iOS Emulator

XCode ships with an iOS simulator/emulator.
In addition to running code, the simulator enables you to test the following with virtual iOS devices:

- Device rotation
- Simulating various GPS coordinates
- Device shake
- Simulating low memory scenarios

Open iOS Simulator/Emulator

Open from Xcode

Select the 'Xcode' menu then 'Open Developer Tool then 'Simulator':

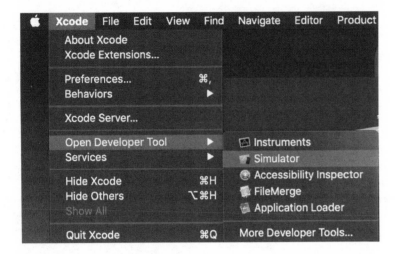

Opening from Command-Line

Use the following command in your terminal.

```
open -a Simulator
```

Run Project

Android Studio

When you have the Simulator(s) open (running), the simulator(s) become available on the main toolbar in the first dropdown, to the left of the run configuration dropdown & run/debug buttons:

If you have more than one simulator running, they will all be displayed in the dropdown on the main toolbar.

Visual Studio Code

When you have the Simulator(s) running, the currently-selected simulator is displayed on the toolbar on the bottom right. The current simulator is the one that will be used when the user selects 'Start Debugging' or 'Start Without Debugging' on the popup menu for a runnable file.

t   Flutter: 0.8.2   iPhone XR (ios Emulator)

If you have multiple simulators running, you can select between simulators by clicking on the simulator displayed on the toolbar on the bottom right. This opens a menu at the top to enable the user to select in between them:

Select a device to use

iPhone XR ios
Current Device

iPad Air 2 ios
Emulator

Command-Line

You start your iOS simulator(s) as required then you use the 'flutter run' command to run your app with an open device or emulator.

No Simulators/Devices Open?

If you invoke 'flutter run' without any devices or emulators, you get a message similar to that below:

```
flutter run
No connected devices.

Run 'flutter emulators' to list and start any available device emulators.

If you expected your device to be detected, please run "flutter doctor" to diagnose
potential issues, or visit https://flutter.io/setup/ for troubleshooting tips.
```

Multiple Simulators/Devices Open?

If you invoke 'flutter run' with multiple devices or emulators open, you get a message similar to that below:

```
flutter run
More than one device connected; please specify a device with the '-d <deviceId>' flag, or use '-d all' to act
on all devices.

iPhone 6s • 34B92793-1355-4E13-857B-D5E7A3FB4F4F • ios • iOS 12.1 (simulator)
iPhone XR • D49E45DA-7D58-473A-B0FA-29E3C4E88455 • ios • iOS 12.1 (simulator)
```

The command below runs the app on the iPhone 6s:

```
flutter run -d 34B92793-1355-4E13-857B-D5E7A3FB4F4F
```

One Simulator/Device Open?

Remember that if you only have one device or emulator open, you just do a 'flutter run':

```
flutter run
```

12.Setup Device & Run Project

Introduction

The purpose of this chapter is to setup a real device, connect it to your computer and run the project. Ensure that you have your newly-created project open in your editor before continuing.

Android Device

Introduction

This is relatively straightforward. You basically do the following:

- Use the device settings app (on your device i.e. your phone) to set yourself up as a developer and enable USB debugging.

- Setup the computer to detect the device. This involves setting up ADB, which is the Android Debug Bridge. This enables an Android app to be debugged on an emulator or actual Android device.

- Connect the device to the computer.
    - Your connected device should become visible in the IDE in the same way as it would for an emulator (see 'Open Android Emulator & Run Your First App').
    - Run the app in the same way as you would for an emulator.

Further Reading / Instructions

Full instructions here: https://developer.android.com/studio/run/device

iOS Device

Check Your Hardware First

- Computer.
    - As per the iOS emulator, this is not going to work on a PC. So, get your Mac computer ready (or virtual Mac ready)!
- Device.
    - Your Flutter app won't just work on any old iOS device. You will need to have an iOS device that is capable of running iOS8 or later. Otherwise you will get an error like this:

The iOS deployment target is set to 5, but the range of supported deployment target versions for this platform is 8.0 to 12.1. (in target 'Runner')

Setup Your XCode Project

Your XCode project resides within the 'ios' folder of your Flutter project.
You will need to open it and set it up:

- Open your XCode project.
- Create a signing team.
- Setup a unique bundle identifier for the project.

Open XCode Project

Android Studio

- Right-click on iOS folder in project.
- Select 'Flutter' in popup menu.
- Select 'Open iOS module in XCode' in popup menu.

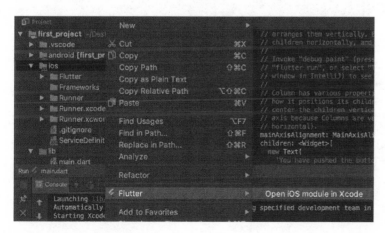

Visual Studio Code

- Right-click on iOS folder in project.
- Select 'Open in XCode' in popup menu

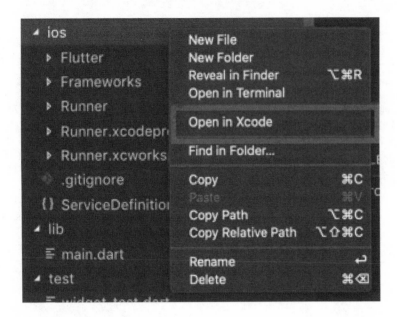

Command-Line

- Open terminal and navigate to the root folder of your project.
- Enter the following command.

```
open ios/Runner.xcworkspace
```

- This command should open the XCode project.

Create Signing Team

- You will need to login to XCode using your Apple ID and setup a signing team.
- In XCode, navigate to the Runner target settings page, then General > Signing > Team.
- The signing workflow is detailed here: https://help.apple.com/xcode/mac/current/ -/dev60b6fbbc7

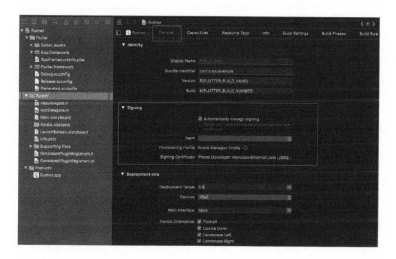

Set Bundle Identifier

- In XCode, navigate to the Runner target settings page, then General > Identity > Bundle Identifier.
- The Bundle Identifier needs to be unique for your project and is quite restrictive in terms of characters, so make sure all of the characters are only alphanumeric (A-Z,a-z,0-9), hypen (-), or period (.).

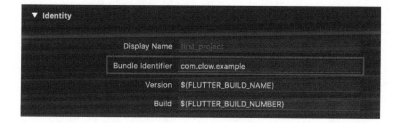

Connect the Device to The Mac & Run

- The first time you connect, you will need to trust both your Mac and the Development Certificate on that device. Select Trust in the dialog prompt (on the iOS device) when first connecting the iOS device to your Mac.

- Your connected device should become visible in the IDE in the same way as it would for an emulator (see 'Run Your App on the iOS Simulator').

- If you see the 'Untrusted Developer' error on the iOS device, then go to Settings and search for Device Management. You can then trust the developer there.
- Run the app in the same way as you would for an emulator.

Further Reading / Instructions

Full instructions here: https://flutter.io/docs/get-started/install/macos

13. Hot Restarting & Reloading

Introduction

This is a very short chapter, but it contains valuable information that you will use all the time. When are running a Flutter app and you make code changes, you can tell your editor to reload them. That is the subject of this chapter.

Hot Reloads

In fact, one of the great things about Dart is its ability to hot reload code.

The Official Documentation Says:

Flutter's hot reload feature helps you quickly and easily experiment, build UIs, add features, and fix bugs. Hot reload works by injecting updated source code files into the running Dart Virtual Machine (VM). After the VM updates classes with the new versions of fields and functions, the Flutter framework automatically rebuilds the widget tree, allowing you to quickly view the effects of your changes.

Two Options

After you have made your code changes, you have two options in regard to reloading:
* Hot restarting.
* Hot reloading.

Hot Restarting

This loads your changed code into the Dart VM and restarts the application. This is the safest thing to do and doesn't take long.

Hot Reloading

If you want to load your changed code into the Dart VM but you don't want to restart the application or change its state, you can do this. The result might be different behavior vs a hot restart. Just remember your code changes may not work with the existing state.

Android Studio

Both hot restart and hot reload are available in the run/debug tool windows.

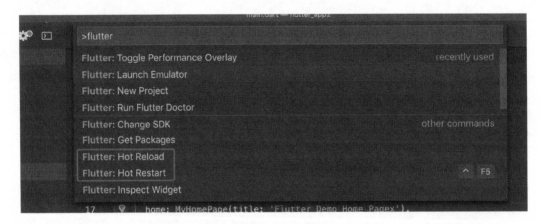

Visual Studio Code

Both hot restart and hot reload are available in the Command Palette.

Command-Line

If you are using 'flutter' run to run the app from the command line, you can use the key 'R' to hot restart and the key 'r' to hot reload.

14. Dependencies & Packages

Introduction

In Dart, you don't have to develop everything from scratch. There is a packaging system where developers can develop packages and publish them. Other people can then use these packages.

The purpose of this chapter is to outline how to use this packaging system.

Website

When someone writes a package and it is published to the https://pub.dartlang.org/ site, developers can declare a dependency to that project and pull it into their project as a dependency. Then the user can add imports at the top the files to import code and use it.

Note that Dart and Flutter packages follow semantic versioning rules.

Core Packages

Flutter comes with many packages by default. These are called Core Packages and you don't need to declare any kind of external dependency to use them.

Non-Core Packages

You could call these 'External Packages'. These are packages that are not setup by default. You need to declare these dependencies and pull them into your project to use them.

Most Useful Non-Core Packages

These are the packages that I have used the most. This may be very different for other Flutter developers.

Name	Description
http	For HTTP communication.
rxdart	Reactive functional programming library.
datetime_picker_formfield	Date / time picker.

image_picker	Image picker. Very useful apps where you take pictures or upload photos.
zoomable_image	For panning and zooming images by touch
shared_preferences	For saving local settings and data in your app.
cached_network_image	A flutter library to show images from the internet and keep them in the cache directory. This helps speed things up. It also lets you display an image placeholder while the image loads.

How to Use an External Package

Declare Dependency in Project

- Open the pubspec.yaml file in the root of your project and add a dependency. For example, the code below declares dependencies to the flutter sdk, cupertino icons and scoped_model. Note how some dependencies specify the version, some don't:

```
flutter:
  sdk: flutter
cupertino_icons: ^0.1.2
scoped_model: ^1.0.1
```

Import Packages

- Once your pubspec.yaml file is setup, you need to install the packages by pulling them from https://pub.dartlang.org/ . Normally your editor will assist you with this.
  - Android Studio
    - Click 'Packages Get' in the action ribbon at the top of pubspec.yaml
  - Visual Studio Code
    - Click 'Get Packages' located in right side of the action ribbon at the top of pubspec.yaml
  - Command-Line
    - Run the command 'flutter packages get'.

Import & Use Package Code

You import the package code in the usual manner using the 'import' statement at the top of your code. For example, the code imports the flutter material package and the scoped model package.

```
import 'package:flutter/material.dart';
import 'package:scoped_model/scoped_model.dart';
```

Restart Your App

You will probably need to restart your app if it is running.
That's it!

Package Version Numbers

Some dependencies specify the version, some don't.
- Version specifiers:
    - ○ 'any' – any version
    - ○ '1.2.3' – only version 1.2.3
    - ○ '>1.8.3' – any version higher than 1.8.3
    - ○ '>=1.8.3' – any version 1.8.3 or higher
    - ○ '<1.8.3' – any version lower than 1.8.3
    - ○ '<=1.8.3' – any version 1.8.3 or lower
- Carat syntax.
    - ○ The '^' means - "the range of all versions guaranteed to be backwards compatible with the specified version".
    - ○ '^1.1.1' is equivalent to versions '>=1.1.1 <2.0.0'
    - ○ '^0.1.2' is equivalent to versions '>=0.1.2 <0.2.0'

Project Files

.packages

This file gets generated when you do a 'packages get'. This file contains a list of dependencies used by your application.

pubspec.lock

Also known as 'package lock file'.
The first time you get a new dependency for your package, pub downloads the latest version of it that's compatible with your other dependencies. It then locks your package to always use that version by creating a lockfile. This is a file named pubspec.lock that pub creates and stores next to your pubspec. It lists the specific versions of each dependency (immediate and transitive) that your package uses.

How to Publish Your Own Packages

Introduction

You can easily write your own packages and share them with the rest of the world.
You can publish to kinds of packages:

- Dart Packages
  - These are packages written in dart.
  - Some of these packages are designed for dart only, others are designed for flutter.
  - We are going to cover these.

- Plugin Packages
  - These are packages written in dart that include platform-specific code, for example Android-specific or iOS-specific.
  - These are beyond the scope of the book.

Setting Up a Dart Package

The Flutter SDK has a command line tool that enables you to quickly setup a dart package:

```
flutter create --template=package <name>
```

This doesn't create a large project, in fact it creates a project with two files:

Folder	Description
[root]	Root folder. Contains pubspec.yaml file, readme file.
android	As the name suggests, the folder contains all the Android-related files and code(s) for the package. This is where Android-specific settings and code resides. When building for Android, Flutter uses Gradle as the dependency manager.
ios	Similar to the 'android' folder, this folder contains the iOS related files and code(s) for the package. This is where iOS-specific settings and generated code resides. When building for iOS, Flutter uses Cocoapods as the dependency manager.
lib	This is where the application code resides. You should see a file 'main.dart', the entry point for the Flutter application. This is the file you select and run. You will add more files and subfolders into this folder.
test	This is where the unit testing code resides. You may add more files and subfolders into this folder.

Now you need to implement the code in your package, including writing unit tests.

Once you have completed code implementation, you need to add documentation.

Adding Documentation

- Add text to the README.md file.
    - This is the first place developers will look.
- Every time you make a change to the package, add text to the CHANGELOG.md file.
- Use the dart documentation tool to generate api documentation.
    - Change directory to the location of your package:

```
cd ~/dev/mypackage
```

    - Add an environment variable to tell the Tell the documentation tool where the Flutter SDK is (change to reflect where you placed it):
        - Mac/Unix

```
export FLUTTER_ROOT=~/dev/flutter
```

        - Windows

```
set FLUTTER_ROOT=~/dev/flutter (on Windows)
```

    - Run the dartdoc tool (comes as part of the Flutter SDK):
        - Mac/Unix

```
$FLUTTER_ROOT/bin/cache/dart-sdk/bin/dartdoc
```

        - Windows

```
%FLUTTER_ROOT%\bin\cache\dart-sdk\bin\dartdoc
```

Final Review

Review the publishing specification file pubspec.yaml.
Review the documentation, make sure it's all ready.

Do a Publish Dry-Run

This is good preparation for the real thing.
Running this command will check all the publishing pre-requisites without actually publishing.

```
flutter packages pub publish --dry-run
```

Publish

If everything went well in the publishing dry-run then do the actual publishing.

```
flutter packages pub publish
```

Further Reading

A lot of this information for this chapter came from here:
https://flutter.io/docs/development/packages-and-plugins/developing-packages

15.Introduction to Widgets

Introduction

The purpose of this chapter is to cover composition.

We mentioned composition earlier. It's how you compose your user interface from Widgets and each one is used to render a part of the UI. Widgets are built by composing other Widgets, which are themselves built out of progressively more basic Widgets. This is known as aggressive composability.

We also mentioned that your app ends up being a hierarchy of Widgets, a Widget Tree:
- Some widgets are parent widgets.
    - For example, Widget #2.
- , Some widgets are child widgets.
    - For example, Widget #3 and Widget #4 are children of Widget #2.

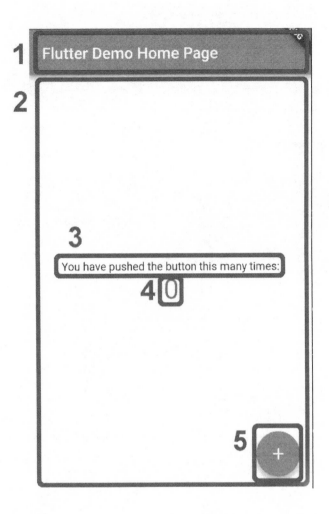

What Are Widgets?

Widgets are really configuration objects rather than graphic objects.

When you write a Widget, it is not just directly rendered on screen, it's not as direct as that. You write them and they *configure the user interface* then Flutter gets them rendered on screen.

User Interface: Material & Cupertino

Google has its own user interface design language called Material, which is used in all Google products. If you look at a program running on an Android phone, chances are that the UI will have that look and feel.

Material Design, According to Google

Material Design is a system for building bold and beautiful digital products. By uniting style, branding, interaction, and motion under a consistent set of principles and components, product teams can realize their greatest design potential.

Most Flutter Widgets Work with Material Design

As Flutter was written by Google, most Flutter widgets support the Material design look and feel. As most people are writing Flutter apps that implement the Material design look and feel, we are going to concentrate on the Flutter widgets that support that look and feel.

User Interface: Cupertino

Apple (based in Cupertono) is the other big player in mobile apps and it has its own user interface design language. Apple does not have a name for its design language (yet). Apple though has something called "Human Interface Guidelines". These guidelines ensure that all iOS applications adhere to Apple's design principles.

Flutter Includes iOS-Styled Widgets

Google has written many iOS-styled Widgets for Flutter developers so that they can emulate native iOS apps. I have not used these Widgets, so I am not going to spend any time on them. However, it is good to know that they exist and are available. Here is a list:

- CupertinoActionSheet
- CupertinoActivityIndicator
- CupertinoAlertDialog
- CupertinoButton
- CupertinoDatePicker
- CupertinoDialog
- CupertinoFullscreenDialogTransition
- CupertinoPageScaffold
- CupertinoPageTransition
- CupertinoPicker
- CupertinoPopupSurface
- CupertinoSegmentedControl
- CupertinoSlider
- CupertinoSwitch
- CupertinoNavigationBar
- CupertinoTabBar
- CupertinoTabScaffold

- CupertinoTabView
- CupertinoTextField
- CupertinoTimerPicker

Building Widgets

Flutter does the job of rendering the widgets on the screen for us (more on change detection & rendering later), but it needs *configuration information for the widget*: what color is it going to be, what is its border, does it contain other widgets....

Build Method

When it needs to know how to render a widget, Flutter calls the 'build' method in your widget. That method returns a Widget object that gives Flutter configuration information about the widget (and any child widgets that it may be composed of).

```
class MyApp extends StatelessWidget {
  // This widget is the root of your application.
  @override
  Widget build(BuildContext context) {
    return MaterialApp(
      title: 'Flutter Demo',
      home: Center(child:Text('Hello World'))
    );
  }
}
```

The 'build' method takes one argument, the BuildContext (more on that later) and returns a Widget object. That returned Widget object contains configuration data that tells Flutter that it needs to render a Material App widget with a title and some centered text.

Build Context

Earlier we mentioned that a widget can contain other widgets, in a tree structure, a hierarchy. This is often called a Widget Tree.

The first argument to the build' method of your Widget is the BuildContext. This gives your 'build' method information about the location of your Widget in the Widget Tree.
It may not seem useful at the moment but will come in very handy later on!

Widgets Have No Mutable State

Before we talk about state, we need to get our terminology straight. In this context, the words 'data' and 'state' mean the same thing – the 'data contained in the widget'.

Flutter Widget data is <u>immutable</u>.
Flutter Widgets can store data, but <u>that data doesn't change</u>.

Later on, we will introduce StatelessWidgets and StatefulWidgets.
It sounds like StatefulWidgets would have mutable data, but Stateful Widgets are only <u>associated</u> with a separate State object that stores the mutable data. They <u>don't store mutable data</u> themselves.

Not All Widgets Are Equal

Ok, we know that a Flutter user interface is composed of Widgets and that each widget has a build method that gives Flutter information on how render it. That's true for all widgets.

We also know that some Widgets can be composed of other widgets, for example a Form widget being composed of text and input boxes.

However, in addition to that, some widgets are <u>simple</u>, others are more <u>dynamic</u>. These dynamic Widgets, they can (appear to) store data (state) and they can <u>react</u> to things happening.

Further Reading

https://medium.com/fluttery/what-even-are-flutter-widgets-ce537a048a7d
https://medium.com/flutter-io/why-flutter-doesnt-use-oem-widgets-94746e812510

16.Stateless Widgets

Introduction

The purpose of this chapter is to introduce stateless widgets and how they can be used.

Not All Widgets Need to be Smart

If you look a user interface, it consists of many Widgets but not many of them have to be smart or interact with the user.

If you look at the default flutter application, there are several widgets but only in fact one Widget with any interactions with the user – the 'MyHomePage' Widget that has a counter that counts up when the user clicks on the floating button.

So, the rest of the widgets are used to display something, not interact with the user. That is what stateless widgets are for.

Minimum Code

Here is the minimum code you need for a Stateless Widget:

```
class EmptyWidget extends StatelessWidget {
  @override
  Widget build(BuildContext context) {
    return <Insert Some Widgets Here>;
  }
}
```

Creation

Stateless widgets are created by a parent widget in its 'build' method. They are given the information they need to do their job when they are created.

Stateless widgets receive arguments (information) from their parent widget in the 'build' method, which they store in final member variables.

Example

```
CarWidget("Bmw", "M3",
```

"https://media.ed.edmunds-media.com/bmw/m3/2018/oem/2018_bmw_m3_sedan_base_fq_oem_4_150.jpg"),

- 'Bmw'
  - o Stored in member variable 'make'.
- 'M3'
  - o Stored in member variable 'model'.
- "https://media.ed.edmunds-media.com/bmw/m3/2018/oem/2018_bmw_m3_sedan_base_fq_oem_4_150.jpg'
  - o Stored in member variable 'imageSrc'.

Rendering

The 'Build' Method

- Stateless Widgets generate their UI in their 'build' method, the result of which is rendered by Flutter.
- They can build their UI using values from their member variables, or from other sources.
- They cannot force themselves to re-render.

Values from Member Variables

When a Stateless Widget is asked to build a UI, it can use the values from these member variables to render the UI (probably with other Stateless Widget children). These values **don't** change, they are set in the constructor and that's it.

Example

The code below builds a UI to display textual info about a car (its make & model) using information from the member variables.

```
@override
Widget build(BuildContext context) {
  return Center(
    child: Column(children: <Widget>[
  Text(make),
  Text(model),
  Image.network(imageSrc)
  ]));
}
```

Values from Other Sources

When a Stateless Widget is asked to build a UI, it can use values from other sources, for example InheritedWidgets (which can store information).

Example

The code below builds a UI to say "Hi There", using information from another source (the 'Theme' inherited widget) to determine text color.

```
@override
Widget build(BuildContext context) {
return Center(
    child: Column(children: <Widget>[
    Text("Hello", style: Theme.of(context).textTheme.display1),
    Text("There", style: Theme.of(context).textTheme.display1)
])); 
}
```

When Does The 'Build' Method Execute?

- The first time the widget is inserted in the tree.
- When the widget's parent changes.
- When the values in another source change, for example when an InheritedWidget it depends on changes.

Lifecycle

These widgets are throw-away widgets, they don't hang around.
You create them in the 'build' method of another widget, and they are re-created every time that 'build' of the parent widget runs.

Exercise – 'first_stateless'

We start off by creating a basic app with Stateless Widgets.
Later on, we enhance it to make it look more attractive.

Step 1 – Create Default Flutter App

Follow the instructions in Generate Your First App
Leave the project open.

Step 2 – Replace Application Code

Replace contents of file 'main.dart' in folder 'lib' with the following:

```
import 'package:flutter/material.dart';

void main() => runApp(new MyApp());

class MyApp extends StatelessWidget {
```

```
  @override
  Widget build(BuildContext context) {
   return new MaterialApp(
    title: 'Flutter Demo',
    theme: new ThemeData(
     primarySwatch: Colors.blue,
    ),
    home: new MyHomePage(title: 'Cars'),
   );
  }
}

class MyHomePage extends StatelessWidget {
  MyHomePage({Key key, this.title}) : super(key: key);

  final String title;

  @override
  Widget build(BuildContext context) {
   return new Scaffold(
     appBar: new AppBar(
      title: new Text(this.title),
     ),
     body: new Column(children: <Widget>[
      CarWidget("Bmw", "M3",
        "https://media.ed.edmunds-
media.com/bmw/m3/2018/oem/2018_bmw_m3_sedan_base_fq_oem_4_150.jpg"),
      CarWidget("Nissan", "GTR",
        "https://media.ed.edmunds-media.com/nissan/gt-r/2018/oem/2018_nissan_gt-
r_coupe_nismo_fq_oem_1_150.jpg"),
      CarWidget("Nissan", "Sentra",
        "https://media.ed.edmunds-media.com/nissan/sentra/2017/oem/2017_nissan_sentra_sedan_sr-
turbo_fq_oem_4_150.jpg"),
     ]));
  }
}

class CarWidget extends StatelessWidget {
  CarWidget(this.make, this.model, this.imageSrc) : super();

  final String make;
  final String model;
  final String imageSrc;

  @override
  Widget build(BuildContext context) {
   return Center(
     child: Column(children: <Widget>[
    Text(make),
    Text(model),
    Image.network(imageSrc)
   ]));
  }
}
```

Step 3 – Open Emulator & Run

Follow the instructions in 'Open Emulator & Run Your First App' to run the app.
You should get something like the following:

Summary So Far

- The MyApp & Material App Widgets are unchanged.
- The MyHomePage Widget is unchanged except for the build method, which now contains a Column Widget (see below) containing 3 Car Widgets. Note how we pass the information to each Car Widget in the constructor.
- We have a new StatelessWidget called CarWidget. It accepts data in the constructor. In the build method it returns a Center Widget (see below) that contains a Column Widget (see below) that contains 3 widgets: a Text Widget for the make, another for the model and an Image Widget for the image.
- Widgets used (more info about widgets in Chapter 'Flutter Widgets').
  - Column Widget
    - Layout Widget that displays its children vertically.
  - Center Widget
    - Layout Widget that centers its child.
  - Text Widget
    - Displays text.
  - Image Widget
    - Displays an image.

Step 4 – Add Some Padding

Now let's add some more vertical padding between each car to spread them out a bit. This is achieved by wrapping the existing Center Widget in the 'build' method in the CarWidget with a Padding Widget. Note how the Padding constructor requires a 'padding' argument and a 'child' argument.

Change the 'build' method in the CarWidget to the following:

```
@override
Widget build(BuildContext context) {
  return Padding(
    padding: EdgeInsets.all(20.0),
    child: Center(
      child: Column(children: <Widget>[
      Text(make),
      Text(model),
      Image.network(imageSrc)
    ]))) ;
}
```

Now the cars are more spaced out.

Step 5 – Add Scrolling

Depending on how your emulator is setup, you may see Chevrons at the bottom. This is because you have run out of vertical space.

The remedy for this is simple. Edit the MyHomePage Widget and change the Column (the one that contains the CarWidgets) to a ListView.

```
@override
 Widget build(BuildContext context) {
  return new Scaffold(
    appBar: new AppBar(
     title: new Text(this.title),
    ),
    body: new ListView(children: <Widget>[
     CarWidget("Bmw", "M3",
        "https://media.ed.edmunds-
media.com/bmw/m3/2018/oem/2018_bmw_m3_sedan_base_fq_oem_4_150.jpg"),
     CarWidget("Nissan", "GTR",
        "https://media.ed.edmunds-media.com/nissan/gt-r/2018/oem/2018_nissan_gt-
r_coupe_nismo_fq_oem_1_150.jpg"),
     CarWidget("Nissan", "Sentra",
        "https://media.ed.edmunds-media.com/nissan/sentra/2017/oem/2017_nissan_sentra_sedan_sr-
turbo_fq_oem_4_150.jpg"),
    ]));
 }
```

Step 6 – Add Border

Let's add a border around each car. This is achieved by wrapping the existing Center Widget in the 'build' method in the CarWidget with a Container Widget which has a border decoration and padding.

```
@override
 Widget build(BuildContext context) {
  return Padding(
    padding: EdgeInsets.all(20.0),
    child: Container(
     decoration: BoxDecoration(border: Border.all()),
     padding: EdgeInsets.all(20.0),
     child: Center(
        child: Column(children: <Widget>[
       Text(make),
       Text(model),
```

```
        Image.network(imageSrc)
    ])))));
}
```

Looks much nicer now:

Step 7 – Final Touch

As a final touch, lets:
- Combine the make and model together using string interpolation.
- Change the make and model text style to be bigger.
- Add some padding between text and image.
  - Wrap image with padding at top.

```
@override
Widget build(BuildContext context) {
  return Padding(
    padding: EdgeInsets.all(20.0),
    child: Container(
      decoration: BoxDecoration(border: Border.all()),
      padding: EdgeInsets.all(20.0),
      child: Center(
        child: Column(children: <Widget>[
        Text('${make} ${model}', style: TextStyle(fontSize: 24.0)),
        Padding(
            padding: EdgeInsets.only(top: 20.0),
            child: Image.network(imageSrc))
      ]))));
```

}

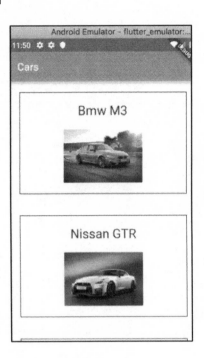

Example – 'stateless_widget_rebuild'

Optional

You don't have to look at this example code at this point as it can get complicated. You might want to come back to this later once you want to look into StatelessWidgets in more detail. So, feel free to skip this and go onto the next chapter.

Purpose

I wrote this example to validate some of what I had written in this chapter was correct. I wanted to prove that a Stateless Widget can be re-rendered (in the 'build' method) when a parent Widget changes, <u>without it being thrown away and reconstructed</u>. This is contrary to some information I had read online that says that Stateless Widgets are only built once.

In this example, this is proven by the 'MyApp' Stateless Widget. I added console logging to the constructor and the 'build' method to see when it is constructed and re-rendered (in the 'build' method).

This app is similar to the default Flutter App except it has a button on the toolbar (top right) to change the theme's brightness. When you hit the toolbar, it updates a model which is part of a parent Widget higher up in the Widget Tree. This doesn't force the 'MyApp' Stateless Widget to be reconstructed but it <u>does</u> force it to invoke the 'build' method to rebuild the UI darker or lighter, as you can see from the Console Output below.

Console Output

Startup

```
I/flutter ( 5858): MyApp - constructor
I/flutter ( 5858): MyApp – build
```

Hit Button on Toolbar

```
I/flutter ( 5858): MyApp - build
```

Source Code

```
import 'package:flutter/material.dart';

void main() => runApp(ModelBinding<ThemeModel>(
   initialModel: ThemeModel(true), child: new MyApp()));

class ThemeModel {
 ThemeModel(this._dark);

  bool _dark = true;

  bool get dark => _dark;

  @override
  bool operator ==(Object other) {
   if (identical(this, other)) {
     return true;
```

```
    } else if (other.runtimeType != runtimeType) {
      return false;
    } else {
      final ThemeModel otherModel = other;
      return dark == otherModel.dark;
    }
  }

  int get hashCode => dark.hashCode;
}

class _ModelBindingScope<T> extends InheritedWidget {
  const _ModelBindingScope({Key key, this.modelBindingState, Widget child})
    : super(key: key, child: child);

  final _ModelBindingState<T> modelBindingState;

  @override
  bool updateShouldNotify(_ModelBindingScope oldWidget) => true;
}

class ModelBinding<T> extends StatefulWidget {
  ModelBinding({Key key, @required this.initialModel, this.child})
    : assert(initialModel != null),
      super(key: key);

  final T initialModel;
  final Widget child;

  _ModelBindingState<T> createState() => _ModelBindingState<T>();

  static Type _typeOf<T>() => T;

  static T of<T>(BuildContext context) {
    final Type scopeType = _typeOf<_ModelBindingScope<T>>();
    final _ModelBindingScope<T> scope =
      context.inheritFromWidgetOfExactType(scopeType);
    return scope.modelBindingState.currentModel;
  }

  static void update<T>(BuildContext context, T newModel) {
    final Type scopeType = _typeOf<_ModelBindingScope<T>>();
    final _ModelBindingScope<dynamic> scope =
      context.inheritFromWidgetOfExactType(scopeType);
    scope.modelBindingState.updateModel(newModel);
  }
}

class _ModelBindingState<T> extends State<ModelBinding<T>> {
  T currentModel;

  @override
  void initState() {
    super.initState();
    currentModel = widget.initialModel;
  }

  void updateModel(T newModel) {
```

```
    if (newModel != currentModel) {
      setState(() {
        currentModel = newModel;
      });
    }
  }

  @override
  Widget build(BuildContext context) {
    return _ModelBindingScope<T>(
      modelBindingState: this,
      child: widget.child,
    );
  }
}

class MyApp extends StatelessWidget {
  MyApp() {
    debugPrint('MyApp - constructor');
  }

  @override
  Widget build(BuildContext context) {
    debugPrint('MyApp - build');
    ThemeModel model = ModelBinding.of(context);
    return MaterialApp(
      title: 'Flutter Demo',
      theme: ThemeData(
          primarySwatch: Colors.blue,
          brightness: model.dark ? Brightness.dark : Brightness.light),
      home: MyHomePage(title: 'Flutter Demo Home Page'),
    );
  }
}

class MyHomePage extends StatefulWidget {
  MyHomePage({Key key, this.title}) : super(key: key);
  final String title;
  @override
  _MyHomePageState createState() => _MyHomePageState();
}

class _MyHomePageState extends State<MyHomePage> {
  int _counter = 0;
  void _incrementCounter() {
    setState(() {
      _counter++;
    });
  }

  @override
  Widget build(BuildContext context) {
    ThemeModel model = ModelBinding.of(context);
    return Scaffold(
      appBar: AppBar(
        title: Text(widget.title),
        actions: <Widget>[
          IconButton(
```

```
      icon: const Icon(Icons.rotate_right),
      tooltip: 'Brightness',
      onPressed: () {
        setState(() {
          ModelBinding.update(context, new ThemeModel(!model.dark));
        });
      },
    )
  ],
),
body: Center(
  child: Column(
    mainAxisAlignment: MainAxisAlignment.center,
    children: <Widget>[
      Text(
        'You have pushed the button this many times:',
      ),
      Text(
        '$_counter',
        style: Theme.of(context).textTheme.display1,
      ),
    ],
  ),
),
floatingActionButton: FloatingActionButton(
  onPressed: _incrementCounter,
  tooltip: 'Increment',
  child: Icon(Icons.add),
), // This trailing comma makes auto-formatting nicer for build methods.
  );
}
}
```

17.Stateful Widgets

Introduction

The purpose of this chapter is to introduce stateful widgets and how they can be used.

Some Widgets Need to be Smart

Stateful widgets are useful when the part of the user interface you are describing can change dynamically. User interfaces need to respond to a variety of things:

- The user doing something in the user interface.
- Receiving data from another computer.
- Time passing.

This is what Stateful Widgets are for. They store data (state) in an associated State class and they can respond when that data (state) changes as the result of the user doing something.

Minimum Code

Here is the minimum code you need for a Stateful Widget:

```
class EmptyWidget extends StatefulWidget {
  EmptyWidget({Key key}) : super(key: key);

  @override
  _EmptyWidgetState createState() => _EmptyWidgetState();
}

class _EmptyWidgetState extends State<EmptyWidget> {

  @override
  Widget build(BuildContext context) {
    return <Insert Some Widgets Here>;
  }
}
```

Two Classes

If you look at the minimum code above you will see that a Stateful Widget is composed of two classes, not one. You have one class that extends StatefulWidget, another that extends State.

Class #1 – the class that extends StatefulWidget

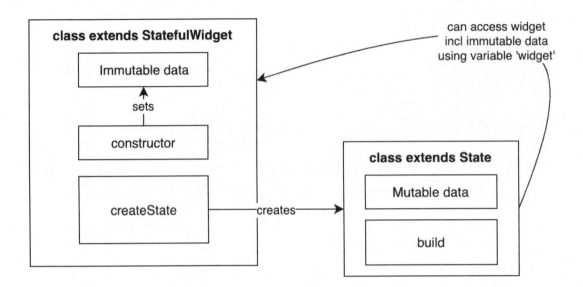

- This is a class that is used to create the State object, class #2 in its 'createState' method.
- An instance of this class is shorter-lived than that for the State object, class #2
- The data in this class cannot change (immutable).
  - It is final and passed in through the constructor, same as for a StatelessWidget.
  - This class is thrown away and replaced when the data needs to change and a new Widget is constructed.

Class #2 – the class that extends State

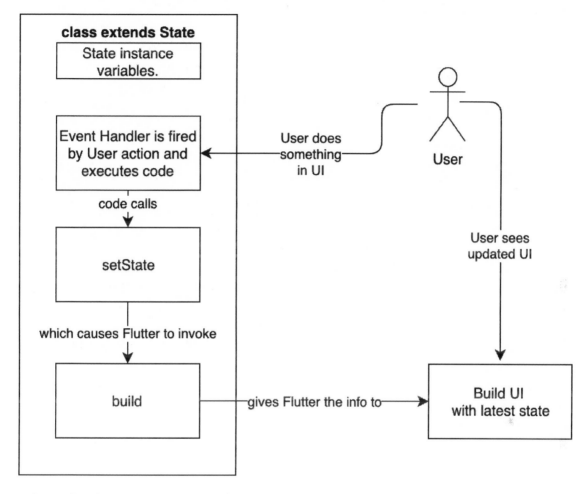

- This is the class that does most of the work.
  - It holds the data that can change (mutable).
  - It builds the UI using the 'build' method.
  - It can respond to events, like the user clicking on a button.
- An instance of this class is longer-lived than that for the StatefulWidget, class #1.
- The data in this class can change.
  - Change the data within a lambda within the 'setState' method and this will ensure the UI is rebuilt.
  - The StatefulWidget class #1 can be thrown away and replaced and this state is then attached to the replacement.
- Code in this class can refer to class #1 using the 'widget' variable.

Creation

When you create a Stateful Widget the following happens.

1. The instance of class #1 (the class that extends StatefulWidget) is constructed.
2. The lifecycle method 'createState' of class #1 (the class that extends StatefulWidget) is invoked by Flutter to create the instance of class #2 (the class that extends State).
3. The instance of class #2 (the class that extends State) is constructed.
4. The method 'build' of the State class (created in 3) is invoked to build the UI.

Rendering

The 'Build' Method

- Stateful Widgets generate their UI in their 'build' method, the result of which is rendered by Flutter.
  - That 'build' method resides in class #2, the class that extends State.
- They can build their UI using values from their member variables, other sources.
- They **can** force themselves to re-render.
- When the Stateful Widget method 'setState' is called in the State class, this invokes regeneration of the UI because it causes Flutter to invoke the 'build' method.
  - If you look at the default Flutter application, you will see this method to increment the counter. Note how it updates the instance variable '_counter' in a lambda inside the 'setState' method. This ensures that the UI will be rebuilt with the new counter value.

```
void _incrementCounter() {
  setState(() {
    _counter++;
  });
}
```

LifeCycle Methods

Class #1 – the class that extends StatefulWidget

createState()

Flutter calls this method. You add code here to an instance of the State class (class #2).

Class #2 – the class that extends State

build()

Flutter calls this method when the Widget has to be re-rendered (rebuilt).

initState()

Flutter calls this method when the widget is created, after the constructor. This is a great place to add animation code to setup your AnimationController. See the Animation chapter for more info.

Example

```
@override
void initState() {
  super.initState();
  animation = new AnimationController(
    vsync: this,
    duration: new Duration(seconds: 3),
  );
  animation.addListener(() {
    this.setState(() {});
  });
}
```

didChangeDependencies ()

Flutter calls this method when Flutter detects that the data from another source has changed, possibly affecting the UI and causing a call to 'build'. This could be caused by some data changing in an InheritedWidget higher up in the Widget tree. This not fired when 'setState()' is fired to rebuild the UI.

didUpdateWidget()

Flutter calls this method when it has to throw away the StatefulWidget (class #1) and replace it with another StatefulWidget (class #1) of the same type but with different data, which is then associated with State (class #2). Now that the State is associated with a different StatefulWidget.

setState()

You call this method to set state in the Widget and ensure it rebuilds the UI using the 'build' method.

deactivate()

Rarely used. Flutter calls this method when State is removed from the tree, but it might be reinserted before the current frame change is finished. This method exists basically because State objects can be moved from one point in a tree to another.

dispose()

Flutter calls this method when 'dispose()' is called when the State object is destroyed. This is a great place to add code to dispose of instance variables, such as AnimationControllers:

```
@override
```

```
void dispose() {
  animation.dispose();
  super.dispose();
}
```

More Reading

https://www.didierboelens.com/2018/06/widget---state---context---inheritedwidget/

Example – 'stateful_widget_flowers'

Optional

You don't have to look at this example code at this point as it can get complicated. You might want to come back to this later once you want to look into StatefulWidgets in more detail. So, feel free to skip this and go onto the next chapter.

App Purpose

This app allows the user to view flowers then blur them.
There is a button on the top right which switches between 'dark' mode and 'bright' mode.

The point of the app is not to view flowers but to let you:

- See the logs when you run the app, so that you can figure out how Stateful Widgets work and when their lifecycle methods are fired.

- Run the code yourself, put breakpoints in and figure out how Stateful Widgets work with their lifecycle events.

App Widgets

This app has two StatefulWidgets:

- AppWidget
  It is the main app and it contains the FlowerWidget.
  It has boolean state over the brightness on/off.

- FlowerWidget
  It displays the flower in a frame with a title bar, a toolbar and an action button.
  It has state over the amount of blurring.

Start App

When you start the app, you will see the following logs:

```
I/flutter (23225): AppWidget - constructor - 261774211
I/flutter (23225): AppWidget - createState - 261774211
I/flutter (23225): _AppWidgetState - build - 160341789
```

```
I/flutter (23225): FlowerWidget - constructor - 1026133623
I/flutter (23225): FlowerWidget - createState - 1026133623
I/flutter (23225): _FlowerWidgetState - constructor - 514586671
I/flutter (23225): _FlowerWidgetState - initState - 514586671
I/flutter (23225): _FlowerWidgetState - didChangeDependencies - 514586671
I/flutter (23225): _FlowerWidgetState - build – 514586671
```

As you can see it creates each Widget first then creates the state using the 'createState' method. Note that 'didChangeDependencies' was invoked because the Theme state was set when the _AppWidgetState was built for the first time. The Theme is an InheritedWidget and used by the _FlowerWidgetState when it builds the UI.

Change the Flower

When you change the flower (on the toolbar), you will see the following UI change occur:

changes to ->

with the following logs:

```
I/flutter (23700): _AppWidgetState - build - 543277124
I/flutter (23700): FlowerWidget - constructor - 814857920
I/flutter (23700): _FlowerWidgetState - didUpdateWidget - 57066142
I/flutter (23700): _FlowerWidgetState - build - 57066142
I/flutter (23700): _FlowerWidgetState - didChangeDependencies - 57066142
I/flutter (23700): _FlowerWidgetState - build - 57066142
I/flutter (23700): _FlowerWidgetState - didChangeDependencies - 57066142
I/flutter (23700): _FlowerWidgetState - build – 57066142
```

Note that this changes the 'bright' state of the AppWidget. This causes the AppWidget UI to be rebuilt with a different theme brightness and a different flower image. The 'build' method in the _AppWidgetState creates a new FlowerWidget, because its constructor value 'imageSrc' has changed. That results in Flutter invoking the 'didUpdateWidget' to indicate that the State is now associated with a different StatefulWidget. Flutter also invokes 'didChangeDependencies' because the Flower object is dependent on the Theme InheritedWidget and that was changed (the theme brightness was changed).

Add Blur

When hit the floating button at the bottom, you will see the flower image blur and you will see the following log:

```
I/flutter (23700): _FlowerWidgetState - build – 57066142
```

Note that Flutter invokes the 'build' in the FlowerWidget State object (see the code below) because the code calls the 'setState' method. No other lifecycle methods are invoked because that code does not affect another other widgets.

```
void _blurMore() {
  setState(() {
    _blur += 5.0;
  });
}
```

Source Code

```
import 'dart:ui';

import 'package:flutter/foundation.dart';
import 'package:flutter/material.dart';

void main() => runApp(AppWidget());

class AppWidget extends StatefulWidget {
  AppWidget() {
    debugPrint("AppWidget - constructor - " + hashCode.toString());
  }

  @override
  _AppWidgetState createState() {
    debugPrint("AppWidget - createState - " + hashCode.toString());
    return _AppWidgetState();
  }
}

class _AppWidgetState extends State<AppWidget> {
  bool _bright = false;

  _brightnessCallback() {
    setState(() => _bright = !_bright);
  }

  @override
  Widget build(BuildContext context) {
    debugPrint("_AppWidgetState - build - " + hashCode.toString());
    return MaterialApp(
      title: 'Flutter Demo',
      theme: ThemeData(
```

```
          primarySwatch: Colors.blue,
          brightness: _bright ? Brightness.light : Brightness.dark),
        home: FlowerWidget(
          imageSrc: _bright
            ? "https://www.viewbug.com/media/mediafiles/" +
              "2015/07/05/56234977_large1300.jpg"
            : "https://images.unsplash.com/" +
              "photo-1531603071569-0dd65ad72d53?ixlib=rb-1.2.1&ixid=" +
              "eyJhcHBfaWQiOjEyMDd9&w=1000&q=80",
          brightnessCallback: _brightnessCallback));
  }
}

class FlowerWidget extends StatefulWidget {
  final String imageSrc;
  final VoidCallback brightnessCallback;

  FlowerWidget({Key key, this.imageSrc, this.brightnessCallback})
    : super(key: key) {
    debugPrint("FlowerWidget - constructor - " + hashCode.toString());
  }

  @override
  _FlowerWidgetState createState() {
    debugPrint("FlowerWidget - createState - " + hashCode.toString());
    return _FlowerWidgetState();
  }
}

class _FlowerWidgetState extends State<FlowerWidget> {
  double _blur = 0;

  _FlowerWidgetState() {
    debugPrint("_FlowerWidgetState - constructor - " + hashCode.toString());
  }

  @override
  initState() {
    debugPrint("_FlowerWidgetState - initState - " + hashCode.toString());
  }

  /**
   * Fired when Flutter detects that the data from another source has changed,
   * possibly affecting the UI and causing a call to 'build'.
   * In this case it is when the Theme changes (its an InheritedWidget).
   */
  @override
  void didChangeDependencies() {
    debugPrint(
      "_FlowerWidgetState - didChangeDependencies - " + hashCode.toString());
  }

  @override
  /**
   * Fired when the widget is reconstructed as its widget data has changed,
   * In this case it is when a new FlowerWidget is created with a different
   * imageSrc.
   */
```

```
void didUpdateWidget(Widget oldWidget) {
  debugPrint("_FlowerWidgetState - didUpdateWidget - " + hashCode.toString());

  // The flower image has changed, so reset the blur.
  _blur = 0;
}

void _blurMore() {
  setState(() {
    _blur += 5.0;
  });
}

@override
Widget build(BuildContext context) {
  debugPrint("_FlowerWidgetState - build - " + hashCode.toString());
  return Scaffold(
    appBar: AppBar(title: Text("Flower"), actions: [
      new IconButton(
          icon: new Icon(Icons.refresh),
          onPressed: () {
            widget.brightnessCallback();
          })
    ]),
    body: new Container(
      decoration: new BoxDecoration(
          // dependency on inherited widget - start
          color: Theme.of(context).backgroundColor,
          // dependency on inherited widget - end
          image: new DecorationImage(
              // dependency on data from widget - start
              image: NetworkImage(widget.imageSrc),
              // dependency on data from widget - end
              fit: BoxFit.cover)),
      child: new BackdropFilter(
        // dependency on state data - start
        filter: new ImageFilter.blur(sigmaX: _blur, sigmaY: _blur),
        // dependency on state data - end
        child: new Container(
          decoration: new BoxDecoration(color: Colors.white.withOpacity(0.0)),
        ),
      ),
    ),
    floatingActionButton: FloatingActionButton(
      onPressed: _blurMore,
      tooltip: 'Blur More',
      child: Icon(Icons.add),
    ),
  );
}
}
```

18. Basic Material Widgets

Introduction

We are going to spend the next few chapters going over Flutter widgets and examples of their use. Reading the example source code may be difficult at this stage because we have not covered all of the techniques used in the examples, for example State Management. However, if you keep going it will all make sense eventually.

The purpose of this chapter is to introduce some of the more commonly-used Flutter Widgets along with some example code that uses them.

Text

The Text widget displays a string of text with single style. Multiple line texts are allowed.
To style the entire text in one way, specify a 'style' property in the constructor of the Text Widget.
To style sections of the text, use child TextSpans (see example below).

Example – 'text'

Every time you hit the '+' a new word comes out in a different color.

Source Code

```dart
import 'package:flutter/material.dart';

void main() => runApp(new MyApp());

class MyApp extends StatelessWidget {
  // This widget is the root of your application.
  @override
  Widget build(BuildContext context) {
    return new MaterialApp(
      title: 'Flutter Styled Text Demo',
      theme: new ThemeData(
        primarySwatch: Colors.blue,
      ),
      home: new MyHomePage(),
    );
  }
}

class TextBlock {
  final Color _color;
  final String _text;

  TextBlock(this._color, this._text);

  String get text => _text;

  Color get color => _color;
}

class MyHomePage extends StatefulWidget {
  MyHomePage({Key key}) : super(key: key);

  @override
  _MyHomePageState createState() => new _MyHomePageState();
}

class _MyHomePageState extends State<MyHomePage> {
  int _index = 0;
  final List<TextBlock> textBlocks = [
    TextBlock(Colors.red, 'every'),
    TextBlock(Colors.redAccent, ' schoolboy'),
    TextBlock(Colors.green, '\nknows'),
    TextBlock(Colors.greenAccent, ' who'),
    TextBlock(Colors.blue, '\nimprisoned'),
    TextBlock(Colors.blueAccent, '\nMontezuma')
  ];

  void _incrementCounter() {
    setState(() {
      if (_index < textBlocks.length) {
        _index++;
      }
    });
  }

  @override
```

```
Widget build(BuildContext context) {
  final List<TextSpan> textSpans = List<TextSpan>();
  for (var i = 0; i < _index; i++) {
    TextBlock textBlock = textBlocks[i];
    textSpans.add(TextSpan(
        text: textBlock.text,
        style: TextStyle(color: textBlock.color, fontSize: 32.0)));
  }
  return new Scaffold(
    body: new Center(
      child: new Column(
        mainAxisAlignment: MainAxisAlignment.center,
        children: <Widget>[Text.rich(TextSpan(children: textSpans))],
      ),
    ),
    floatingActionButton: new FloatingActionButton(
      onPressed: _incrementCounter,
      tooltip: 'Increment',
      child: new Icon(Icons.note_add),
    ), // This trailing comma makes auto-formatting nicer for build methods.
  );
}
}
```

Image

Introduction

This is a widget used to show an image. When displaying an image, you specify the image source in the constructor:

- image provider
- asset
- network
- file
- memory

The downside of the Image widget is the lack of placeholder (for example 'loading…' text). It shows nothing then shows the image. This doesn't really cut it, so you need to use the FadeInImage to wrap this Widget.

The Flutter Image Widget has a fit property will enables developers to determine how the image graphics are fitted into the available area. This fit property can really change how the image is presented! See the BoxFit class documentation here:
https://docs.flutter.io/flutter/painting/BoxFit-class.html

Exercise – 'loading_image'

Load a large into an app. Display an image placeholder while it loads.

Step 1 – Create Default Flutter App

Follow the instructions in <u>Generate Your First App</u>
Leave project open.

Step 2 – Get Loading Image

- Download: <u>https://digitalsynopsis.com/wp-content/uploads/2016/06/loading-animations-preloader-gifs-ui-ux-effects-10.gif</u>
- Create new folder 'assets' in your project.
- Rename image file to 'loading.gif'.
- Copy image file into 'assets' folder in your project.

Step 3 – Include the Loading Image in Your Project as an Asset

When you add a reference to an asset (an image or something similar) in the pubspec file, Flutter ensures that it is bundled into the app when it builds. So no round trip will be required to load the image.

- Edit the pubspec.yaml file and change the lines below from:

```
# To add assets to your application, add an assets section, like this:
```

```
# assets:
#  - images/a_dot_burr.jpeg
#  - images/a_dot_ham.jpeg
```

- **to:**

```
assets:
 - assets/loading.gif
```

Step 4 – Replace Application Code

Replace contents of file 'main.dart' in folder 'lib' with the following:

```dart
import 'package:flutter/material.dart';

void main() => runApp(new LoadingImageApp());

class LoadingImageApp extends StatelessWidget {
  // This widget is the root of your application.
  @override
  Widget build(BuildContext context) {
    return new MaterialApp(
      title: 'Image',
      theme: new ThemeData(
        primarySwatch: Colors.blue,
      ),
      home: new HomeWidget(),
    );
  }
}

class HomeWidget extends StatelessWidget {
  HomeWidget({Key key}) : super(key: key);

  @override
  Widget build(BuildContext context) {
    return new Scaffold(
      appBar: new AppBar(
        title: new Text("Image"),
      ),
      body: new Center(
        child: FadeInImage.assetNetwork(
        placeholder: 'assets/loading.gif',
        image:
          'http://archivision.com/educational/samples/files/1A2-F-P-I-2-C1_L.jpg',
      )));
  }
}
```

Step 5 – Open Emulator & Run

Follow the instructions in Open Android Emulator & Run Your First App
When you run this example, you see a loading icon (which very quickly goes away) then a computer.

Icon

Introduction

The icon widget allows you to quickly build icon widgets using a pre-built list of material icons, available in the Icons class. You can specify the icon size and color.

Example - 'icon'

This app simply displays 3 icons with different sizes and colors.

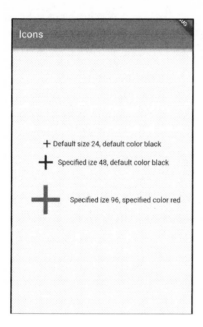

Source Code

```
import 'package:flutter/material.dart';

void main() => runApp(new IconApp());

class IconApp extends StatelessWidget {
  @override
  Widget build(BuildContext context) {
    return new MaterialApp(
      title: 'Flutter Demo',
      theme: new ThemeData(
        primarySwatch: Colors.blue,
      ),
      home: new HomeWidget(),
    );
  }
}

class HomeWidget extends StatelessWidget {
```

```
@override
Widget build(BuildContext context) {
  Row row1 = Row(
    mainAxisAlignment: MainAxisAlignment.center, // center horizontally
    children: <Widget>[
      const Icon(Icons.add),
      const Text("Default size 24, default color black")
    ]);
  Row row2 =
    Row(mainAxisAlignment: MainAxisAlignment.center, // center horizontally
      children: <Widget>[
      const Icon(Icons.add, size: 48.0),
      const Text("Specified ize 48, default color black")
    ]);
  Row row3 =
    Row(mainAxisAlignment: MainAxisAlignment.center, // center horizontally
      children: <Widget>[
      const Icon(Icons.add, size: 96.0, color: Colors.red),
      const Text("Specified size 96, specified color red")
    ]);
  return new Scaffold(
    appBar: new AppBar(title: const Text("Icons")),
    body: new Column(
      mainAxisAlignment: MainAxisAlignment.center, // center vertically
      children: <Widget>[row1, row2, row3]));
  }
}
```

Further Reading

You can use tools available on the internet to build your own icon library, with constants available (similar to the Icons constants). Here is a link to the article:
https://steemit.com/utopian-io/@psyanite/how-to-use-custom-icons-in-flutter

Buttons

Introduction

Flutter offers a bunch of different button widgets:
- FlatButton - material
    - Useful for buttons that don't need a border, for example those that are already in a toolbar or menu (something that provides a ui context).
    - Flashes background when clicked on.
- RaisedButton - Material
    - Useful if you want a button made more visible in a 'sea of content'.
    - Flashes shadow when clicked on.
- IconButton - material

- o Flashes background circle when clicked on.
- OutlineButton - material
  - o A bordered button whose elevation increases and whose background becomes opaque when the button is pressed.
  - o Flashes background and border when clicked on.
- DropdownButton - material
  - o Used for selecting from a list of items
  - o Shows menu when clicked on.
  - o You can supply existing value as constructor argument.
- BackButton
  - o An IconButton setup for use as a back button.
  - o Flashes background circle when clicked on.
- CloseButton
  - o An IconButton setup for use as a close button to close modals (or any other closeable content).
  - o Flashes background circle when clicked on.
- FloatingActionButton - material
  - o A button that hovers in a layer above content.
  - o Advisable that you only ever use one at a time.
  - o You can change background and foreground colors.
  - o You can use the 'extended' named constructor to make a larger, wider Floating Action Button.

```
FloatingActionButton.extended(
  onPressed: () {},
  icon: Icon(Icons.save),
  label: Text("Save"),
)
```

- o Flashes when clicked on.

Enabling

You can enable or disable buttons using the 'onPressed' constructor argument.
Setting it to null disables the button, otherwise it is enabled.
The code below uses a ternary operator for this.

```
OutlineButton(
onPressed: _enabled ? _onPressed : null,
  child: const Text('Register'),
)
```

Example – 'buttons'

This app displays different types of buttons so you can see what they look like.

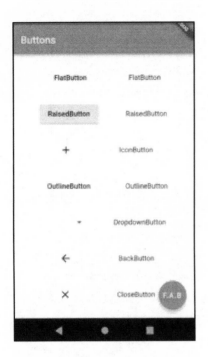

Source Code

```
import 'package:flutter/material.dart';

void main() => runApp(new ButtonApp());

class ButtonApp extends StatelessWidget {
  // This widget is the root of your application.
  @override
  Widget build(BuildContext context) {
    return new MaterialApp(
      title: 'Flutter Demo',
      theme: new ThemeData(
        primarySwatch: Colors.blue,
      ),
      home: const HomeWidget(),
    );
  }
}

class HomeWidget extends StatelessWidget {
  const HomeWidget({Key key}) : super(key: key);

  @override
  Widget build(BuildContext context) {
    Row flatButtonRow = Row(
      mainAxisAlignment: MainAxisAlignment.spaceEvenly,
      children: <Widget>[
        FlatButton(
          onPressed: () => debugPrint('FlatButton pressed'),
          child: Text('FlatButton')),
        const Text("FlatButton")
      ]);
    Row raisedButtonRow = Row(
```

```
      mainAxisAlignment: MainAxisAlignment.spaceEvenly,
      children: <Widget>[
        RaisedButton(
          onPressed: () => debugPrint('RaisedButton pressed'),
          child: Text('RaisedButton')),
        const Text("RaisedButton")
      ]);
  Row iconButtonRow = Row(
      mainAxisAlignment: MainAxisAlignment.spaceEvenly,
      children: <Widget>[
        IconButton(
          icon: Icon(Icons.add),
          onPressed: () => debugPrint('IconButton pressed')),
        const Text("IconButton")
      ]);
  Row outlineButtonRow = Row(
      mainAxisAlignment: MainAxisAlignment.spaceEvenly,
      children: <Widget>[
        OutlineButton(
          onPressed: () => debugPrint('OutlineButton pressed'),
          child: Text("OutlineButton")),
        const Text("OutlineButton")
      ]);
  Row dropdownButtonRow = Row(
      mainAxisAlignment: MainAxisAlignment.spaceEvenly,
      children: <Widget>[
        new DropdownButton<String>(
          items: <String>['Mens', 'Womans'].map((String value) {
            return new DropdownMenuItem<String>(
              value: value,
              child: Text(value),
            );
          }).toList(),
          onChanged: (value) => debugPrint('Changed: ${value}')),
        const Text("DropdownButton")
      ]);

  Row backButtonRow = Row(
      mainAxisAlignment: MainAxisAlignment.spaceEvenly,
      children: <Widget>[BackButton(), const Text("BackButton")]);

  Row closeButtonRow = Row(
      mainAxisAlignment: MainAxisAlignment.spaceEvenly,
      children: <Widget>[CloseButton(), const Text("CloseButton")]);

  return new Scaffold(
    appBar: new AppBar(
      title: const Text("Buttons"),
    ),
    body: new Center(
      child: new Column(
        mainAxisAlignment: MainAxisAlignment.spaceEvenly,
        children: <Widget>[
          flatButtonRow,
          raisedButtonRow,
          iconButtonRow,
          outlineButtonRow,
          dropdownButtonRow,
```

```
        backButtonRow,
        closeButtonRow,
      ],
    ),
  ),
  floatingActionButton: FloatingActionButton(
      onPressed: () => debugPrint('FloatingActionButton pressed'),
      child: const Text("F.A.B")),
  );
  }
}
```

19. Multi-Child Layout Widgets

Introduction

Layout Widgets are used that affect the positioning and presentation of their child widgets.

There are two main kinds of Layout Widgets: Single-Child Layout Widgets and Multi-Child Layout Widgets.

The purpose of this chapter is to cover Multi-Child Layout Widgets.

Multi-Child Layout Widgets

Multi-Child Layout Widgets and they are used to determine what UI elements go where - where the elements of the user interface are going to be presented. They are very important as you can break almost 90% of the layout designs into Rows and Columns.

Obviously, you can combine/nest these Widgets. You could have a Row that contains 2 Columns that contains 3 Custom Widgets. Then each Custom Widget could contain a Row of an Icon Widget, a Text Widget then a Button.

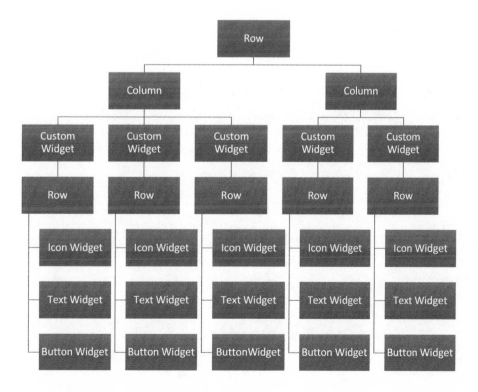

These layouts work really well when they are used to layout components to which you already know the size, such as buttons, textboxes etc. They also work when you have widgets that don't overflow the screen space available and you expand them to use all the space available up. When you need to use up extra screen space you can use the MainAxisAlignment property to space child Widgets out or use Expanded Widgets to expand those child Widgets.

These layouts don't work well when they are used to layout components with very dynamic sizing requirements, for example Text widgets that are generated from user data, with some wide texts, some narrow texts. In this case, you are probably better off using the Table. It can handle the text overflows without any additional complications.

When using these Widgets, you may sometimes encounter the times when the child Widgets don't fit in the screen space. This often results in visible chevrons (the yellow and black stripes) such as you see below, along with a console error:

Column

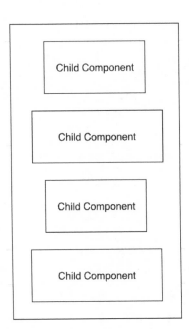

- Enables you to lay out Widgets Vertically.
- Use the MainAxisAlignment to specify vertical layout.
- Use the CrossAxisAlignment to specify horizontal alignment.
- Will try to take up as much space as it needs for children but no more.
  - To use all available space, wrap in Expanded widget.
- Does not provide scrolling.
  - If you run out of vertical space, you may get an error.
  - If you need to include scrolling, use a ListView instead.

Spacing Out Children Using MainAxisAlignment

The MainAxisAlignment widget allows you to determine how the Widgets are laid out vertically. Take a look at the example below to see how this affects the horizontal layouts.

Example – 'column_spaced_evenly'

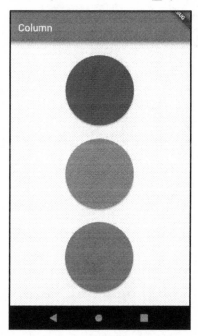

Source Code

```
import 'package:flutter/material.dart';

void main() => runApp(new ColumnSpacedEvenly());

class ColumnSpacedEvenly extends StatelessWidget {
  @override
  Widget build(BuildContext context) {
    return new MaterialApp(
      title: 'Flutter Demo',
      theme: new ThemeData(
        primarySwatch: Colors.blue,
      ),
```

```
      home: new HomeWidget(),
    );
  }
}

class HomeWidget extends StatelessWidget {
  HomeWidget({Key key}) : super(key: key);

  @override
  Widget build(BuildContext context) {
    RawMaterialButton redButton = RawMaterialButton(
      constraints: const BoxConstraints(minWidth: 188.0, minHeight: 136.0),
      onPressed: () {},
      shape: new CircleBorder(),
      elevation: 2.0,
      fillColor: Colors.red,
      padding: const EdgeInsets.all(15.0),
    );
    RawMaterialButton greenButton = new RawMaterialButton(
      constraints: const BoxConstraints(minWidth: 188.0, minHeight: 136.0),
      onPressed: () {},
      shape: new CircleBorder(),
      elevation: 2.0,
      fillColor: Colors.green,
      padding: const EdgeInsets.all(15.0),
    );
    RawMaterialButton blueButton = new RawMaterialButton(
      constraints: const BoxConstraints(minWidth: 188.0, minHeight: 136.0),
      onPressed: () {},
      shape: new CircleBorder(),
      elevation: 2.0,
      fillColor: Colors.blue,
      padding: const EdgeInsets.all(15.0),
    );
    return new Scaffold(
        appBar: new AppBar(
          title: new Text("Column"),
        ),
        body: new Center(
          child: new Column(
            mainAxisAlignment: MainAxisAlignment.spaceEvenly,
            children: <Widget>[redButton, greenButton, blueButton],
          ),
        ));
  }
}
```

Expanding Children Using Expanded Widget

If you use an Expanded Widget (Single-Child Layout Widget) around each of your child Widgets, this allows them to expand to fit the available space.

Example – 'column_expanded'

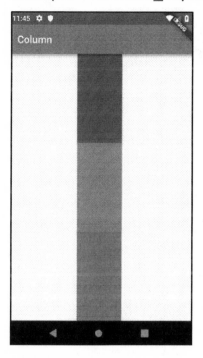

Source Code

```
import 'package:flutter/material.dart';

void main() => runApp(new ColumnSpacedEvenly());

class ColumnSpacedEvenly extends StatelessWidget {
 @override
 Widget build(BuildContext context) {
   return new MaterialApp(
     title: 'Flutter Demo',
     theme: new ThemeData(
       primarySwatch: Colors.blue,
     ),
     home: new HomeWidget(),
   );
 }
}

class HomeWidget extends StatelessWidget {
 HomeWidget({Key key}) : super(key: key);

 @override
 Widget build(BuildContext context) {
  RawMaterialButton redButton = RawMaterialButton(
    onPressed: () {}, elevation: 2.0, fillColor: Colors.red);
  RawMaterialButton greenButton = new RawMaterialButton(
    onPressed: () {},
    elevation: 2.0,
    fillColor: Colors.green,
  );
  RawMaterialButton blueButton = new RawMaterialButton(
```

```
  onPressed: () {},
  elevation: 2.0,
  fillColor: Colors.blue,
);
return new Scaffold(
  appBar: new AppBar(
    title: new Text("Column"),
  ),
  body: new Center(
    child: new Column(
      mainAxisAlignment: MainAxisAlignment.start,
      children: <Widget>[
        Expanded(child: redButton),
        Expanded(child: greenButton),
        Expanded(child: blueButton)
      ],
    ),
  ));
}
}
```

Row

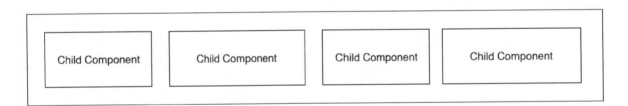

- Enables you to lay out Widgets Horizontally.
- Use the MainAxisAlignment to specify layout.
- If you run out of horizontal space, you may get an error and chevrons may appear.

Spacing Out Children Using MainAxisAlignment

The MainAxisAlignment widget allows you to determine how the Widgets are laid out horizontally. Take a look at the example below to see how this affects the horizontal layouts.

Example – 'row_main_axis_alignment'

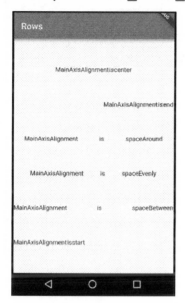

Source Code

```dart
import 'package:flutter/material.dart';

void main() => runApp(new RowMainAxisAlignmentApp());

class RowMainAxisAlignmentApp extends StatelessWidget {
  @override
  Widget build(BuildContext context) {
    return new MaterialApp(
      title: 'Flutter Demo',
      theme: new ThemeData(
        primarySwatch: Colors.blue,
      ),
      home: new HomeWidget(),
    );
  }
}

class HomeWidget extends StatelessWidget {
  HomeWidget({Key key}) : super(key: key);

  @override
  Widget build(BuildContext context) {
    return new Scaffold(
      appBar: new AppBar(title: new Text("Rows")),
      body: new Column(
        mainAxisAlignment: MainAxisAlignment.spaceEvenly,
        children: <Widget>[
          Row(
            mainAxisAlignment: MainAxisAlignment.center,
            children: <Widget>[
              const Text("MainAxisAlignment"),
              const Text("is"),
              const Text("center")
```

```
      ],
    ),
    Row(
      mainAxisAlignment: MainAxisAlignment.end,
      children: <Widget>[
        const Text("MainAxisAlignment"),
        const Text("is"),
        const Text("end")
      ],
    ),
    Row(
      mainAxisAlignment: MainAxisAlignment.spaceAround,
      children: <Widget>[
        const Text("MainAxisAlignment"),
        const Text("is"),
        const Text("spaceAround")
      ],
    ),
    Row(
      mainAxisAlignment: MainAxisAlignment.spaceEvenly,
      children: <Widget>[
        const Text("MainAxisAlignment"),
        const Text("is"),
        const Text("spaceEvenly")
      ],
    ),
    Row(
      mainAxisAlignment: MainAxisAlignment.spaceBetween,
      children: <Widget>[
        const Text("MainAxisAlignment"),
        const Text("is"),
        const Text("spaceBetween")
      ],
    ),
    Row(
      mainAxisAlignment: MainAxisAlignment.start,
      children: <Widget>[
        const Text("MainAxisAlignment"),
        const Text("is"),
        const Text("start")
      ],
    ),
  ],
));
}
}
```

Expanding Children Using Expanded Widget

If you use an Expanded Widget (Single-Child Layout Widget) around some of your child
Widgets, that allows them to expand to fit the available space.

Example – 'row_with_expanded'

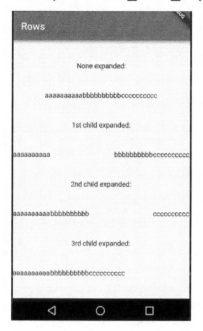

Source Code

```
import 'package:flutter/material.dart';

void main() => runApp(new RowWithExpandedApp());

class RowWithExpandedApp extends StatelessWidget {
 @override
 Widget build(BuildContext context) {
  return new MaterialApp(
   title: 'Flutter Demo',
   theme: new ThemeData(
    primarySwatch: Colors.blue,
   ),
   home: new HomeWidget(),
  );
 }
}

class HomeWidget extends StatelessWidget {
 HomeWidget({Key key}) : super(key: key);

 @override
 Widget build(BuildContext context) {
  return new Scaffold(
    appBar: new AppBar(title: new Text("Rows")),
    body: new Column(
     mainAxisAlignment: MainAxisAlignment.spaceEvenly,
     children: <Widget>[
      const Text("None expanded:"),
      Row(
       mainAxisAlignment: MainAxisAlignment.center,
       children: <Widget>[
```

```
            const Text("aaaaaaaaaa"),
            const Text("bbbbbbbbbb"),
            const Text("cccccccccc")
        ],
    ),
    const Text("1st child expanded:"),
    Row(
      children: <Widget>[
        const Expanded(child: const Text("aaaaaaaaaa")),
        const Text("bbbbbbbbbb"),
        const Text("cccccccccc")
      ],
    ),
    const Text("2nd child expanded:"),
    Row(
      children: <Widget>[
        const Text("aaaaaaaaaa"),
        const Expanded(child: const Text("bbbbbbbbbb")),
        const Text("cccccccccc")
      ],
    ),
    const Text("3rd child expanded:"),
    Row(
      children: <Widget>[
        const Text("aaaaaaaaaa"),
        const Text("bbbbbbbbbb"),
        const Expanded(child: const Text("cccccccccc"))
      ],
    ),
  ],
));
}
}
```

Flex

The Flex Widget is similar to Row and Column widget, except that it can act as both when you specify the mainAxis.

Example – 'flex'

This app uses the Flex layout for the main content – three rectangles. It has a toolbar with two buttons. The first button allows the user to toggle the Flex axis between vertical and horizontal. The second button allows the user to change the value of the main axis alignment.

Source Code

```dart
import 'package:flutter/material.dart';

void main() => runApp(new MyApp());

class MyApp extends StatelessWidget {
  @override
  Widget build(BuildContext context) {
    return new MaterialApp(
      title: 'Flutter Demo',
      theme: new ThemeData(
        primarySwatch: Colors.blue,
      ),
      home: new HomeWidget(title: 'Flex'));
  }
}

class HomeWidget extends StatefulWidget {
  HomeWidget({Key key, this.title}) : super(key: key);

  final String title;

  @override
  _MyHomePageState createState() => new _MyHomePageState();
}

class _MyHomePageState extends State<HomeWidget> {
  List<MainAxisAlignment> _alignments = [
    MainAxisAlignment.start,
    MainAxisAlignment.end,
    MainAxisAlignment.center,
    MainAxisAlignment.spaceBetween,
    MainAxisAlignment.spaceEvenly,
    MainAxisAlignment.spaceAround
```

```
];
List<String> _alignmentsText = [
  "Start",
  "End",
  "Center",
  "Soace Between",
  "Space Evenly",
  "Space Around"
];

bool _vertical = true;
int _alignmentIndex = 0;

RawMaterialButton redButton = RawMaterialButton(
   onPressed: () {}, elevation: 2.0, fillColor: Colors.red);
RawMaterialButton greenButton = new RawMaterialButton(
 onPressed: () {},
 elevation: 2.0,
 fillColor: Colors.green,
);
RawMaterialButton blueButton = new RawMaterialButton(
 onPressed: () {},
 elevation: 2.0,
 fillColor: Colors.blue,
);

@override
Widget build(BuildContext context) {
  return new Scaffold(
    appBar: new AppBar(
      title: new Text(widget.title),
      actions: <Widget>[
       IconButton(
        icon: const Icon(Icons.rotate_right),
        tooltip: 'Direction',
        onPressed: () {
          setState(() {
            _vertical = !_vertical;
          });
        },
       ),
       Padding(
          padding: EdgeInsets.only(top: 20.0),
          child: Text(_vertical ? "Vertical" : "Horizontal")),
       IconButton(
        icon: const Icon(Icons.aspect_ratio),
        tooltip: 'Main axis',
        onPressed: () {
          setState(() {
            _alignmentIndex++;
            if (_alignmentIndex >= _alignments.length) {
              _alignmentIndex = 0;
            }
          });
        },
       ),
       Padding(
          padding: EdgeInsets.only(top: 20.0),
```

```
            child: Text(_alignmentsText[_alignmentIndex])),
          Padding(
            padding: EdgeInsets.all(10.0),
          )
        ],
      ),
    body: new Flex(
      direction: _vertical ? Axis.vertical : Axis.horizontal,
      mainAxisAlignment: _alignments[_alignmentIndex],
      children: <Widget>[redButton, greenButton, blueButton],
    ));
  }
}
```

ListView & ListTiles

The ListView Widget is similar to the Flex widget in that it can act as both a horizontal list and a vertical list. The difference is that it provides scrolling out of the box.

Example - 'horizontal_list'

This app displays a list of Widgets horizontally rather than vertically. You can scroll by swiping to the left or to the right.

Source Code

```
import 'package:flutter/material.dart';

void main() => runApp(HorizontalListApp());
```

```
class HorizontalListApp extends StatelessWidget {
  @override
  Widget build(BuildContext context) {
    final title = 'Horizontal List';
    return MaterialApp(
      title: title,
      home: Scaffold(
        appBar: AppBar(
          title: Text(title),
        ),
        body: Container(
          margin: EdgeInsets.symmetric(vertical: 20.0),
          child: ListView(
            scrollDirection: Axis.horizontal,
            children: <Widget>[
              Container(
                width: 160.0,
                color: Colors.red,
              ),
              Container(
                width: 160.0,
                color: Colors.blue,
              ),
              Container(
                width: 160.0,
                color: Colors.green,
              ),
              Container(
                width: 160.0,
                color: Colors.yellow,
              ),
              Container(
                width: 160.0,
                color: Colors.orange,
              ),
            ],
          ),
        ),
      ),
    );
  }
}
```

ListTile

A list tile contains one to three lines of text optionally flanked by icons or other widgets, such as check boxes. So, you can have text in the middle and a widget on each side. Here is an example of a ListTile:

Many people combine ListViews and ListTiles together because ListTiles are great for building great-looking selection lists.

Example – 'settings'

Source Code

```
import 'package:flutter/material.dart';

void main() => runApp(new ListViewListTileApp());

class ListViewListTileApp extends StatelessWidget {
  // This widget is the root of your application.
  @override
  Widget build(BuildContext context) {
    return new MaterialApp(
      title: 'Flutter Demo',
      theme: new ThemeData(
        primarySwatch: Colors.blue,
      ),
      home: new HomeWidget(title: 'ListView & ListTile'),
    );
  }
}

class HomeWidget extends StatefulWidget {
  HomeWidget({Key key, this.title}) : super(key: key);

  final String title;

  @override
  _HomeWidgetState createState() => new _HomeWidgetState();
}

class _HomeWidgetState extends State<HomeWidget> {
  int _selectedIndex = 0;
  static const TEXT_STYLE_NORMAL = const TextStyle(
    color: Colors.black, fontSize: 18.0, fontWeight: FontWeight.normal);
```

```
static const TEXT_STYLE_SELECTED = const TextStyle(
  color: Colors.black, fontSize: 18.0, fontWeight: FontWeight.bold);
final TextFormField _fontSizeTextField = TextFormField(
  decoration: InputDecoration(
    icon: const Icon(Icons.format_size),
    hintText: 'Font Size',
    labelText: 'Enter the font size'));
final TextFormField _historyTextFormField = TextFormField(
  decoration: InputDecoration(
    icon: const Icon(Icons.history),
    hintText: 'Days',
    labelText: 'Enter days'));
final TextFormField _languageTextFormField = TextFormField(
  decoration: InputDecoration(
    icon: const Icon(Icons.language),
    hintText: 'Language',
    labelText: 'Enter your language'));

select(index) {
  setState(() {
    _selectedIndex = index;
  });
}

@override
Widget build(BuildContext context) {
  final ListTile accessibilityListTile = ListTile(
    leading: Icon(Icons.accessibility),
    title: Text("Accessibility",
      style:
        _selectedIndex == 0 ? TEXT_STYLE_SELECTED : TEXT_STYLE_NORMAL),
    subtitle: const Text("Accesibility Settings"),
    trailing: Icon(Icons.settings),
    onTap: () => select(0));

  final ListTile historyListTile = ListTile(
    leading: Icon(Icons.history),
    title: Text("History",
      style:
        _selectedIndex == 1 ? TEXT_STYLE_SELECTED : TEXT_STYLE_NORMAL),
    subtitle: const Text("History Settings"),
    trailing: Icon(Icons.settings),
    onTap: () => select(1));

  final ListTile languageListTile = ListTile(
    leading: Icon(Icons.language),
    title: Text("Language",
      style:
        _selectedIndex == 2 ? TEXT_STYLE_SELECTED : TEXT_STYLE_NORMAL),
    subtitle: const Text("Language Settings"),
    trailing: Icon(Icons.settings),
    onTap: () => select(2));

  final String selectionTitle = (_selectedIndex == 0
      ? "Accessibility"
      : _selectedIndex == 1 ? "History" : "Language") +
    " Settings";
```

```
final TextFormField selectionTextFormField = _selectedIndex == 0
  ? _fontSizeTextField
  : _selectedIndex == 1 ? _historyTextFormField : _languageTextFormField;

return new Scaffold(
  appBar: new AppBar(
    title: new Text(widget.title),
  ),
  body: ListView(children: <Widget>[
    accessibilityListTile,
    historyListTile,
    languageListTile
  ]),
  bottomSheet: Container(
    color: Color(0xFFB3E5FC),
    padding: EdgeInsets.all(20.0),
    child: Container(
      constraints: BoxConstraints(maxHeight: 200.0),
      child: Column(children: <Widget>[
        Icon(Icons.settings),
        Text(selectionTitle),
        Expanded(child: selectionTextFormField)
      ]))));
  }
}
```

Stack

The Stack Layout Widget is useful for overlaying Widgets on top of each other. Each child of a Stack Layout Widget is either positioned or non-positioned. Positioned children are those wrapped in a Positioned widget that has at least one non-null property.

The stack paints its children in order with the first child being at the bottom. If you want to change the order in which the children paint, you can rebuild the stack with the children in the new order. In this case, ensure each child has a key to prevent it from being rebuilt every-time.

Example – 'stack_please_wait'

Many applications need to show a 'please wait' indicator which something is loading. For example, when the user logs in, the app needs to contact the server and verify your information asynchronously. This app enables the user to toggle a 'please wait' indicato on or off.

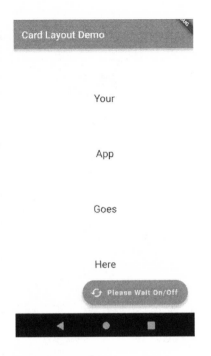 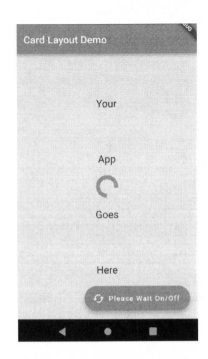

Source Code

```dart
import 'package:flutter/material.dart';

void main() => runApp(new StackPleaseWaitAppWidget());

class StackPleaseWaitAppWidget extends StatelessWidget {
  @override
  Widget build(BuildContext context) {
    return new MaterialApp(
      title: 'Flutter Demo',
      theme: new ThemeData(
        primarySwatch: Colors.blue,
      ),
      home: new HomeWidget(title: 'Card Layout Demo'),
    );
  }
}

class HomeWidget extends StatefulWidget {
  HomeWidget({Key key, this.title}) : super(key: key);
  final String title;
  final PleaseWaitWidget _pleaseWaitWidget =
    PleaseWaitWidget(key: ObjectKey("pleaseWaitWidget"));
  final AppWidget _appWidget = AppWidget(key: ObjectKey("appWidget"));

  @override
  _HomeWidgetState createState() => new _HomeWidgetState();
}

class _HomeWidgetState extends State<HomeWidget> {
  bool _pleaseWait = false;

  void _togglePleaseWait() {
    setState(() {
```

```
      _pleaseWait = !_pleaseWait;
    });
  }

  @override
  Widget build(BuildContext context) {
    List<Widget> childWidgets = _pleaseWait
      ? [widget._pleaseWaitWidget, widget._appWidget]
      : [widget._appWidget];
    return new Scaffold(
      appBar: new AppBar(
        title: new Text(widget.title),
      ),
      body: new Center(
        child: Stack(key: ObjectKey("stack"), children: childWidgets)),
      floatingActionButton: new FloatingActionButton.extended(
        onPressed: _togglePleaseWait,
        label: Text('Please Wait On/Off'),
        icon: new Icon(Icons.cached)));
  }
}

class PleaseWaitWidget extends StatelessWidget {
  PleaseWaitWidget({
    Key key,
  }) : super(key: key);

  @override
  Widget build(BuildContext context) {
    return Container(
      child: Center(
        child: CircularProgressIndicator(strokeWidth: 8.0),
      ),
      color: Colors.grey.withOpacity(0.3));
  }
}

class AppWidget extends StatelessWidget {
  AppWidget({
    Key key,
  }) : super(key: key);

  @override
  Widget build(BuildContext context) {
    return Center(
      child: new Column(
        mainAxisAlignment: MainAxisAlignment.spaceEvenly,
        children: <Widget>[
          const Text('Your', style: TextStyle(fontSize: 20.0)),
          const Text('App', style: TextStyle(fontSize: 20.0)),
          const Text('Goes', style: TextStyle(fontSize: 20.0)),
          const Text('Here', style: TextStyle(fontSize: 20.0))
        ],
      ),
    );
  }
}
```

20.Single-Child Layout Widgets

Introduction

Layout Widgets are used that affect the positioning and presentation of their child widgets. Earlier we mentioned that there are two main kinds of Layout Widgets: Single-Child Layout Widgets and Multi-Child Layout Widgets.

We covered Multi-Child Layout Widgets in the previous chapter.

The purpose of this chapter is to cover Single-Child Layout Widgets. These are Widgets that affect the layout of only one child Widget. They are used to wrap a single child Widget and affect its presentation.

The Padding Widget is probably used most of all these and is used to affect the padding around its child widget.

Padding

Used all the time to add padding around a child Widget. It uses EdgeInset objects to specify the padding metrics around the child Widget.

Example – 'padding'

This app allows the user click on an icon on the right side of the toolbar to cycle through the border insets.

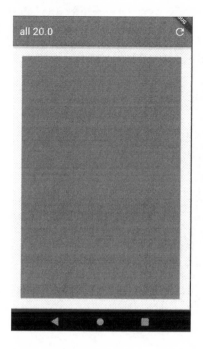 

Source Code

```
import 'package:flutter/material.dart';

void main() => runApp(new MyApp());

class MyApp extends StatelessWidget {
  // This widget is the root of your application.
  @override
  Widget build(BuildContext context) {
    return new MaterialApp(
      title: 'Flutter Demo',
      theme: new ThemeData(
        primarySwatch: Colors.blue,
      ),
      home: new HomeWidget(),
    );
  }
}

class HomeWidget extends StatefulWidget {
  HomeWidget({Key key}) : super(key: key);

  @override
  _HomeWidgetState createState() => new _HomeWidgetState();
}

class _HomeWidgetState extends State<HomeWidget> {
  static const double TWENTY = 20.0;
  static const List<String> _titles = [
    "all 20.0",
    "left 20.0",
    "right 20.0",
    "top 20.0",
    "bottom 20.0",
```

```
  "sym horiz 20.0",
  "sym vert 20.0"
];
static const List<EdgeInsets> _edgeInsets = [
  const EdgeInsets.all(TWENTY),
  const EdgeInsets.only(left: TWENTY),
  const EdgeInsets.only(right: TWENTY),
  const EdgeInsets.only(top: TWENTY),
  const EdgeInsets.only(bottom: TWENTY),
  const EdgeInsets.symmetric(horizontal: TWENTY),
  const EdgeInsets.symmetric(vertical: TWENTY)
];
int _index = 0;
final Container _childContainer = Container(color: Colors.blue);

void _next() {
  setState(() {
    _index++;
    if (_index >= _titles.length) {
      _index = 0;
    }
  });
}

@override
Widget build(BuildContext context) {
  Padding padding =
      Padding(padding: _edgeInsets[_index], child: _childContainer);
  return Scaffold(
    appBar: AppBar(
      title: Text(_titles[_index]),
      actions: [
        new IconButton(
          icon: new Icon(Icons.refresh), onPressed: () => _next()
        ),
      ],
    ),
    body: Center(
      child: Container(
        child: padding,
        decoration: BoxDecoration(
          border: new Border.all(color: Colors.blueAccent)))));
  }
}
```

Container

A convenience widget that combines common painting, positioning, and sizing widgets. Often used to contain wrap child widgets and apply styling.

Example – 'container'

This example app shows an aircraft in a container Widget with a border and a background. The user can hit the button on the bottom right to spin the aircraft. Ignore the animation code for the moment.

Source Code

```
import 'package:flutter/material.dart';

void main() => runApp(new ContainerApp());

class ContainerApp extends StatelessWidget {
  // This widget is the root of your application.
  @override
  Widget build(BuildContext context) {
    return new MaterialApp(
      title: 'Flutter Demo',
      theme: new ThemeData(
        primarySwatch: Colors.blue,
      ),
      home: new HomeWidget(title: 'Flutter Demo Home Page'),
    );
  }
}

class HomeWidget extends StatefulWidget {
  HomeWidget({Key key, this.title}) : super(key: key);
  final String title;

  @override
  _HomeWidgetState createState() => new _HomeWidgetState();
```

```
}
class _HomeWidgetState extends State<HomeWidget>
   with SingleTickerProviderStateMixin {
 Animation<double> _animation;
 AnimationController _controller;

 @override
 void initState() {
  super.initState();
  _controller =
    AnimationController(duration: const Duration(seconds: 2), vsync: this);
  _animation = Tween<double>(begin: 0.0, end: 1.0).animate(_controller)
   ..addListener(() {
    setState(() {});
   });
 }

 @override
 Widget build(BuildContext context) {
  return new Scaffold(
    appBar: new AppBar(
     title: new Text(widget.title),
    ),
    body: new Center(
      child: new Container(
       child: new RotationTransition(
        turns: new AlwaysStoppedAnimation(_animation.value),
        child: new Icon(Icons.airplanemode_active, size: 150.0)),
       decoration: BoxDecoration(
        border: Border.all(width: 2.0, color: Colors.black),
        borderRadius: BorderRadius.all(Radius.circular(8.0)),
        color: Colors.redAccent))),
    floatingActionButton: new FloatingActionButton(
      onPressed: _spin,
      tooltip: 'Increment',
      child: new Icon(Icons.rotate_right)));
 }

 void _spin() {
  _controller.forward(from: 0.0);
 }
}
```

Further Reading

https://medium.com/flutter-community/flutters-container-this-ain-t-your-daddy-s-div-100817339610

Card

Material UI uses cards. They are used contain content and actions about a single subject. According to the Google Documentation:

- A card is identifiable as a single, contained unit.
- A card can stand alone, without relying on surrounding elements for context.
- A card cannot merge with another card, or divide into multiple cards.

Example – 'cards'

This app displays a news feed using Cards.
Note that this example uses a stream 'map' function to convert News data objects into Widgets.

Source Code

```
import 'package:flutter/material.dart';

void main() => runApp(new MyApp());

class MyApp extends StatelessWidget {
  // This widget is the root of your application.
  @override
  Widget build(BuildContext context) {
    return new MaterialApp(
      title: 'Flutter Demo',
      theme: new ThemeData(
        primarySwatch: Colors.blue,
      ),
      home: new NewsfeedWidget(title: 'News Feed'),
    );
  }
}

class News {
```

```dart
  DateTime _dt;
  String _title;
  String _text;

  News(this._dt, this._title, this._text);
}

class NewsCard extends StatelessWidget {
  News _news;

  NewsCard(this._news);

  @override
  Widget build(BuildContext context) {
    return Padding(
      padding: EdgeInsets.only(bottom: 20.0),
      child: Card(
        child: Padding(
          padding: EdgeInsets.all(20.0),
          child: Column(
            crossAxisAlignment: CrossAxisAlignment.start,
            children: <Widget>[
              Image.network("https://www.bbc.co"
                ".uk/news/special/2015/newsspec_10857/bbc_news_logo.png?cb=1"),
              Padding(
                padding: EdgeInsets.only(top: 20.0, bottom: 10.0),
                child: Text(
                  "${_news._dt.month}//${_news._dt.day}/${_news._dt.year}",
                  style: TextStyle(
                    fontSize: 10.0, fontStyle: FontStyle.italic),
                )),
              Padding(
                padding: EdgeInsets.only(bottom: 10.0),
                child: Text("${_news._title}",
                  style: TextStyle(
                    fontSize: 20.0, fontWeight: FontWeight.bold))),
              Text(
                "${_news._text}",
                maxLines: 2,
                style: TextStyle(fontSize: 14.0),
                overflow: TextOverflow.fade,
              ),
              Row(children: [
                FlatButton(child: Text("Share"), onPressed: () => {}),
                FlatButton(child: Text("Bookmark"), onPressed: () => {}),
                FlatButton(child: Text("Link"), onPressed: () => {})
              ])
            ],
          ))));
  }
}

class NewsfeedWidget extends StatelessWidget {
  NewsfeedWidget({Key key, this.title}) : super(key: key);

  final String title;
  List<News> _newsList = [
    News(
```

```
    DateTime(2018, 12, 1),
    "Mass shooting in Atlanta",
    "Lorem ipsum dolor sit amet, consectetur adipiscing elit. Proin sit amet " +
      "tortor pretium, interdum magna sed, pulvinar ligula."),
  News(
    DateTime(2019, 1, 12),
    "Carnival clown found drunk in Misisippi",
    "Lorem ipsum dolor sit amet, consectetur adipiscing elit. Proin sit amet " +
      "tortor pretium, interdum magna sed, pulvinar ligula."),
  News(
    DateTime(2019, 2, 12),
    "Walrus found in family pool in Florida",
    "Lorem ipsum dolor sit amet, consectetur adipiscing elit. Proin sit amet " +
      "tortor pretium, interdum magna sed, pulvinar ligula."),
];

@override
Widget build(BuildContext context) {
  List<Widget> newsCards = _newsList.map((news) => NewsCard(news)).toList();
  return new Scaffold(
    appBar: new AppBar(
      title: new Text("News Feed"),
    ),
    body: new ListView(padding: EdgeInsets.all(20.0), children: newsCards));
  }
}
```

Expanded

A widget that expands a child of a Row, Column, or Flex.

Using an Expanded widget makes a child of a Row, Column, or Flex expand to fill the available space in the main axis (e.g., horizontally for a Row or vertically for a Column). If multiple children are expanded, the available space is divided among them according to the flex factor.

Example – 'expanded'

This app shows how two widgets in a column behave when they are contained in a parent Expanded widget (or not).

- If both widgets are expanded, both share the available vertical space evenly.
- If only one is expanded, the expanded one takes up all the available vertical space.
- If neither is expanded, the available vertical space goes unfilled

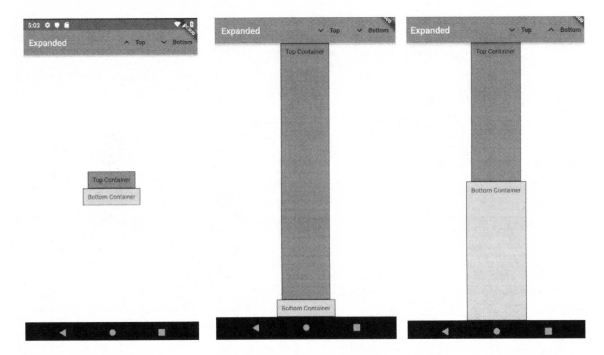

Source Code

```
import 'package:flutter/material.dart';

void main() => runApp(new MyApp());

class MyApp extends StatelessWidget {
  @override
  Widget build(BuildContext context) {
    return new MaterialApp(
      title: 'Flutter Demo',
      theme: new ThemeData(
        primarySwatch: Colors.blue,
      ),
      home: new HomeWidget(),
    );
  }
}

class HomeWidget extends StatefulWidget {
  HomeWidget({Key key}) : super(key: key);

  @override
  _HomeWidgetState createState() => new _HomeWidgetState();
}

class _HomeWidgetState extends State<HomeWidget> {
  bool _topExpanded = false;
  bool _bottomExpanded = false;

  toggleTop() {
    setState(() => _topExpanded = !_topExpanded);
  }
```

```
toggleBottom() {
  setState(() => _bottomExpanded = !_bottomExpanded);
}

@override
Widget build(BuildContext context) {
  Container topContainer = Container(
    child: new Text(
      'Top Container',
    ),
    decoration: BoxDecoration(
      border: Border.all(color: Colors.black, width: 1.0),
      color: Colors.blue),
    padding: EdgeInsets.all(10.0),
  );
  Container bottomContainer = Container(
    child: new Text(
      'Bottom Container',
    ),
    decoration: BoxDecoration(
      border: Border.all(color: Colors.black, width: 1.0),
      color: Colors.yellow),
    padding: EdgeInsets.all(10.0),
  );
  Widget topWidget =
    _topExpanded ? Expanded(child: topContainer) : topContainer;
  Widget bottomWidget =
    _bottomExpanded ? Expanded(child: bottomContainer) : bottomContainer;
  return new Scaffold(
    appBar: new AppBar(title: new Text("Expanded"), actions: <Widget>[
      FlatButton.icon(
        icon: Icon(_topExpanded ? Icons.expand_more : Icons.expand_less),
        label: Text("Top"),
        onPressed: () => toggleTop()),
      FlatButton.icon(
        icon:
          Icon(_bottomExpanded ? Icons.expand_less : Icons.expand_more),
        label: Text("Bottom"),
        onPressed: () => toggleBottom())
    ]),
    body: new Center(
      child: new Column(
        mainAxisAlignment: MainAxisAlignment.center,
        children: <Widget>[topWidget, bottomWidget],
      ),
    ));
}
}
```

Flexible

This widget is similar to the Expanded widget in that it expands the child Widget, except that it is a little more flexible in regard to Constraints.

When child widgets have Constraints (for example minimum, maximum dimension) then:

Single-Child Layout Widgets

- Expanded Widgets always respect those Constraints, never overriding them.
- Flexible Widgets have the following fit options:
  - Fit 'expanded': expands to fit the available screen space, overriding the Constraints.
  - Fit 'loose' expands to fit the available screen space, respecting those Constraints, never overriding them.

Example – 'flexible'

This app shows two Widgets that have a min size of 100 x 100 and a max size of 200 x 200. There are two toolbar buttons to control the use of the available space.

- The top container is expanded / contracted by using a Flexible with a fit that toggles between loose (the child can be at most as large as the available space but is allowed to be smaller). and tight (expands tightly to available space).
- The bottom container is expanded / contacted by using / not using an Expanded widget.

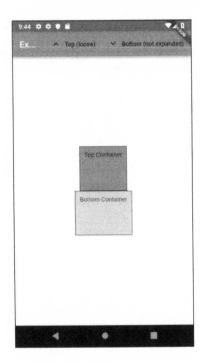

Source Code

```
import 'package:flutter/material.dart';

void main() => runApp(new MyApp());

class MyApp extends StatelessWidget {
  @override
  Widget build(BuildContext context) {
    return new MaterialApp(
      title: 'Flutter Demo',
      theme: new ThemeData(
```

```
      primarySwatch: Colors.blue,
    ),
    home: new HomeWidget(),
  );
 }
}

class HomeWidget extends StatefulWidget {
 HomeWidget({Key key}) : super(key: key);

 @override
 _HomeWidgetState createState() => new _HomeWidgetState();
}

class _HomeWidgetState extends State<HomeWidget> {
 bool _topTightFit = false;
 bool _bottomExpanded = false;

 toggleTop() {
  setState(() => _topTightFit = !_topTightFit);
 }

 toggleBottom() {
  setState(() => _bottomExpanded = !_bottomExpanded);
 }

 @override
 Widget build(BuildContext context) {
  Container topContainer = Container(
    child: new Text(
     'Top Container',
    ),
    constraints: BoxConstraints(
      minHeight: 100.0, minWidth: 100.0, maxHeight: 200.0, maxWidth: 200.0),
    decoration: BoxDecoration(
      border: Border.all(color: Colors.black, width: 1.0),
      color: Colors.blue),
    padding: EdgeInsets.all(10.0),
  );
  Container bottomContainer = Container(
    child: new Text(
     'Bottom Container',
    ),
    constraints: BoxConstraints(
      minHeight: 100.0, minWidth: 100.0, maxHeight: 200.0, maxWidth: 200.0),
    decoration: BoxDecoration(
      border: Border.all(color: Colors.black, width: 1.0),
      color: Colors.yellow),
    padding: EdgeInsets.all(10.0),
  );
  Widget topWidget = Flexible(
    child: topContainer, fit: _topTightFit ? FlexFit.tight : FlexFit.loose);
  Widget bottomWidget =
    _bottomExpanded ? Expanded(child: bottomContainer) : bottomContainer;
  String toolbarTextTop = "Top (" + (_topTightFit ? "tight" : "loose") + ")";
  String toolbarTextBottom =
    "Bottom (" + (_bottomExpanded ? "expanded" : "not expanded") + ")";
  return new Scaffold(
```

```
    appBar: new AppBar(title: new Text("Expanded"), actions: <Widget>[
      FlatButton.icon(
        icon: Icon(_topTightFit
          ? Icons.keyboard_arrow_up
          : Icons.keyboard_arrow_up),
        label: Text(toolbarTextTop),
        onPressed: () => toggleTop()),
      FlatButton.icon(
        icon: Icon(_bottomExpanded
          ? Icons.keyboard_arrow_down
          : Icons.keyboard_arrow_down),
        label: Text(toolbarTextBottom),
        onPressed: () => toggleBottom()
    ]),
    body: new Center(
      child: new Column(
        mainAxisAlignment: MainAxisAlignment.center,
        children: <Widget>[topWidget, bottomWidget],
      ),
    ));
  }
}
```

Center

This widget is used to center a Widget within its parent Widget.

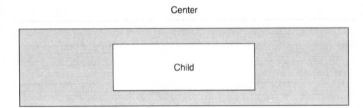

GestureDetector

A widget that detects gestures.
Often used to add event listeners (like 'onTop') onto Widgets that don't have that capability.

Example – 'gesture_app'

This app allows the user to try out gestures on a piece of text, logging the recorded gestures in a scrollable textbox below. The user can click on the 'Clear' button to clear the textbox.

Source Code

```
import 'package:flutter/material.dart';

void main() => runApp(new GestureApp());

class GestureApp extends StatelessWidget {
  // This widget is the root of your application.
  @override
  Widget build(BuildContext context) {
    return new MaterialApp(
      title: 'Flutter Demo',
      theme: new ThemeData(
        primarySwatch: Colors.blue,
      ),
      home: new HomeWidget(title: 'Gestures'),
    );
  }
}

class HomeWidget extends StatefulWidget {
  HomeWidget({Key key, this.title}) : super(key: key);

  final String title;

  @override
  _HomeWidgetState createState() => new _HomeWidgetState();
}

class _HomeWidgetState extends State<HomeWidget> {
  String _log = '';

  void _clear() {
    setState(() {
```

```
    _log = '';
  });
}

void _logGesture(String logText) {
 setState(() {
  _log += "\n";
  _log += logText;
 });
}

@override
Widget build(BuildContext context) {
 return new Scaffold(
    appBar: new AppBar(
     title: new Text(widget.title),
    ),
    body: new Center(
     child: new Column(
      mainAxisAlignment: MainAxisAlignment.spaceEvenly,
      children: <Widget>[
       GestureDetector(
          child: Text(
           'Gesture Me',
          ),
          onTap: () => _logGesture('tap'),
          onTapDown: (details) => _logGesture('onTapDown: ${details}'),
          onTapUp: (details) => _logGesture('onTapUp: ${details}'),
          onTapCancel: () => _logGesture('onTapCancel'),
          onDoubleTap: () => _logGesture('onDoubleTap'),
          onLongPress: () => _logGesture('onLongPress'),
          onVerticalDragDown: (details) =>
            _logGesture('onVerticalDragDown: ${details}'),
          onVerticalDragStart: (details) =>
            _logGesture('onVerticalDragStart: ${details}'),
          onVerticalDragUpdate: (details) =>
            _logGesture('onVerticalDragUpdate'),
          onVerticalDragEnd: (details) =>
            _logGesture('onVerticalDragEnd: ${details}'),
          onVerticalDragCancel: () =>
            _logGesture('onVerticalDragCancel'),
          onHorizontalDragDown: (details) =>
            _logGesture('onHorizontalDragDown: ${details}'),
          onHorizontalDragStart: (details) =>
            _logGesture('onHorizontalDragStart: ${details}'),
          onHorizontalDragUpdate: (details) =>
            _logGesture('onHorizontalDragUpdate: ${details}'),
          onHorizontalDragEnd: (details) =>
            _logGesture('onHorizontalDragEnd: ${details}'),
          onHorizontalDragCancel: () =>
            _logGesture('onHorizontalDragCancel')),
        Container(
          child: SingleChildScrollView(child: Text('$_log')),
          constraints: BoxConstraints(maxHeight: 200.0),
          decoration: BoxDecoration(
            border: Border.all(
             color: Colors.grey,
             width: 1.0,
```

```
      )),
        margin: EdgeInsets.all(10.0),
        padding: EdgeInsets.all(10.0)),
      RaisedButton(child: Text('Clear'), onPressed: () => _clear())
    ],
    ),
  ));
  }
}
```

Positioned

Used to wrap a child Widget to control where it is positioned when added to a group of Widgets stacked using the Stack layout widget.

Example – 'positioned'

This app allows the user to add another square on top of the existing squares, positioned each time further down and further to the right.

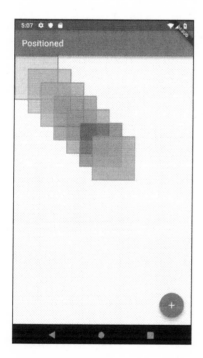

Source Code

```
import 'package:flutter/material.dart';
import 'dart:math';

void main() => runApp(new MyApp());

class MyApp extends StatelessWidget {
  @override
```

```
  Widget build(BuildContext context) {
   return new MaterialApp(
    title: 'Flutter Demo',
    theme: new ThemeData(
     primarySwatch: Colors.blue,
    ),
    home: new MyHomePage(),
   );
  }
}

class MyHomePage extends StatefulWidget {
 MyHomePage({Key key}) : super(key: key);

 @override
 _MyHomePageState createState() => new _MyHomePageState();
}

class _MyHomePageState extends State<MyHomePage> {
 double _top = 0.0;
 double _left = 0.0;
 List<Widget> widgetList = [];

 final _random = new Random();

 int next(int min, int max) => min + _random.nextInt(max - min);

 void _addLayer() {
  setState(() {
   widgetList.add(Positioned(
     left: _left,
     top: _top,
     child: Container(
       width: 100.0,
       height: 100.0,
       decoration: BoxDecoration(
        border: Border.all(
         color: Colors.grey,
         width: 2.0,
        ),
        color: Color.fromRGBO(
          next(0, 255), next(0, 255), next(0, 255), 0.5,
        ))));
  });
  _top += 30;
  _left += 30;
 }

 @override
 Widget build(BuildContext context) {
  return new Scaffold(
   appBar: new AppBar(
    title: new Text("Positioned"),
   ),
   body: new Stack(children: widgetList),
   floatingActionButton: new FloatingActionButton(
    onPressed: _addLayer,
    tooltip: 'Increment',
```

```
      child: new Icon(Icons.add),
    ), // This trailing comma makes auto-formatting nicer for build methods.
  );
 }
}
```

SafeArea

When you wrap a child Widget with a Safe Area, it adds any necessary padding needed to keep your widget from being blocked by the system status bar, notches, holes, rounded corners and other "creative" features by manufactures.

Example: Non-Safe Area

Example: Safe Area

Example: Safe Area with Minimum Padding Set

SingleChildScrollView

This Widget is used to show a child Widget even if there is not enough space to view the entirety of the child Widget.

Constructor Arguments Include:

Argument	Description
child	Child Widget
scrollDirection	Direction of scrolling. Can be either horizontal or vertical. Cannot be both.
scrollPhysics	How the scroll view continues to animate after the user stops dragging the scroll view.

Exercise – 'single_child_scroll_view'

This app that displays a very large multicolored globe and allows the user to scroll over it.

Step 1 – Create Default Flutter App

Follow the instructions in <u>Generate Your First App</u>
Leave project open.

Step 2 – Replace Application Code

Replace contents of file 'main.dart' in folder 'lib' with the following:

```
import 'dart:math';
```

```dart
import 'package:flutter/material.dart';

void main() => runApp(new MyApp());

class MyApp extends StatelessWidget {
  // This widget is the root of your application.
  @override
  Widget build(BuildContext context) {
    return new MaterialApp(
      title: 'Flutter Demo',
      theme: new ThemeData(
        primarySwatch: Colors.blue,
      ),
      home: new MyHomePage(),
    );
  }
}

class CirclePainter extends CustomPainter {
  final _random = new Random();
  List<Color> _colors = [];

  CirclePainter() {
    for (int i = 0; i < 100; i++) {
      _colors.add(Colors.green
        .withRed(next(0, 255))
        .withGreen(next(0, 255))
        .withBlue(next(0, 255)));
    }
  }

  int next(int min, int max) => min + _random.nextInt(max - min);

  @override
  void paint(Canvas canvas, Size size) {
    for (int i = 0; i < 100; i++) {
      var radius = (i * 10).toDouble();
      canvas.drawCircle(
        new Offset(1000.0, 1000.0),
        radius,
        new Paint()
          ..color = _colors[i]
          ..strokeCap = StrokeCap.round
          ..style = PaintingStyle.stroke
          ..strokeWidth = 15.0);
    }
  }

  @override
  bool shouldRepaint(CirclePainter oldDelegate) {
    return false;
  }
}

class MyHomePage extends StatelessWidget {
  CirclePainter circlePainter = new CirclePainter();
  MyHomePage({Key key}) : super(key: key);
```

```
  @override
  Widget build(BuildContext context) {
   return new Scaffold(
     appBar: new AppBar(
      title: new Text("Scroll"),
     ),
     body: new SingleChildScrollView(
       scrollDirection: Axis.vertical,
       physics: AlwaysScrollableScrollPhysics(),
       child: CustomPaint(
        size: Size(2000.0, 2000.0),
        foregroundPainter: circlePainter,
       )));
  }
}
```

Step 3 – Open Emulator & Run

Follow the instructions in <u>Open Android Emulator & Run Your First App</u>
You should be able to scroll vertically but not horizontally over the globe.

Step 4 – Change the 'ScrollDirection'

Change the 'scrollDirection' constructor Argument of the SingleChildScrollView from Axis.vertical to Axis.horizontal.

```
  @override
  Widget build(BuildContext context) {
   return new Scaffold(
     appBar: new AppBar(
      title: new Text("Scroll"),
     ),
     body: new SingleChildScrollView(
       scrollDirection: Axis.horizontal,
       physics: AlwaysScrollableScrollPhysics(),
       child: CustomPaint(
        size: Size(2000.0, 2000.0),
        foregroundPainter: circlePainter,
       )));
  }
```

Step 5 – Reload the Changes

You should be able to scroll horizontally but not vertically over the globe.

Step 6 – Edit the 'build' Method and Change the SingleChildScrollView to a ListView

```
return new Scaffold(
    appBar: new AppBar(
      title: new Text("Scroll"),
    ),
    body: new Center(
      child: new SingleChildScrollView(
        child: Column(
      children: childWidgetList,
    ))));
```

21.App Scaffolding Widgets

Introduction

Flutter makes it easy to generate a default mobile app and you quickly end up with something sophisticated with Color themes, an App Bar, a Content Area with a Count and a Floating Button.

The reason you get something sophisticated so quickly is that the Default App uses Flutter Widgets that were specially designed to scaffold an app as quickly as possible.

The purpose of this chapter is to cover these Widgets.

When your code entry point runs (i.e. the main method), it calls runApp to initialize a given widget (an App Widget). The build method of the App Widget is invoked and it returns a MaterialApp object, which gives Flutter the information it needs to generate the widget and display it on the screen, along with its child Widgets.

So, your App Widget returns a MaterialApp that you have initialized with the title, theme and home properties initialized. It's called a Material App because this class builds the foundations for an app that uses Google's Material Design UI.

MaterialApp

Builds the foundations for a cross-platform app that uses Google's Material Design UI.
It introduces built-in objects such as the Navigator, Themes and Locales to help you develop your app.

Navigator

We will cover the Navigator in a later chapter.

Themes

When you build a Flutter app, you build a root Widget. That Widget usually returns a MaterialApp, which builds the foundations for the app. One of the constructor arguments for MaterialApp is the Theme object. This object specifies the colors to be used in the application's Widgets. As you can see below the user can pass in Theme data into the MaterialApp constructor using a ThemeData object.

Default Flutter App Uses Blue Theme

```
class MyApp extends StatelessWidget {
 // This widget is the root of your application.
 @override
 Widget build(BuildContext context) {
  return new MaterialApp(
   title: 'Flutter Demo',
   theme: new ThemeData(
    primarySwatch: Colors.blue,
   ),
   home: new MyHomePage(title: 'Flutter Demo Home Page'),
   debugShowMaterialGrid: true,
   debugShowCheckedModeBanner: false,
   showPerformanceOverlay: true,
  );
 }
}
```

Example of Darkening Theme

Source Code

This is the default Flutter app with just a change to the accent color and the brightness.

```
class MyApp extends StatelessWidget {
  // This widget is the root of your application.
  @override
  Widget build(BuildContext context) {
    return new MaterialApp(
      title: 'Flutter Demo',
      theme: new ThemeData(
        accentColor: Colors.redAccent,
        brightness: Brightness.dark),
      home: new MyHomePage(title: 'Flutter Demo Home Page'),
    );
  }
}
```

Locales

In computing, a locale is a set of parameters that defines the user's language, region and any special variant preferences that the user wants to see in their user interface. Usually a locale identifier consists of at least a language code and a country/region code. The MaterialApp Widget defaults the apps Locale to that of the device it is running on. However, there are locale constructor arguments that let you override the default Locale behavior.

Debugging Constructor Arguments

In addition, the MaterialApp constructor lets you specify additional arguments to enable you to turn on Service Extensions, such as the following:

- debugShowMaterialGrid
- showPerformanceOverlay
- checkerboardRasterCacheImages
- checkerboardOffscreenLayers
- showSemanticsDebugger
- debugShowCheckedModeBanner

We will cover these later on here: Debugging & Performance Profiling

Scaffold

Provides a pre-determined, standard layout structure for your App on which you can add child Widgets. For more information take a look at the Scaffold Widget exercise in this chapter.

AppBar

App bar with title, icons and menu functionality. Used to display a title plus some icons, which the user can tap on to initiate actions.
You can add an AppBar to your app by specifying the'appBar' constructor argument when creating the Scaffold.

Body

Here is where you add the widget that is displayed in the content area of the app.

BottomNavigationBar

Good place to put bottom navigation buttons. The bottom navigation bar is rendered at the bottom, below the Body, BottomSheet and PersistentFooterButtons Widgets. Uses BottomNavigationBarItem items to allow the user to tap on an icon to navigate.

You can add an BottomNavigationBar to your app by specifying the 'bottomNavigationBar' constructor argument when creating the Scaffold.

Drawer

A drawer is an invisible side screen which generally contain menu items and occupies around half of the screen when displayed

You can add a Drawer to the left side of your app by specifying the 'drawer' constructor argument when creating the Scaffold. This gives you the Hamburger menu on the AppBar.

You can add a Drawer to the right side your app by specifying the 'endDrawer' constructor argument when creating the Scaffold. This does not show a Hamburger menu though.

BottomSheet

Used to show the user information or additional commands without changing the context of what the user is viewing. Used to display content at the bottom of the screen to the user.

Note that there are also ModalBottomSheets that can block the user interface (stop the user from interacting with other content within your application) until the user makes a selection.

You can add a BottomSheet to your app by specifying the 'bottomSheet' constructor argument when creating the Scaffold.

PersistentFooterButtons

Used to show a set of widgets at the bottom of the scaffold above the BottomNavigationBar but below the Body and the BottomSheet. Usually FlatButton widgets. These widgets will be wrapped in a ButtonBar. These buttons are persistently visible, even if the body of the scaffold scrolls.

You can add PersistentFooterButtons to your app by specifying the 'persistentFooterButtons' constructor argument when creating the Scaffold.

Exercise – 'scaffold'

This exercise attempts to use all of the functionality available in the Scaffold Widget.
In doing so it uses all the Widgets that were introduced in this chapter.

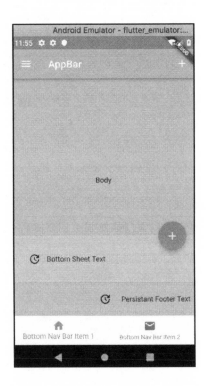

Step 1 – Create Default Flutter App

Follow the instructions in Generate Your First App
Leave project open.

Step 2 – Replace Application Code

Replace contents of file 'main.dart' in folder 'lib' with the following:

```dart
import 'package:flutter/material.dart';

void main() => runApp(new MyApp());

class MyApp extends StatelessWidget {
 // This widget is the root of your application.
 @override
 Widget build(BuildContext context) {
  return new MaterialApp(
    title: 'Flutter Demo',
    theme: new ThemeData(
     primarySwatch: Colors.blue,
    ),
    home: new MyHomePage(),
  );
 }
}

class MyHomePage extends StatelessWidget {
 MyHomePage({Key key}) : super(key: key);
```

```
@override
Widget build(BuildContext context) {
 return new Scaffold(
    appBar: new AppBar(
     backgroundColor: Colors.amber,
     title: new Text("AppBar"),
     actions: <Widget>[
      IconButton(
         icon: Icon(Icons.add),
         onPressed: () {
          print("Add IconButton Pressed...");
         })
    ],
    ),
    backgroundColor: Colors.lightBlueAccent,
    body: new Center(
     child: new Column(
      mainAxisAlignment: MainAxisAlignment.center,
      children: <Widget>[
       new Text(
        'Body',
        )
      ],
     ),
    ),
    bottomNavigationBar: BottomNavigationBar(
     type: BottomNavigationBarType.fixed,
     onTap: (index) => debugPrint("Bottom Navigation Bar onTap: ${index}"),
     items: [
      BottomNavigationBarItem(
       icon: new Icon(Icons.home),
       title: new Text('Bottom Nav Bar Item 1'),
      ),
      BottomNavigationBarItem(
       icon: new Icon(Icons.mail),
       title: new Text('Bottom Nav Bar Item 2'),
      )
     ],
    ),
    bottomSheet: Container(
     color: Colors.amberAccent,
     padding: EdgeInsets.all(20.0),
     child: Row(children: <Widget>[
      IconButton(
        icon: Icon(Icons.update),
        onPressed: () {
         print("Bottom Sheet Icon Pressed");
        }),
      Text('Bottom Sheet Text')
     ])),
    drawer: Drawer(
     child: ListView(children: <Widget>[
     Row(children: <Widget>[
      IconButton(
        icon: Icon(Icons.add),
        onPressed: () {
         print("Drawer Item 1 Pressed");
        }),
```

```
      Text('Drawer Item 1')
    ]),
    Row(children: <Widget>[
     IconButton(
        icon: Icon(Icons.add),
        onPressed: () {
         print("Drawer Item 2 Pressed");
        }),
     Text('Drawer Item 2')
    ])
   ])),

   /*

 For swiping in from right-side.

 endDrawer: Drawer(
    child: ListView(children: <Widget>[
   Row(children: <Widget>[
    IconButton(
       icon: Icon(Icons.add),
       onPressed: () {
        print("Drawer Item 1");
       }),
    Text('Drawer Item 1 Pressed')
   ]),
    Row(children: <Widget>[
     IconButton(
        icon: Icon(Icons.add),
        onPressed: () {
         print("Drawer Item 2 Pressed");
        }),
     Text('Drawer Item 2')
    ])
   ])),
   */
   floatingActionButton: new FloatingActionButton(
      onPressed: () {
       print("FloatingActionButton Pressed");
      },
      tooltip: 'Increment',
      child: new Icon(Icons.add)),
   persistentFooterButtons: <Widget>[
    IconButton(
       icon: Icon(Icons.update),
       onPressed: () {
        print("Persistant Footer Icon Pressed");
       }),
    Text('Persistant Footer Text')
   ]);
 }
}
```

Step 3 – Open Emulator & Run

Follow the instructions in <u>Open Android Emulator & Run Your First App</u>
You should get something like the following:

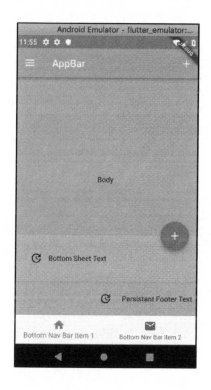

If you touch the
hamburger menu
on the top left,
that opens up
the drawer
shown to the
right.

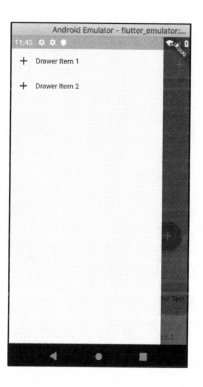

22.Other Widgets

Introduction

The purpose of this chapter is to cover left-over commonly-used Widgets that have not been covered yet. This does not include Widgets that are used on Forms to enter information. Those will be covered in this chapter: Forms.

Dialog

Dialogs are temporary windows that appear as overlays over the existing application. They are very useful to display something to the user or get user input. When a dialog is displayed, the rest of the app is unavailable. Flutter comes with two boilerplate dialog widgets: Alert Dialog and SimpleDialog. However, you can build custom dialogs quite easily.

AlertDialog

A material design dialog used to display an alert message to the user, with buttons underneath.

To show such a dialog in Flutter, you invoke the 'showDialog' method. This method then displays a dialog above the current contents of the app. This method takes a builder, which in this case returns an instance of the SimpleDialog. This method also returns a [Future] that resolves to the value (if any) that was selected on the dialog. Remember that Futures are covered in the 'More Advanced Dart' Chapter.

AlertDialog Constructor Properties

All these properties are optional. However, if you don't supply anything then nothing will come up!

Name	Description
title	Title.
content	Message or content.
actions	Buttons

Example – 'alert_dialog'

This app is the same as the default Flutter app, except that it asks you to confirm when you hit the '+' floating button.

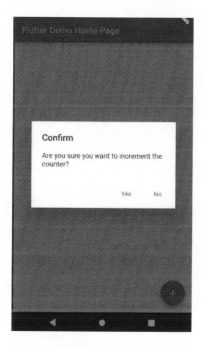

Source Code

```
import 'dart:async';

import 'package:flutter/material.dart';

void main() => runApp(new MyApp());

class MyApp extends StatelessWidget {
  // This widget is the root of your application.
  @override
  Widget build(BuildContext context) {
    return new MaterialApp(
      title: 'Flutter Demo',
      theme: new ThemeData(
        primarySwatch: Colors.blue,
      ),
      home: new HomeWidget(title: 'Flutter Demo Home Page'),
    );
  }
}

class HomeWidget extends StatefulWidget {
  HomeWidget({Key key, this.title}) : super(key: key);

  final String title;

  @override
  _HomeWidgetState createState() => new _HomeWidgetState();
}

class _HomeWidgetState extends State<HomeWidget> {
  int _counter = 0;

  Future<bool> _showConfirmDialog() async {
```

```
return await showDialog<bool>(
  context: context,
  builder: (BuildContext context) {
    return AlertDialog(
      title: const Text('Confirm'),
      content: const Text('Are you sure you want to increment the '
        'counter?'),
      actions: <Widget>[
        FlatButton(
          onPressed: () {
            Navigator.pop(context, true);
          },
          child: const Text('Yes'),
        ),
        FlatButton(
          onPressed: () {
            Navigator.pop(context, false);
          },
          child: const Text('No'),
        )
      ],
    );
  });
}

void _incrementCounter() {
  _showConfirmDialog().then((result) {
    if (result == true) {
      setState(() {
        _counter++;
      });
    }
  });
}

@override
Widget build(BuildContext context) {
  return new Scaffold(
    appBar: new AppBar(
      title: new Text(widget.title),
    ),
    body: new Center(
      child: new Column(
        mainAxisAlignment: MainAxisAlignment.center,
        children: <Widget>[
          new Text(
            'You have pushed the button this many times:',
          ),
          new Text(
            '$_counter',
            style: Theme.of(context).textTheme.display1,
          ),
        ],
      ),
    ),
    floatingActionButton: new FloatingActionButton(
      onPressed: _incrementCounter,
      tooltip: 'Increment',
```

```
      child: new Icon(Icons.add),
    ), // This trailing comma makes auto-formatting nicer for build methods.
  );
 }
}
```

SimpleDialog

A simple material design dialog used to offer the user a choice between several options. A simple dialog has an optional title that is displayed above the choices.

To show such a dialog in Flutter, you invoke the 'showDialog' method. This method then displays a dialog above the current contents of the app. This method takes a builder, which in this case returns an instance of the SimpleDialog. This method also returns a [Future] that resolves to the value (if any) that was selected on the dialog. Remember that Futures are covered in the 'More Advanced Dart' Chapter.

SimpleDialog Constructor Properties

All these properties are optional. However, if you don't supply anything then nothing will come up!

Name	Description
title	Title.
children	List of Widgets, typically SimpleDialogOptions.

Example – 'simple_dialog'

This app shows a GridView with kitten images. It allows the user to select how the kitten images are fitted into their available screen space.

Source Code

```dart
import 'dart:async';

import 'package:flutter/material.dart';

void main() => runApp(new MyApp());

class MyApp extends StatelessWidget {
  // This widget is the root of your application.
  @override
  Widget build(BuildContext context) {
    return new MaterialApp(
      title: 'Simple Dialog',
      theme: new ThemeData(
        primarySwatch: Colors.blue,
      ),
      home: new HomeWidget(title: 'Simple Dialog'),
    );
  }
}

class HomeWidget extends StatefulWidget {
  HomeWidget({Key key, this.title}) : super(key: key);
  final String title;

  @override
  _HomeWidgetState createState() => new _HomeWidgetState();
}

class _HomeWidgetState extends State<HomeWidget> {
  BoxFit _boxFit = BoxFit.cover;

  void _showBoxFitDialog() async {
    BoxFit boxFit = await showDialog<BoxFit>(
```

```
      context: context,
      builder: (BuildContext context) {
        return SimpleDialog(
          title: const Text('Select Box Fit'),
          children: <Widget>[
            SimpleDialogOption(
              onPressed: () {
                Navigator.pop(context, BoxFit.cover);
              },
              child: const Text('Cover'),
            ),
            SimpleDialogOption(
              onPressed: () {
                Navigator.pop(context, BoxFit.contain);
              },
              child: const Text('Contain'),
            ),
            SimpleDialogOption(
              onPressed: () {
                Navigator.pop(context, BoxFit.fill);
              },
              child: const Text('Fill'),
            ),
            SimpleDialogOption(
              onPressed: () {
                Navigator.pop(context, BoxFit.fitHeight);
              },
              child: const Text('Fit Height'),
            ),
            SimpleDialogOption(
              onPressed: () {
                Navigator.pop(context, BoxFit.fitWidth);
              },
              child: const Text('Fit Width'),
            ),
            SimpleDialogOption(
              onPressed: () {
                Navigator.pop(context, BoxFit.scaleDown);
              },
              child: const Text('Scale Down'),
            ),
            SimpleDialogOption(
              onPressed: () {
                Navigator.pop(context, BoxFit.none);
              },
              child: const Text('None'),
            ),
          ],
        );
      });
  if (boxFit != null) {
    // not cancelled
    setState(() {
      _boxFit = boxFit;
    });
  }
}
```

```
@override
Widget build(BuildContext context) {
  List<Widget> kittenTiles = [];
  for (int i = 200; i < 1000; i += 100) {
    String imageUrl = "http://placekitten.com/200/${i}";
    kittenTiles.add(GridTile(child: Image.network(imageUrl, fit: _boxFit)));
  }
  return Scaffold(
    appBar: AppBar(
      title: Text("${widget.title}: ${_boxFit}"),
    ),
    body: OrientationBuilder(builder: (context, orientation) {
      return GridView.count(
          crossAxisCount: (orientation == Orientation.portrait) ? 2 : 3,
          childAspectRatio: 1.0,
          mainAxisSpacing: 1.0,
          crossAxisSpacing: 1.0,
          children: kittenTiles);
    }),
    floatingActionButton: new FloatingActionButton(
      onPressed: _showBoxFitDialog,
      child: new Icon(Icons.select_all),
    ), // This trailing comma makes auto-formatting nicer for build methods.
  );
}
}
```

Custom Dialog Widget

You can build your own Widget and make it visible the 'showDialog' method.
Your custom dialog widget will be the child of the boilerplate Dialog Widget:

```
GridOptions gridOptions = await showDialog<GridOptions>(
    context: context,
    builder: (BuildContext context) {
      return Dialog(child: CustomDialogWidget(this._gridOptions));
    });
```

Remember that your code will need to wait for the dialog's Future to complete in order to get data back from it. Your code in the custom dialog Widget will call Navigator.pop(data) to pass this data back once the it's closed.

One thing I have noticed from doing custom dialogs in Flutter is that sometimes TextFields do not work well in them. You tap into a TextField and it flashes the keyboard then it disappears. If this happens then the fix for this is changing:

```
final _formKey = GlobalKey<FormState>();
```

to

```
static final _formKey = GlobalKey<FormState>();
```

Example – 'custom_dialog_gridview_settings'

This app shows the grid of cats. It has a button that opens a dialog of the grid options so that the user can change the appearance of the grid.

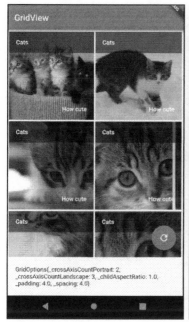  

Source Code

```
import 'dart:async';

import 'package:flutter/material.dart';

void main() => runApp(new GridViewApp());

class GridOptions {
 int _crossAxisCountPortrait;
 int _crossAxisCountLandscape;
 double _childAspectRatio;
 double _padding;
 double _spacing;

 GridOptions(this._crossAxisCountPortrait, this._crossAxisCountLandscape,
    this._childAspectRatio, this._padding, this._spacing);

 GridOptions.copyOf(GridOptions gridOptions) {
  this._crossAxisCountPortrait = gridOptions._crossAxisCountPortrait;
  this._crossAxisCountLandscape = gridOptions._crossAxisCountLandscape;
  this._childAspectRatio = gridOptions._childAspectRatio;
  this._padding = gridOptions._padding;
  this._spacing = gridOptions._spacing;
 }

 @override
```

```
 String toString() {
    return 'GridOptions{_crossAxisCountPortrait: $_crossAxisCountPortrait, _crossAxisCountLandscape:
$_crossAxisCountLandscape, _childAspectRatio: $_childAspectRatio, _padding: $_padding, _spacing:
$_spacing}';
  }
}

class GridViewApp extends StatelessWidget {
  // This widget is the root of your application.
  @override
  Widget build(BuildContext context) {
   return new MaterialApp(
     title: 'Flutter Demo',
     theme: new ThemeData(
      primarySwatch: Colors.blue,
     ),
     home: new HomeWidget(),
   );
  }
}

class CustomDialogWidget extends StatefulWidget {
  GridOptions _gridOptions;
  CustomDialogWidget(this._gridOptions) : super();

  @override
  _CustomDialogWidgetState createState() =>
     new _CustomDialogWidgetState(GridOptions.copyOf(this._gridOptions));
}

class _CustomDialogWidgetState extends State<CustomDialogWidget> {
  GridOptions _gridOptions;

  _CustomDialogWidgetState(this._gridOptions);

  @override
  Widget build(BuildContext context) {
   return Container(
      height: 400.0,
      width: 250.0,
      child:
        Column(mainAxisAlignment: MainAxisAlignment.spaceAround, children: <
           Widget>[
        Text("Grid Options",
          style: TextStyle(fontSize: 20.0, fontWeight: FontWeight.bold)),
        Row(mainAxisAlignment: MainAxisAlignment.center, children: <Widget>[
         Spacer(),
         Text("Cross Axis Count Portrait"),
         Spacer(),
         new DropdownButton<int>(
          value: _gridOptions._crossAxisCountPortrait,
          items: <int>[2, 3, 4, 5, 6].map((int value) {
            return new DropdownMenuItem<int>(
              value: value,
              child: new Text(value.toString()),
            );
          }).toList(),
          onChanged: (newValue) {
```

```
        setState(() {
          _gridOptions._crossAxisCountPortrait = newValue;
        });
      },
    ),
    Spacer(),
  ]),
  Row(mainAxisAlignment: MainAxisAlignment.center, children: <Widget>[
    Spacer(),
    Text("Cross Axis Count Landscape"),
    Spacer(),
    new DropdownButton<int>(
      value: _gridOptions._crossAxisCountLandscape,
      items: <int>[2, 3, 4, 5, 6].map((int value) {
        return new DropdownMenuItem<int>(
          value: value,
          child: new Text(value.toString()),
        );
      }).toList(),
      onChanged: (newValue) {
        setState(() {
          _gridOptions._crossAxisCountLandscape = newValue;
        });
      },
    ),
    Spacer(),
  ]),
  Row(mainAxisAlignment: MainAxisAlignment.center, children: <Widget>[
    Spacer(),
    Text("Aspect Ratio"),
    Spacer(),
    new DropdownButton<double>(
      value: _gridOptions._childAspectRatio,
      items: <double>[1.0, 1.5, 2.0, 2.5].map((double value) {
        return new DropdownMenuItem<double>(
          value: value,
          child: new Text(value.toString()),
        );
      }).toList(),
      onChanged: (newValue) {
        setState(() {
          _gridOptions._childAspectRatio = newValue;
        });
      },
    ),
    Spacer(),
  ]),
  Row(mainAxisAlignment: MainAxisAlignment.center, children: <Widget>[
    Spacer(),
    Text("Padding"),
    Spacer(),
    new DropdownButton<double>(
      value: _gridOptions._padding,
      items:
          <double>[1.0, 2.0, 4.0, 8.0, 16.0, 32.0].map((double value) {
        return new DropdownMenuItem<double>(
          value: value,
          child: new Text(value.toString()),
```

```
          );
        }).toList(),
        onChanged: (newValue) {
          setState(() {
            _gridOptions._padding = newValue;
          });
        },
      ),
      Spacer(),
    ]),
    Row(mainAxisAlignment: MainAxisAlignment.center, children: <Widget>[
      Spacer(),
      Text("Spacing"),
      Spacer(),
      new DropdownButton<double>(
        value: _gridOptions._spacing,
        items:
          <double>[1.0, 2.0, 4.0, 8.0, 16.0, 32.0].map((double value) {
          return new DropdownMenuItem<double>(
            value: value,
            child: new Text(value.toString()),
          );
        }).toList(),
        onChanged: (newValue) {
          setState(() {
            _gridOptions._spacing = newValue;
          });
        },
      ),
      Spacer(),
    ]),
    FlatButton(
        child: Text("Apply"),
        onPressed: () => Navigator.pop(context, _gridOptions))
    ]));
  }
}

class HomeWidget extends StatefulWidget {
  HomeWidget({Key key}) : super(key: key);

  @override
  _HomeWidgetState createState() => new _HomeWidgetState();
}

class _HomeWidgetState extends State<HomeWidget> {
  List<Widget> _kittenTiles = [];
  GridOptions _gridOptions = GridOptions(2, 3, 1.0, 4.0, 4.0);

  _HomeWidgetState() : super() {
    for (int i = 200; i < 1000; i += 100) {
      String imageUrl = "http://placekitten.com/200/${i}";
      _kittenTiles.add(GridTile(
        header: GridTileBar(
          title: Text("Cats", style: TextStyle(fontWeight: FontWeight.bold)),
          backgroundColor: Color.fromRGBO(0, 0, 0, 0.5),
        ),
        footer: GridTileBar(
```

```
        title: Text("How cute",
          textAlign: TextAlign.right,
          style: TextStyle(fontWeight: FontWeight.bold))),
      child: Image.network(imageUrl, fit: BoxFit.cover)));
  }
}

void _showGridOptionsDialog() async {
  GridOptions gridOptions = await showDialog<GridOptions>(
    context: context,
    builder: (BuildContext context) {
      return Dialog(child: CustomDialogWidget(this._gridOptions));
    });
  if (gridOptions != null) {
    setState(() {
      _gridOptions = gridOptions;
    });
  }
}

@override
Widget build(BuildContext context) {
  return Scaffold(
    appBar: AppBar(
      title: Text("GridView"),
    ),
    body: OrientationBuilder(builder: (context, orientation) {
      return GridView.count(
        crossAxisCount: (orientation == Orientation.portrait)
          ? _gridOptions._crossAxisCountPortrait
          : _gridOptions._crossAxisCountLandscape,
        childAspectRatio: _gridOptions._childAspectRatio,
        padding: EdgeInsets.all(_gridOptions._padding),
        mainAxisSpacing: _gridOptions._spacing,
        crossAxisSpacing: _gridOptions._spacing,
        children: _kittenTiles);
    }),
    bottomNavigationBar: Container(
      child: Text(_gridOptions.toString()), padding: EdgeInsets.all(20.0)),
    floatingActionButton: new FloatingActionButton(
      onPressed: _showGridOptionsDialog,
      tooltip: 'Try more grid options',
      child: new Icon(Icons.refresh),
    ), // This trailing comma makes auto-formatting nicer for build methods.
  );
}
}
```

Dismissible

This Widget is useful if you want to be able to swipe left on lists to delete items.
You can also specify other swiping directions in the constructor.

Example – 'dismissible'

This app shows a list of cats. You can swipe left on a cat to delete him/her.

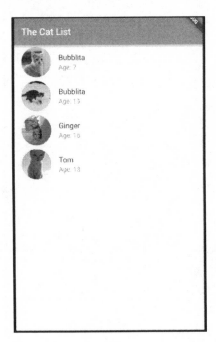 

Source Code

```
import 'dart:math';

import 'package:flutter/material.dart';

void main() => runApp(MyApp());

class Cat {
  String imageSrc;
  String name;
  int age;
  int votes;

  Cat(this.imageSrc, this.name, this.age, this.votes);

  operator ==(other) => (other is Cat) && (imageSrc == other.imageSrc);

  int get hashCode => imageSrc.hashCode;
}

class MyApp extends StatelessWidget {
  // This widget is the root of your application.
  @override
  Widget build(BuildContext context) {
    return MaterialApp(
      title: 'Cat List',
      theme: ThemeData(
        primarySwatch: Colors.blue,
```

```
        ),
      home: MyHomePage(title: 'The Cat List'),
    );
  }
}

class MyHomePage extends StatefulWidget {
  MyHomePage({Key key, this.title}) : super(key: key);

  final String title;

  @override
  _MyHomePageState createState() => _MyHomePageState();
}

class _MyHomePageState extends State<MyHomePage> {
  final GlobalKey<AnimatedListState> _listKey = GlobalKey();
  List<String> CAT_NAMES = [
    "Tom",
    "Oliver",
    "Ginger",
    "Pontouf",
    "Madison",
    "Bubblita",
    "Bubbles"
  ];

  Random _random = Random();
  List<Cat> _cats = [];

  int next(int min, int max) => min + _random.nextInt(max - min);

  _MyHomePageState() : super() {
    for (int i = 200; i < 250; i += 10) {
      _cats.add(Cat("http://placekitten.com/200/${i}", CAT_NAMES[next(0, 6)],
        next(1, 32), 0));
    }
  }

  _buildItem(Cat cat, {int index = -1}) {
    return ListTile(
        key: Key("ListTile:${cat.hashCode.toString()}"),
        leading: CircleAvatar(
          backgroundImage: NetworkImage(cat.imageSrc), radius: 32.0),
        title: Text(cat.name, style: TextStyle(fontSize: 25.0)),
        subtitle: Text("This little thug is ${cat.age} year(s) old.",
          style: TextStyle(fontSize: 15.0)));
  }

  _onDismissed(int index) {
    // If you do the code below
    // setState(() {
    //   _cats.remove(index);
    // });
    // then you get the following error:
    // This MyHomePage widget cannot be marked as needing to build because the framework is already in
the
    // process of building widgets. A widget can be marked as needing to be built during the build phase
```

```
    // only if one of its ancestors is currently building. This exception is allowed because the framework
    // builds parent widgets before children, which means a dirty descendant will always be built.
    // Otherwise, the framework might not visit this widget during this build phase.
    //
    // This works:
    _cats.remove(index);

  }

  Future<bool> _confirmDismiss(DismissDirection direction) async{
    return await showDialog<bool>(
      context: context,
      builder: (BuildContext context) {
        return AlertDialog(
          title: const Text('Confirm'),
          content: Text('Are you sure you want to delete this cat?\n\nHe is cute you know...'),
          actions: <Widget>[
            FlatButton(
              onPressed: () {
                Navigator.pop(context, true);
              },
              child: const Text('Yes'),
            ),
            FlatButton(
              onPressed: () {
                Navigator.pop(context, false);
              },
              child: const Text('No'),
            )
          ],
        );
      });
  }

  @override
  Widget build(BuildContext context) {
    return Scaffold(
      appBar: AppBar(
        title: Text(widget.title),
      ),
      body: ListView.builder(
        itemCount: _cats != null ? _cats.length : 0,
        itemBuilder: (context, index) {
          Cat cat = _cats[index];
          return Dismissible(
            confirmDismiss: _confirmDismiss,
            direction: DismissDirection.endToStart,
            onDismissed: _onDismissed(index),
            key: ValueKey(cat.hashCode.toString()),
            child: ListTile(
              leading: CircleAvatar(
                backgroundImage: NetworkImage(cat.imageSrc),
                radius: 32.0),
              title: Text('${cat.name}'),
              subtitle: Text('Age: ${cat.age}')));
        }));
  }
}
```

ExpansionPanelList & ExpansionPanel

These two widgets are designed to work together to present a list of expandable panels to the user. They help you build a UI with expanding lists but they **don't** hold the state for you.

You have to manage the state of what was expanded / collapsed and rebuild the ExpansionPanelList & ExpansionPanels everytime the state changes. This sounds slow but it's not! Check out the example below to see an example of this.

ExpansionPanelList

This does the following:
- Lays out the child ExpansionPanels.
- Provides expansionCallback constructor argument to which you can add provide to respond to the user attempting to expand / collapse panels, managing the state and forcing a repaint once a panel is expanded or collapsed.
- Animations.

ExpansionPanel

This does the following:
- Display the header with an arrow next to it.
- Displays the body if the 'isExpanded' constructor argument is set to true.
- When the user clicks on header arrow to expand or collapse, this fires the expansionCallback in the ExpansionPanelList.

Example – 'expansion_panel'

This app shows Frequently Asked Questions with arrows. When the user taps the arrow on a question, the panel is expanded to show the answer.

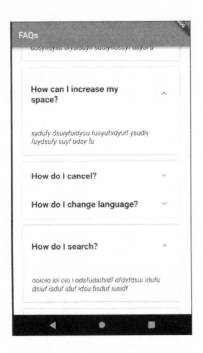

Source Code

```
import 'package:flutter/material.dart';

void main() => runApp(new MyApp());

class ExpansionPanelData {
  String _title;
  String _body;
  bool _expanded;

  ExpansionPanelData(this._title, this._body, this._expanded);

  String get title => _title;

  @override
  String toString() {
    return 'ExpansionPanelData{_title: $_title, _body: $_body, _expanded: $_expanded}';
  }

  String get body => _body;

  bool get expanded => _expanded;

  set expanded(bool value) {
    _expanded = value;
  }
}

class MyApp extends StatelessWidget {
  // This widget is the root of your application.
  @override
  Widget build(BuildContext context) {
    return new MaterialApp(
      title: 'Flutter Demo',
```

```
      theme: new ThemeData(
        primarySwatch: Colors.green,
      ),
      home: new HomeWidget(),
      showPerformanceOverlay: true);
  }
}

class HomeWidget extends StatefulWidget {
  @override
  _HomeWidgetState createState() => new _HomeWidgetState([
      ExpansionPanelData(
        "Can I backup my data?",
        "dsfuysdiu fudsy fiusdyf "
        "usdyf iudsyf udsyfiuysd ufyuisdyfi sduiyfiusdyf dsyui u",
        false),
      ExpansionPanelData(
        "How can I increase my space?",
        "sydufy "
        "dsuiyfuidysu fusyufsdyuif ysudiy fuydsufy suyf udsy fu",
        false),
      ExpansionPanelData(
        "How do I cancel?",
        "ddsufysd yfds fsduyf sdyf "
        "sudyuy fsudyf sydyf dsy fdsuyf udsufy udsyfdsfyuysdf uyud",
        false),
      ExpansionPanelData(
        "How do I change language?",
        "udsuf sdifuu fdsuif "
        "uf dsufdisu fius wewqw qeqweqwyiquuiqweqwewqe weewe wewe",
        false),
      ExpansionPanelData(
        "How do I search?",
        "ooioio ioi oio i odsfudsifsdf"
        " dfdsfdsui idufu dsiuf isduf iduf idsu fisduf iusidf ",
        false),
      ExpansionPanelData(
        "How do I view on other devices?",
        "idusdf isu "
        "idsu idsu fisduf usyfuedy ewuyduyed uyeu dyeudy uweyu",
        false),
      ExpansionPanelData(
        "How do I view my history",
        "iirewy syfudy fu "
        "yfsduyfds yfdsuyf udsfydsufy sduyf dsuyf udsyf udsyuee",
        false),
      ExpansionPanelData(
        "Is my subscription cost going to go up?",
        "wieureiy dys udsyyf "
        "dsufy dusyfudsy fuysdu udsyuyfudsyfuewyrwreooioou  uiy",
        false),
    ]);
}

class _HomeWidgetState extends State<HomeWidget> {
 // Track expansion panels, including expanded true/false;
 List<ExpansionPanelData> _expansionPanelData;
```

```
_HomeWidgetState(this._expansionPanelData);

_onExpansion(int panelIndex, bool isExpanded) {
 // Toggle the expanded state. Using setState will force 'build' to fire.
 setState(() {
  _expansionPanelData[panelIndex].expanded =
   !(_expansionPanelData[panelIndex].expanded);
 });
}

@override
Widget build(BuildContext context) {
 // Build the expansion panels from scratch every time the ui builds.
 // This is not as expensive as it sounds.
 List<ExpansionPanel> expansionPanels = [];
 for (int i = 0, ii = _expansionPanelData.length; i < ii; i++) {
  var expansionPanelData = _expansionPanelData[i];
  expansionPanels.add(ExpansionPanel(
    headerBuilder: (BuildContext context, bool isExpanded) {
     return Padding(
        padding: EdgeInsets.all(20.0),
        child: Text(expansionPanelData.title,
          style: TextStyle(
            fontSize: 20.0, fontWeight: FontWeight.bold)));
    },
    body: Padding(
      padding: EdgeInsets.all(20.0),
      child: Text(expansionPanelData.body,
        style:
          TextStyle(fontSize: 16.0, fontStyle: FontStyle.italic))),
    isExpanded: expansionPanelData.expanded));
 }
 return new Scaffold(
   appBar: new AppBar(
    title: new Text("FAQs"),
   ),
   body: SingleChildScrollView(
     child: Container(
     margin: const EdgeInsets.all(24.0),
     child: new ExpansionPanelList(
       children: expansionPanels, expansionCallback: _onExpansion),
   )));
 }
}
```

GridView

Grids are very commonly-used on devices to present many items of information in a small screen area in a clear manner. Typically, your launch (or home) screen will be presented using a grid, see below.

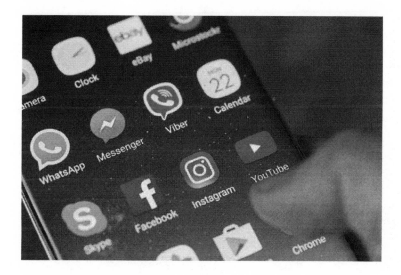

Notice how each Grid item is of a uniform size (unlike a staggered grid, see below). Grids are often fluid – users can view a certain number of items per grid row in portrait mode and a different number of items per grid row in landscape mode.

The Flutter GridView Widget enables developers to quickly build grids. The GridView Widget is very flexible and here are some of the more popular options that are available as properties in the constructor:

- crossAxisCount – number of items per grid row
- childAspectRatio – sets the aspect ratio of each item in the grid
- padding – padding around the grid
- mainAxisSpacing – spacing between items in the grid on main axix
- crossAxisSpacing – spacing between items in the grid on cross axis
- children – array of child widgets to be displayed as items

Builder

The GridView has a builder to improve the performance of the Grid when you have to display many items. This is covered in the Builder chapter.

GridTile

You don't have to use GridTiles with GridViews but they are useful because they can display headers and footers (using GridTileBars) for each item. Really useful when you want to add some text, description or price to each item.

GridTileBar

Used to show headers or footers on grid tiles.

Example – 'gridview_app'

This is an app that shows kittens on a grid. It has a refresh button that enables you to cycle through some example grid options and see how they affect the appearance of the grid. Also note that the grid always works responsively, changing the number of items per grid row when the device changes from portrait to landscape and visa-versa. This app also uses GridTile and Grid TileBar widgets.

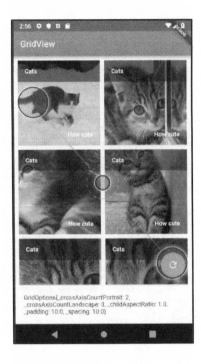

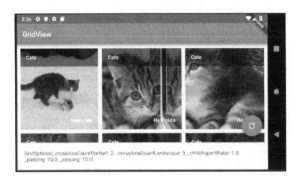

Source Code

```
import 'package:flutter/material.dart';

void main() => runApp(new GridViewApp());

class GridOptions {
  int _crossAxisCountPortrait;
  int _crossAxisCountLandscape;
  double _childAspectRatio;
  double _padding;
  double _spacing;

  GridOptions(this._crossAxisCountPortrait, this._crossAxisCountLandscape,
      this._childAspectRatio, this._padding, this._spacing);

  @override
  String toString() {
    return 'GridOptions{_crossAxisCountPortrait: $_crossAxisCountPortrait, _crossAxisCountLandscape:
$_crossAxisCountLandscape, _childAspectRatio: $_childAspectRatio, _padding: $_padding, _spacing:
$_spacing}';
  }
}
```

```
class GridViewApp extends StatelessWidget {
  // This widget is the root of your application.
  @override
  Widget build(BuildContext context) {
    return new MaterialApp(
      title: 'Flutter Demo',
      theme: new ThemeData(
        primarySwatch: Colors.blue,
      ),
      home: new HomeWidget(title: 'Flutter Demo Home Page'),
    );
  }
}

class HomeWidget extends StatefulWidget {
  HomeWidget({Key key, this.title}) : super(key: key);

  final String title;

  @override
  _HomeWidgetState createState() => new _HomeWidgetState();
}

class _HomeWidgetState extends State<HomeWidget> {
  List<Widget> _kittenTiles = [];
  int _gridOptionsIndex = 0;
  List<GridOptions> _gridOptions = [
    GridOptions(2, 3, 1.0, 10.0, 10.0),
    GridOptions(3, 4, 1.0, 10.0, 10.0),
    GridOptions(4, 5, 1.0, 10.0, 10.0),
    GridOptions(2, 3, 1.0, 10.0, 10.0),
    GridOptions(2, 3, 1.5, 10.0, 10.0),
    GridOptions(2, 3, 2.0, 10.0, 10.0),
    GridOptions(2, 3, 1.0, 10.0, 10.0),
    GridOptions(2, 3, 1.5, 20.0, 10.0),
    GridOptions(2, 3, 2.0, 30.0, 10.0),
    GridOptions(2, 3, 1.0, 10.0, 10.0),
    GridOptions(2, 3, 1.5, 10.0, 20.0),
    GridOptions(2, 3, 2.0, 10.0, 30.0),
  ];

  _HomeWidgetState() : super() {
    for (int i = 200; i < 1000; i += 100) {
      String imageUrl = "http://placekitten.com/200/${i}";
      _kittenTiles.add(GridTile(
        header: GridTileBar(
          title: Text("Cats", style: TextStyle(fontWeight: FontWeight.bold)),
          backgroundColor: Color.fromRGBO(0, 0, 0, 0.5),
        ),
        footer: GridTileBar(
          title: Text("How cute",
            textAlign: TextAlign.right,
            style: TextStyle(fontWeight: FontWeight.bold))),
        child: Image.network(imageUrl, fit: BoxFit.cover)));
    }
  }
```

```
void _tryMoreGridOptions() {
  setState(() {
    _gridOptionsIndex++;
    if (_gridOptionsIndex >= (_gridOptions.length - 1)) {
      _gridOptionsIndex = 0;
    }
  });
}

@override
Widget build(BuildContext context) {
  GridOptions options = _gridOptions[_gridOptionsIndex];
  return Scaffold(
    appBar: AppBar(
      title: Text("GridView"),
    ),
    body: OrientationBuilder(builder: (context, orientation) {
      return GridView.count(
        crossAxisCount: (orientation == Orientation.portrait)
          ? options._crossAxisCountPortrait
          : options._crossAxisCountLandscape,
        childAspectRatio: options._childAspectRatio,
        padding: EdgeInsets.all(options._padding),
        mainAxisSpacing: options._spacing,
        crossAxisSpacing: options._spacing,
        children: _kittenTiles);
    }),
    bottomNavigationBar: Container(
      child: Text(options.toString()), padding: EdgeInsets.all(20.0)),
    floatingActionButton: new FloatingActionButton(
      onPressed: _tryMoreGridOptions,
      tooltip: 'Try more grid options',
      child: new Icon(Icons.refresh),
    ), // This trailing comma makes auto-formatting nicer for build methods.
  );
}
}
```

Further Reading

- This is an excellent article about writing staggered gridviews. These are excellent at displaying items of different sizes.
  https://medium.com/@lets4r/flutorial-create-a-staggered-gridview-9c881a9b0b98

PopupMenuButton

Displays a menu when pressed and calls 'onSelected' when the menu is dismissed because an item was selected. The value passed to 'onSelected' is the value of the selected menu item.

Example – 'popup_menu_button'

This app is similar to the default Flutter app except that it enables the user to increment the counter using the menu. The menu also has an exit option to close the app.

Source Code

```
import 'package:flutter/material.dart';
import 'package:flutter/services.dart';

void main() => runApp(new MyApp());

enum PopupMenuAction { add1, add10, add100, exit }

class MyApp extends StatelessWidget {
  // This widget is the root of your application.
  @override
  Widget build(BuildContext context) {
    return new MaterialApp(
      title: 'Flutter Demo',
      theme: new ThemeData(
        primarySwatch: Colors.blue,
      ),
      home: new HomeWidget(title: 'Flutter Demo Home Page'),
    );
  }
}

class HomeWidget extends StatefulWidget {
  HomeWidget({Key key, this.title}) : super(key: key);
  final String title;
```

```
  @override
  _HomeWidgetState createState() => new _HomeWidgetState();
}

class _HomeWidgetState extends State<HomeWidget> {
  int _counter = 0;

  void _increment(int by) {
    setState(() {
      _counter += by;
    });
  }

  void _onPopupMenuSelected(PopupMenuAction item) {
    if (PopupMenuAction.exit == item) {
      SystemChannels.platform.invokeMethod('SystemNavigator.pop');
    } else {
      _increment(PopupMenuAction.add1 == item
        ? 1
        : PopupMenuAction.add10 == item ? 10 : 100);
    }
  }

  @override
  Widget build(BuildContext context) {
    return new Scaffold(
      appBar: new AppBar(
        title: new Text(widget.title),
        actions: <Widget>[
          PopupMenuButton<PopupMenuAction>(
            onSelected: _onPopupMenuSelected,
            itemBuilder: (BuildContext context) =>
                <PopupMenuEntry<PopupMenuAction>>[
                  const PopupMenuItem<PopupMenuAction>(
                    value: PopupMenuAction.add1,
                    child: Text('+1'),
                  ),
                  const PopupMenuItem<PopupMenuAction>(
                    value: PopupMenuAction.add10,
                    child: Text('+10'),
                  ),
                  const PopupMenuItem<PopupMenuAction>(
                    value: PopupMenuAction.add100,
                    child: Text('+100'),
                  ),
                  const PopupMenuDivider(),
                  const PopupMenuItem<PopupMenuAction>(
                    value: PopupMenuAction.exit,
                    child: Text('Exit'),
                  ),
                ],
          )
        ],
      ),
      body: new Center(
        child: new Column(
          mainAxisAlignment: MainAxisAlignment.center,
          children: <Widget>[
```

```
      new Text(
        'You have pushed the button this many times:',
      ),
      new Text(
        '$_counter',
        style: Theme.of(context).textTheme.display1,
      ),
    ],
  ),
));
  }
}
```

Radio

This is a material design button that allows the user to select one item from a group of items. We will cover this in detail in the Forms chapter.

SnackBar

Very useful for showing quick messages to the user, things like:
- Customer deleted.
- Error messages.

Snackbars close themselves, so they don't leave any unnecessary clutter in the UI.

Example – 'snack_bar'

This app has a button to simulate an error being displayed with a Snack Bar.

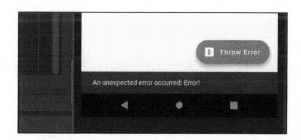

Other Widgets

Source Code

```dart
import 'package:flutter/material.dart';

void main() => runApp(new MyApp());

class MyApp extends StatelessWidget {
  // This widget is the root of your application.
  @override
  Widget build(BuildContext context) {
    return new MaterialApp(
      title: 'Flutter Demo',
      theme: new ThemeData(
        primarySwatch: Colors.blue,
      ),
      home: new HomePageWidget(),
    );
  }
}

class HomePageWidget extends StatelessWidget {
  HomePageWidget({Key key}) : super(key: key);
  final GlobalKey<ScaffoldState> _scaffoldKey = GlobalKey<ScaffoldState>();

  _showSnackBar() {
    _scaffoldKey.currentState.showSnackBar(SnackBar(
      content: Text('An unexpected error occurred: Error!'),
    ));
  }

  @override
  Widget build(BuildContext context) {
    return Scaffold(
      key: _scaffoldKey,
      appBar: new AppBar(
        title: new Text("Snackbar"),
      ),
      body: new Center(
        child: new Column(
          mainAxisAlignment: MainAxisAlignment.center,
          children: <Widget>[
            new Text(
              'Content goes here.',
            ),
          ],
        ),
      ),
      floatingActionButton: new FloatingActionButton.extended(
        icon: Icon(Icons.explicit),
        label: Text("Throw Error"),
        onPressed: () => _showSnackBar(),
        tooltip: 'Throw Error'));
  }
}
```

Spacer

Spacers can be used to tune the spacing between widgets in a Flex container, like Row or Column. Spacers can be used vertically or horizontally.

Spacers sometimes behavior differently from expected as they are not of a fixed width. They attempt to use up all the available space, using the flex property in a similar manner to other Widgets.

Flex Property

The 'flex' property (and constructor argument) lets you specify their relative size. Example: a Spacer(flex:5) will be 5 times wider than a Spacer(flex:1).

Exercise – 'spacer'

We create a basic app with the toolbar icons spaced out using the Spacer Widget.

- You can specify the 'title' as a toolbar property. However, if you specify the 'actions' property in the toolbar then the title passed in by the 'title' property becomes invisible. So, we add the title text to the list of widgets in 'actions' property.
- We use several Spacers in the list of widgets in 'actions' property. Note that all the spacers are the same size, except the one after the title text, which has a flex of 5. This value tells it to make it 5 times as wide as the others.

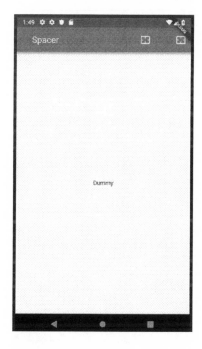

Source Code

```
import 'package:flutter/material.dart';
```

```
void main() => runApp(new MyApp());

class MyApp extends StatelessWidget {
  // This widget is the root of your application.
  @override
  Widget build(BuildContext context) {
    return new MaterialApp(
      title: 'Flutter Demo',
      theme: new ThemeData(
        primarySwatch: Colors.blue,
      ),
      home: new HomePageWidget(),
    );
  }
}

class HomePageWidget extends StatelessWidget {
  HomePageWidget({Key key}) : super(key: key);

  @override
  Widget build(BuildContext context) {
    return new Scaffold(
      appBar: new AppBar(actions: <Widget>[
        Spacer(),
        Center(
          child: Text(
          "Spacer",
          style: TextStyle(fontSize: 20.0),
        )),
        Spacer(flex: 5),
        IconButton(icon: Icon(Icons.settings_overscan), onPressed: () => {}),
        Spacer(),
        IconButton(icon: Icon(Icons.settings_overscan), onPressed: () => {})
      ]),
      body: new Center(
        child: new Column(
          mainAxisAlignment: MainAxisAlignment.center,
          children: <Widget>[
            new Text(
              'Dummy',
            )
          ],
        ),
      ));
  }
}
```

Switch

This is a material design widget that allows the user to select a yes / no.
We will cover this in detail in the Forms chapter.

TabBar, Tabs and TabBarView Widgets

These Widgets are great for quickly building tabbed user-interfaces. Flutter gives all the Widgets we need to get started with a tabbed interface in just a couple of minutes.

However, you need to bear in mind that these tabs will probably not match you are expecting to see on iOS devices, as these Widgets follow the Google Material design language:

TabBar & TabBarView vs iOS Tabs

	TabBar & TabBarView	iOS Tabs
Selected item text color	None	Blue
Selected line (indicator)	Blue	None
Padding	More	Less

Instructions:

1. Add a TabController. The Controller serves to link the TabBar and TabBarView together. When creating a TabBar, you must either provide a TabController using the "controller" property, or you must ensure that there is a DefaultTabController above the TabBar in the Widget hierarchy.
2. Add a TabBar at the top or the bottom of the Widget. This is the Widget that displays its child Widgets (Tabs) in a bar for selection purposes.
3. Add a TabBarView to the main area of the Widget.

Exercise – 'tabs_simple'

Let's build the simplest possible app with a simple tabbed interface containing 3 cat pictures. Then we will modify the tab bar.

Step 1 – Create Default Flutter App

Follow the instructions in Generate Your First App
Leave project open.

Step 2 – Replace Application Code

Replace contents of file 'main.dart' in folder 'lib' with the following:

```dart
import 'package:flutter/material.dart';

void main() => runApp(new MyApp());

class MyApp extends StatelessWidget {
  @override
  Widget build(BuildContext context) {
    return new MaterialApp(
      title: 'Flutter Demo',
      theme: new ThemeData(
        primarySwatch: Colors.blue,
      ),
      home: new HomeWidget(),
    );
  }
}

class Tab1 extends StatelessWidget {
  @override
  Widget build(BuildContext context) {
    return Image.network("https://cdn2.thecatapi.com/images/MTY1NDA3OA.jpg");
  }
}
```

```
class Tab2 extends StatelessWidget {
  @override
  Widget build(BuildContext context) {
    return Image.network("https://cdn2.thecatapi.com/images/68j.jpg");
  }
}

class Tab3 extends StatelessWidget {
  @override
  Widget build(BuildContext context) {
    return Image.network("https://cdn2.thecatapi.com/images/ece.jpg");
  }
}

class HomeWidget extends StatelessWidget {
  HomeWidget({Key key}) : super(key: key);

  @override
  Widget build(BuildContext context) {
    return DefaultTabController(
      length: 3,
      child: new Scaffold(
        appBar: new AppBar(
          title: new Text("Cat Tabs"),
          bottom: TabBar(
            tabs: <Widget>[
              Tab(text: 'Cat #1', icon: Icon(Icons.keyboard_arrow_left)),
              Tab(text: 'Cat #2', icon: Icon(Icons.keyboard_arrow_up)),
              Tab(text: 'Cat #3', icon: Icon(Icons.keyboard_arrow_right))
            ],
          ),
        ),
        body: TabBarView(
          children: <Widget>[Tab1(), Tab2(), Tab3()],
        )));
  }
}
```

Step 3 – Open Emulator & Run

Follow the instructions in <u>Open Android Emulator & Run Your First App</u>
Your tabbed interface should appear at the top and look like this:

Step 4 – Move Tabs to Bottom

Now let's amend the 'build' code to show the tabs at the bottom to make it look a bit more like the iOS tabs.
Change the 'build' method to the following:

```
@override
Widget build(BuildContext context) {
 return DefaultTabController(
    length: 3,
    child: new Scaffold(
      appBar: new AppBar(
       title: new Text("Cat Tabs"),
      ),
      body: TabBarView(
       children: <Widget>[Tab1(), Tab2(), Tab3()],
      ),
      bottomNavigationBar: Container(
        child: TabBar(labelColor: Colors.black, tabs: <Widget>[
      Tab(text: 'Cat #1', icon: Icon(Icons.keyboard_arrow_left)),
      Tab(text: 'Cat #2', icon: Icon(Icons.keyboard_arrow_up)),
      Tab(text: 'Cat #3', icon: Icon(Icons.keyboard_arrow_right))
      ]))));
}
```

Hot-reload your app and your tabbed interface should appear at the bottom and look like this:

Step 5 – Change Tab Styles To Look More Like iOS

Now let's amend the 'build' code to make the tabs at the bottom look even more similar to those on iOS tabs, without using the Cupertino Widgets.

Change the 'build' method to the following:

```
@override
Widget build(BuildContext context) {
 return DefaultTabController(
    length: 3,
    child: new Scaffold(
      appBar: new AppBar(
       title: new Text("Cat Tabs"),
      ),
      body: TabBarView(
       children: <Widget>[Tab1(), Tab2(), Tab3()],
      ),
      bottomNavigationBar: Container(
        child: TabBar(
          labelColor: Colors.blue,
          unselectedLabelColor: Colors.grey,
          labelStyle: TextStyle(
            color: Colors.blue, fontWeight: FontWeight.w800),
          indicatorColor: Colors.white,
          tabs: <Widget>[
```

```
        Tab(text: 'Cat #1', icon: Icon(Icons.keyboard_arrow_left)),
        Tab(text: 'Cat #2', icon: Icon(Icons.keyboard_arrow_up)),
        Tab(text: 'Cat #3', icon: Icon(Icons.keyboard_arrow_right))
      ])))));
}
```

Hot-reload your app and your tabbed interface at the bottom should now look like this:

Table

Introduction

The Table Widget works well when you have dynamically-sized components, generated from user data, some wide, some narrow. This widget gives you a great deal of control over column widths (see below).

Column Width Specifiers

The Table Widget has a 'columnWidths' argument available in the constructor, which you can populate with a map of column indexes and TableColumnWidth objects. Table Column Width objects can be any of the following:

- FixedColumnWidth
- FlexColumnWidth (attempts to take up a share of the spare width)
- FractionColumnWidth (takes a fraction of the width)
- IntrinsicColumnWidth (sizes the column according to the intrinsic dimensions of all the cells in that column).
- MaxColumnWidth
- MinColumnWidth

Example – 'table'

This example shows a table with differently sized columns, text wrapping, as well as scrolling.

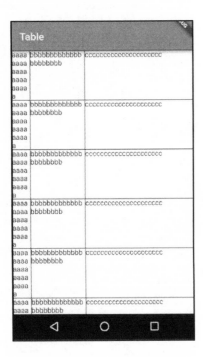

Source Code

```
import 'package:flutter/material.dart';

void main() => runApp(new TableApp());

class TableApp extends StatelessWidget {
  @override
  Widget build(BuildContext context) {
    return new MaterialApp(
      title: 'Flutter Demo',
      theme: new ThemeData(
        primarySwatch: Colors.blue,
      ),
      home: new HomeWidget(),
    );
  }
}

class HomeWidget extends StatelessWidget {
  HomeWidget({Key key}) : super(key: key);

  @override
  Widget build(BuildContext context) {
    const TableRow tableRow = TableRow(children: [
      const Text("aaaaaaaaaaaaaaaaaaaaaaa", overflow: TextOverflow.fade),
      const Text("bbbbbbbbbbbbbbbbbbbbbb", overflow: TextOverflow.fade),
      const Text("ccccccccccccccccccccc", overflow: TextOverflow.ellipsis)
    ]);
    return new Scaffold(
      appBar: new AppBar(title: new Text("Table")),
      body: new Table(
        children: [
          tableRow,
          tableRow,
```

```
      tableRow,
      tableRow,
      tableRow,
      tableRow,
      tableRow,
      tableRow,
      tableRow,
    ],
    columnWidths: const <int, TableColumnWidth>{
      0: FlexColumnWidth(0.1),
      1: FlexColumnWidth(0.3),
      2: FlexColumnWidth(0.6),
    },
    border: TableBorder.all(),
  ) // end table,
  );
 }
}
```

23. Builders

Introduction

The purpose of this chapter is to learn how to use Flutter builder classes.

If you go to the official Flutter documentation for the builder class you see it has the following description:

"A platonic widget that calls a closure to obtain its child widget."

What does that mean? ☺

What is a Builder?

The term closure is just another name for a lambda function, an anonymous method.
So, builder is really a lambda that acts similarly to the Widget's build method:
- You pass it a BuildContext and any other variables you need to.
- It returns a Widget.

How Do You Use a Builder?

Instead of passing a Widget back from your build method, instead you pass back an anonymous builder function that takes whatever parameters are required (including the BuildContext) and spits out a Widget.

Nested Builders

You can nest builders inside builders and this (although sometimes complicated) works very well. There is an example in this Chapter called 'Multiple Builders', which uses nested builders.

Common Builders

AnimatedBuilder

We will cover this builder in the Animations chapter.

GridView Builder

Similar to the ListView builder. Quite often you will end up with large dynamic data grids and you need to display them onscreen using a Grid, even though the user may not scroll all the way to the bottom.

If you simply add a Widget for each item in the grid, you end up with a huge amount of child Widgets, most of which will never be seen. This is not efficient.

This is where the GridView builder comes in. When the user scrolls down through the grid, the GridView builder is invoked to create the child widgets when they are needed, not ahead of time. Much more efficient.

You write a GridView builder and specify it to the GridView in the 'itemBuilder' argument in the constructor. In the builder method, you accept BuildContext and index arguments and you spit out a Widget. This is perfect if your data is held in array – all you do is get the data for that item from the array using that index.

There is an example in this Chapter called 'Multiple Builders'. It uses the GridView builder, amongst other builders!

FutureBuilder

FutureBuilder is a widget that returns another widget based on the Future's execution result. It serves as a bridge between Futures and the Widget's UI.

Example – 'future_builder_app'

This app uses a FutureBuilder to calculates a bunch of timestamps using a Future computation and display it. The screen is blank for a few seconds then it displays a list of times. It's not terribly pretty!

Source Code:

```dart
import 'dart:async';

import 'package:flutter/material.dart';

void main() => runApp(new MyApp());

class MyApp extends StatelessWidget {
  // This widget is the root of your application.
  @override
  Widget build(BuildContext context) {
    return new MaterialApp(
      title: 'Future Builder App',
      theme: new ThemeData(
        primarySwatch: Colors.blue,
      ),
      home: new HomeWidget(),
    );
  }
}

class HomeWidget extends StatefulWidget {
  String computeListOfTimestamps(int count) {
    StringBuffer sb = new StringBuffer();
    for (int i = 0; i < count; i++) {
      sb.writeln("${i + 1} : ${DateTime.now()}");
    }
    return sb.toString();
  }

  Future<String> createFutureCalculation(int count) {
    return new Future(() {
```

```dart
      return computeListOfTimestamps(count);
    });
  }

  HomeWidget({Key key}) : super(key: key);

  @override
  _HomeWidgetState createState() => new _HomeWidgetState();
}

class _HomeWidgetState extends State<HomeWidget> {
  bool _showCalculation = false;

  void _onInvokeFuturePressed() {
    setState(() {
      _showCalculation = !_showCalculation;
    });
  }

  @override
  Widget build(BuildContext context) {
    Widget child = _showCalculation
      ? FutureBuilder(
          future: widget.createFutureCalculation(10000),
          builder: (BuildContext context, AsyncSnapshot snapshot) {
            return Expanded(
                child: SingleChildScrollView(
                    child: Text(
                        '${snapshot.data == null ? "" : snapshot.data}',
                        style: TextStyle(fontSize: 20.0))));
          })
      : Text('hit the button to show calculation');
    return new Scaffold(
      appBar: new AppBar(
        title: new Text("Future"),
      ),
      body: new Center(
          child: new Column(
              mainAxisAlignment: MainAxisAlignment.center,
              children: <Widget>[child])),
      floatingActionButton: new FloatingActionButton(
        onPressed: _onInvokeFuturePressed,
        tooltip: 'Invoke Future',
        child: new Icon(Icons.refresh),
      ), // This trailing comma makes auto-formatting nicer for build methods.
    );
  }
}
```

ListView Builder:

Similar to the GridView builder. Quite often you will end up with large dynamic lists of data and you need to display them onscreen using a ListView, even though the user may not scroll through the list.

If you simply add a Widget for each item in the list, you end up with a huge amount of child Widgets, most of which will never be seen. This is not efficient.

This is where the ListView builder comes in. When the user scrolls through the list, the ListView builder is invoked to create the child widgets when they are needed, not ahead of time. Much more efficient.

You write a ListView builder and specify it to the ListView in the 'itemBuilder' argument in the constructor. In the builder method, you accept BuildContext and index arguments and you spit out a Widget. This is perfect if your data is held in array – all you do is get the data for that item from the array using that index.

Example – 'listview_builder'

This app shoes a list of NASA offices in the US. The app sorts the list of NASA offices by name in the constructor and prints to the console everytime the ListView builder is invoked, so you can see how the child widgets are built 'on demand'. It also displays each Nasa Office in a ListTile.

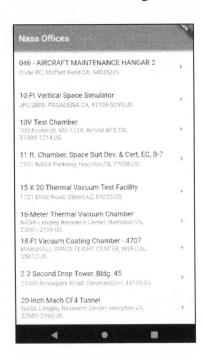

Source Code

```
import 'package:flutter/material.dart';

void main() => runApp(new MyApp());

class MyApp extends StatelessWidget {
  @override
  Widget build(BuildContext context) {
    return new MaterialApp(
      title: 'Flutter Demo',
      theme: new ThemeData(
        primarySwatch: Colors.blue,
```

Builders

```
      ),
      home: new MyHomeWidget(),
    );
  }
}

class MyHomeWidget extends StatelessWidget {
  List<dynamic> _nasaOffices = [
    {
      "Name": "Mach 6, High Reynolds Number Facility",
      "Address": "1864 4th St",
      "City": "Wright-Patterson AFB",
      "State": "OH",
      "ZIP": "45433-7541",
      "Country": "US"
    },
```

... edited for bevity ...

```
    {
      "Name": "N206A - 12 FOOT PRESSURE WIND TUNNEL AUXILIARIES (PAPAC)",
      "Address": "Code RC",
      "City": "Moffett Field",
      "State": "CA",
      "ZIP": "94035",
      "Country": "US"
    }
  ];

  MyHomeWidget({Key key}) : super(key: key) {
    _nasaOffices.sort((a, b) => a['Name'].compareTo(b['Name']));
  }

  @override
  Widget build(BuildContext context) {
    ListView builder = ListView.builder(
        itemCount: _nasaOffices.length,
        itemBuilder: (context, index) {
          print('invoking itemBuilder for row ${index}');
          var nasaOffice = _nasaOffices[index];
          return ListTile(
            title: Text('${nasaOffice['Name']}'),
            subtitle: Text('${nasaOffice['Address']}, ${nasaOffice['City']},'
              '${nasaOffice['State']}, ${nasaOffice['ZIP']},'
              '${nasaOffice['Country']}'),
            trailing: Icon(Icons.arrow_right));
        });
    return new Scaffold(
      appBar: new AppBar(
        title: new Text("Nasa Offices"),
      ),
      body: new Center(child: builder));
  }
}
```

OrientationBuilder

Sometime the user will rotate their screen from portrait mode to landscape mode and visa-versa. You may wish to change the layout to take advantage of the extra space. For example, you may want to show a grid with 2 items across in portrait, 3 items across in landscape.

This is where the OrientationBuilder comes in. Wrap your builder code in an OrientationBuilder and it can react to orientation changes.

There is an example in this Chapter called 'Multiple Builders'. It uses the OrientationBuilder, amongst other builders!

PageRoutebuilder

We will cover this builder in the Routing & Navigation chapter.

StreamBuilder

StreamBuilder

StreamBuilders listen for changes in streams and build Widgets when the stream data changes. Thus, your Widgets can update when the state changes and the state change is pushed to a stream.

Some of the state management patterns (such as the BLoC, covered later on in its own chapter) use this builder to update the ui when a stream value changes.

There is an example in this Chapter called 'Multiple Builders'. It uses the StreamBuilder, amongst other builders!

Example – 'nested_builders'

This app shows some colored squares: 3 across in portrait, 4 across in landscape. It also allows you to hit the '+' button to add more squares. To do this, the app stores its state (the squares) in a BLoC (don't worry about this too much, we will cover this in another chapter) and uses the following builders in the HomeWidget, nested within each other:

- StreamBuilder – update ui when state changes
  - OrientationBuilder – update ui when orientation changes
    - GridView Builder – builds ui for grid.

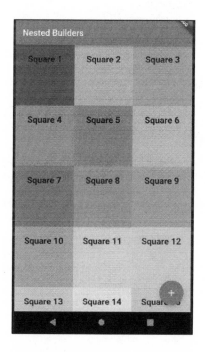

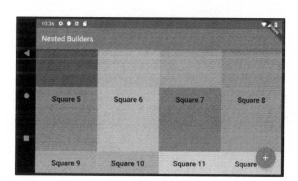

Source Code

```
import 'dart:async';
import 'dart:math';

import 'package:flutter/material.dart';
import 'package:rxdart/rxdart.dart';

class Square {
  String _text;
  Color _color;

  Square(this._text, this._color);

  operator ==(other) =>
    (other is Square) && (_text == other._text) && (_color == other._color);

  int get hashCode => _text.hashCode ^ _color.hashCode;
  Color get color => _color;
  String get text => _text;
}

class Bloc {
  // BLoC stands for Business Logic Component.
  final _random = new Random();
  List<Square> _squareList = [];

  Bloc() {
    _addActionStreamController.stream.listen(_handleAdd);
  }

  int next(int min, int max) => min + _random.nextInt(max - min);

  List<Square> initSquareList() {
    _squareList = [new Square("Square 1", Colors.red)];
    return _squareList;
  }

  void dispose() {
    _addActionStreamController.close();
  }

  Square createSquare() {
    String nextSquareNumberAsString = (_squareList.length + 1).toString();
    return Square("Square " + nextSquareNumberAsString.toString(),
      Color.fromRGBO(next(0, 255), next(0, 255), next(0, 255), 0.5));
  }

  void _handleAdd(void v) {
    _squareList.add(createSquare());
    _squareListSubject.add(_squareList);
  }

  // Streams for State Updates
  Stream<List<Square>> get squareListStream => _squareListSubject.stream;
  final _squareListSubject = BehaviorSubject<List<Square>>();

  // Sinks for Actions
```

```
  Sink get addAction => _addActionStreamController.sink;
  final _addActionStreamController = StreamController();
}

class BlocProvider extends InheritedWidget {
  final Bloc bloc;

  BlocProvider({
    Key key,
    @required this.bloc,
    Widget child,
  }) : super(key: key, child: child);

  @override
  bool updateShouldNotify(InheritedWidget oldWidget) => true;

  static Bloc of(BuildContext context) =>
      (context.inheritFromWidgetOfExactType(BlocProvider) as BlocProvider).bloc;
}

void main() => runApp(new NestedBuildersAppWidget());

class NestedBuildersAppWidget extends StatelessWidget {
  final Bloc _bloc = new Bloc();

  @override
  Widget build(BuildContext context) {
    return new MaterialApp(
      title: 'Nested Builders',
      theme: new ThemeData(
        primarySwatch: Colors.blue,
      ),
      home: BlocProvider(
        bloc: _bloc,
        child: new HomeWidget(title: 'Nested Builders'),
      ),
    );
  }
}

class HomeWidget extends StatelessWidget {
  HomeWidget({Key key, this.title}) : super(key: key);

  final String title;

  @override
  Widget build(BuildContext context) {
    final bloc = BlocProvider.of(context);
    return new Scaffold(
      appBar: new AppBar(
        title: new Text(title),
        actions: <Widget>[],
      ),
      body: StreamBuilder<List<Square>>(
        stream: bloc.squareListStream,
        initialData: bloc.initSquareList(),
        builder: (context, snapshot) {
          List<Square> squares = snapshot.data;
```

```
      return OrientationBuilder(builder: (context, orientation) {
        return GridView.builder(
          itemCount: squares.length,
          gridDelegate: new SliverGridDelegateWithFixedCrossAxisCount(
            crossAxisCount:
              (orientation == Orientation.portrait) ? 3 : 4),
          itemBuilder: (BuildContext context, int index) {
            return new GridTile(
              child: Container(
                color: squares[index].color,
                child: Padding(
                  padding: EdgeInsets.all(20.0),
                  child: Text(squares[index]._text,
                    style: TextStyle(
                      fontSize: 20.0,
                      fontWeight: FontWeight.bold),
                    textAlign: TextAlign.center))));
          });
      });
    }),
  floatingActionButton: new FloatingActionButton(
    onPressed: () => bloc.addAction.add(null),
    tooltip: 'Add',
    child: new Icon(Icons.add),
  ), // This trailing comma makes auto-formatting nicer for build methods.
  );
  }
}
```

24. Routing & Navigation

Introduction

Navigation is a key part of any mobile app as users will constantly be navigating between different screens, for example, from a customer list to a customer detail screen.

The purpose of this chapter is to learn how to write Flutter apps that include navigation.

Navigator Class

Flutter provides a Navigator class to help us perform navigation in our app.
We can provide Navigation between Widgets with or without named routes.

Stack of Routes

When you start using the Navigator class, you realize that it manages a stack of Routes, a history of visited screens/pages. When you navigate back, you pop a Route off the stack.

Navigating Forward

When you navigate forward (for example to a new part of the app), you push a Route to the stack.

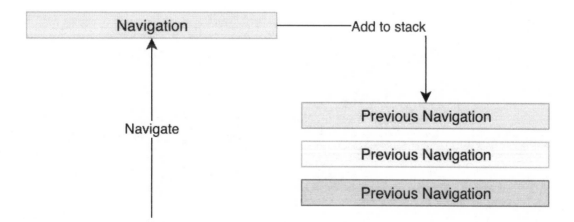

Results In:

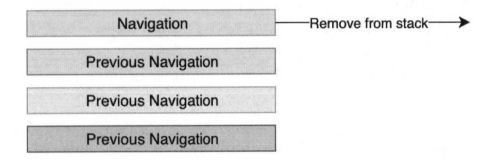

Navigating Back:

Results In:

Invoking Navigation without Named Routes

This is simple and is a great option, especially for smaller apps without too many Widgets. However, this can result in code duplication if we use this method to navigate to the same Widget in more than one place.

Navigating Forward

Note how we navigate forward in the example:

```
Navigator.push(
    context,
```

```
   MaterialPageRoute(builder: (context) => CustomerWidget(customer)),
);
```

We create a new MaterialPageRoute object with a builder that will create the new target Widget to navigate to.

This is another way to do the same thing with a PageRouteBuilder instead creating a MaterialPageRoute:

```
PageRouteBuilder pageRouteBuilder = PageRouteBuilder(pageBuilder:
   (BuildContext context, Animation animation,
      Animation secondaryAnimation) {
 return CustomerWidget(customer);
});
Navigator.push(
 context,
 pageRouteBuilder,
);
```

Animation

When navigating, MaterialPageRoutes automatically perform animations for us. Different animations that follow the design language of the target platform. PageRouteBuilder gives us more control over the animations.

Dialog

Note that the MaterialPageRoute also has a 'fullScreenDialog' constructor argument. This makes the new target Widget appear as a dialog rather than another Widget. As such it displays a 'Close' button instead of a back arrow button.

Navigating Backwards

Note how we don't need to do anything for the back arrow button to appear on the toolbar. Very nice! That back button simply does a Navigator.pop to navigate the user backwards to the previous navigation.

Data

Passing Data to Target Navigation

We pass the Customer and Order data between widgets using constructors that accept the Customer or Order data. We then push that object to the Navigator stack to navigate forward.

Returning Data from Target Navigation

You can Navigate to a Widget and have that Widget return data back to where it was opened. We are not doing this in the Example but it's good to know you can do this. Take a look at some of the Dialog examples.

If you remember how Dialogs worked, they would close by calling Navigator.pop with a data argument (data to be returned). The 'push' method of the Navigator returns a Future, so you can wait for the future to complete to get the data returned from the target Navigation once the user has navigated back.

Example – 'routes_simple'

This example app allows you to navigate from Customers to Customer Info including Orders to Order Info.

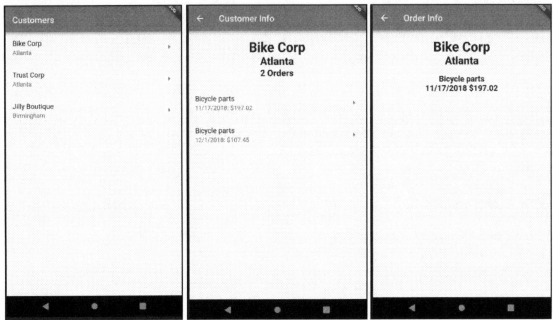

Source Code

```dart
import 'package:flutter/material.dart';

void main() => runApp(new MyApp());

class Order {
  DateTime _dt;
  String _description;
  double _total;

  Order(this._dt, this._description, this._total);

  double get total => _total;
  String get description => _description;
  DateTime get dt => _dt;
}

class Customer {
  String _name;
  String _location;
```

```dart
  List<Order> _orders;

  Customer(this._name, this._location, this._orders);

  List<Order> get orders => _orders;
  String get location => _location;
  String get name => _name;
}
class MyApp extends StatelessWidget {
  // This widget is the root of your application.
  @override
  Widget build(BuildContext context) {
    return new MaterialApp(
      title: 'Flutter Demo',
      theme: new ThemeData(
        primarySwatch: Colors.blue,
      ),
      home: new HomePageWidget(),
    );
  }
}

class HomePageWidget extends StatelessWidget {
  List<Customer> _customerList = [
    Customer("Bike Corp", "Atlanta", [
      Order(DateTime(2018, 11, 17), "Bicycle parts", 197.02),
      Order(DateTime(2018, 12, 1), "Bicycle parts", 107.45),
    ]),
    Customer("Trust Corp", "Atlanta", [
      Order(DateTime(2017, 1, 3), "Shredder parts", 97.02),
      Order(DateTime(2018, 3, 13), "Shredder blade", 7.45),
      Order(DateTime(2018, 5, 2), "Shredder blade", 7.45),
    ]),
    Customer("Jilly Boutique", "Birmingham", [
      Order(DateTime(2018, 1, 3), "Display unit", 97.01),
      Order(DateTime(2018, 3, 3), "Desk unit", 12.25),
      Order(DateTime(2018, 3, 21), "Clothes rack", 97.15),
    ]),
  ];

  HomePageWidget({Key key}) : super(key: key);

  void navigateToCustomer(BuildContext context, Customer customer) {
    Navigator.push(
      context,
      MaterialPageRoute(builder: (context) => CustomerWidget(customer)),
    );
  }

  ListTile createCustomerWidget(BuildContext context, Customer customer) {
    return new ListTile(
      title: Text(customer.name),
      subtitle: Text(customer.location),
      trailing: Icon(Icons.arrow_right),
      onTap: () => navigateToCustomer(context, customer));
  }
```

```
  @override
  Widget build(BuildContext context) {
   List<Widget> customerList = List.from(_customerList
     .map((Customer customer) => createCustomerWidget(context, customer)));
   return new Scaffold(
     appBar: new AppBar(
      title: new Text("Customers"),
     ),
     body: new Center(
      child: new ListView(
       children: customerList,
      ),
     ));
  }
}

class CustomerWidget extends StatelessWidget {
  Customer _customer;

  CustomerWidget(this._customer);

  void navigateToOrder(BuildContext context, Customer customer, Order order) {
   Navigator.push(
    context,
    MaterialPageRoute(builder: (context) => OrderWidget(customer, order)),
   );
  }

  ListTile createOrderListWidget(
     BuildContext context, Customer customer, Order order) {
   return new ListTile(
     title: Text(order.description),
     subtitle: Text("${order.dt.month}/${order.dt.day}/${order.dt.year}: "
       "\$${order.total}"),
     trailing: Icon(Icons.arrow_right),
     onTap: () => navigateToOrder(context, customer, order));
  }

  @override
  Widget build(BuildContext context) {
   List<Widget> widgetList = List.from(_customer.orders.map(
     (Order order) => createOrderListWidget(context, _customer, order)));
   widgetList.insert(
     0,
     Container(
       child: Column(
        children: <Widget>[
         Text(
           _customer.name,
           style: TextStyle(fontSize: 30.0, fontWeight: FontWeight.bold),
         ),
         Text(
           _customer.location,
           style: TextStyle(fontSize: 24.0, fontWeight: FontWeight.bold),
         ),
         Text(
           "${_customer.orders.length} Orders",
           style: TextStyle(fontSize: 20.0, fontWeight: FontWeight.bold),
```

```dart
              )
            ],
          ),
          padding: EdgeInsets.all(20.0)));
    return new Scaffold(
      appBar: new AppBar(
        title: new Text("Customer Info"),
      ),
      body: new Center(
        child: new ListView(
          children: widgetList,
        ),
      ));
  }
}

class OrderWidget extends StatelessWidget {
  Customer _customer;
  Order _order;

  OrderWidget(this._customer, this._order);

  @override
  Widget build(BuildContext context) {
    return new Scaffold(
      appBar: new AppBar(
        title: new Text("Order Info"),
      ),
      body: new Padding(
        padding: EdgeInsets.all(20.0),
        child: new ListView(
          children: <Widget>[
            Text(_customer.name,
              style: TextStyle(
                fontSize: 30.0,
                fontWeight: FontWeight.bold,
              ),
              textAlign: TextAlign.center),
            Text(_customer.location,
              style: TextStyle(fontSize: 24.0, fontWeight: FontWeight.bold),
              textAlign: TextAlign.center),
            Text(""),
            Text(_order.description,
              style: TextStyle(fontSize: 18.0, fontWeight: FontWeight.bold),
              textAlign: TextAlign.center),
            Text(
              "${_order.dt.month}/${_order.dt.day}/${_order.dt.year}: "
              "\$${_order.total}",
              style: TextStyle(fontSize: 18.0, fontWeight: FontWeight.bold),
              textAlign: TextAlign.center)
          ],
        ),
      ));
  }
}
```

Invoking Navigation with Named Routes #1

Named routes enable us to use routes that are defined just once, avoiding code duplication. These are very easy to use!

Define Routes

We define the routes when we build the MaterialApp at the top of the Widget tree:

```
class MyApp extends StatelessWidget {
  // This widget is the root of your application.
  @override
  Widget build(BuildContext context) {
    return new MaterialApp(
          ... [other constructor arguments] ...
routes: <String, WidgetBuilder>{
      '/customer': (context) => CustomerWidget(),
      '/order': (context) => OrderWidget(),
    },
  );
  }
}
```

Navigating Forward

Note how we navigate forward using a name that matches a route defined in the MaterialApp:

```
Navigator.pushNamed(context, "/order");
```

See the problem yet?

The problem is that this approach is great for simple Navigation without passing parameters. It doesn't work really work when you have parameters. Use this approach only when you have simple Widget navigation.

Example – 'routes_named'

This app looks and feels the same as the previous example but it does not pass around parameters. It just shows dummy data.

Source Code

```
import 'package:flutter/material.dart';

void main() => runApp(new MyApp());

class Order {
  DateTime _dt;
  String _description;
  double _total;
```

```
  Order(this._dt, this._description, this._total);

  double get total => _total;

  String get description => _description;

  DateTime get dt => _dt;
}

class Customer {
  String _name;
  String _location;
  List<Order> _orders;

  Customer(this._name, this._location, this._orders);

  List<Order> get orders => _orders;

  String get location => _location;

  String get name => _name;
}

class MyApp extends StatelessWidget {
  // This widget is the root of your application.
  @override
  Widget build(BuildContext context) {
    return new MaterialApp(
      title: 'Flutter Demo',
      theme: new ThemeData(
        primarySwatch: Colors.blue,
      ),
      home: new HomePageWidget(),
      routes: <String, WidgetBuilder>{
        '/customer': (context) => CustomerWidget(), // only simple routes work
        '/order': (context) => OrderWidget(), // only simple routes work
      },
    );
  }
}

class HomePageWidget extends StatelessWidget {
  List<Customer> _customerList = [
    Customer("Bike Corp", "Atlanta", []),
    Customer("Trust Corp", "Atlanta", []),
    Customer("Jilly Boutique", "Birmingham", []),
  ];

  HomePageWidget({Key key}) : super(key: key);

  void navigateToCustomer(BuildContext context, Customer customer) {
    Navigator.pushNamed(context, "/customer"); // only simple routes work
  }

  ListTile createCustomerWidget(BuildContext context, Customer customer) {
    return new ListTile(
      title: Text(customer.name),
```

```
          subtitle: Text(customer.location),
          trailing: Icon(Icons.arrow_right),
          onTap: () => navigateToCustomer(context, customer));
  }

  @override
  Widget build(BuildContext context) {
   List<Widget> customerList = List.from(_customerList
      .map((Customer customer) => createCustomerWidget(context, customer)));
    return new Scaffold(
      appBar: new AppBar(
        title: new Text("Customers"),
      ),
      body: new Center(
        child: new ListView(
          children: customerList,
        ),
      ));
  }
}

class CustomerWidget extends StatelessWidget {
  List<Order> _orderList = [
    Order(DateTime(2018, 11, 17), "Bicycle parts", 197.00),
    Order(DateTime(2018, 12, 1), "Bicycle parts", 107.45),
  ];

  CustomerWidget({Key key}) : super(key: key);

  void navigateToOrder(BuildContext context, Order order) {
    Navigator.pushNamed(context, "/order"); // only simple routes work
  }

  ListTile createOrderWidget(BuildContext context, Order order) {
    return new ListTile(
      title: Text(order.description),
      subtitle: Text("${order.dt.month}/${order.dt.day}/${order.dt.year}: "
        "\$${order.total}"),
      trailing: Icon(Icons.arrow_right),
      onTap: () => navigateToOrder(context, order));
  }

  @override
  Widget build(BuildContext context) {
   List<Widget> widgetList = List.from(
      _orderList.map((Order order) => createOrderWidget(context, order)));
    widgetList.insert(
      0,
      Container(
        child: Column(
          children: <Widget>[
            Text(
              "BikeCorp",
              style: TextStyle(fontSize: 30.0, fontWeight: FontWeight.bold),
            ),
            Text(
              "Atlanta",
              style: TextStyle(fontSize: 24.0, fontWeight: FontWeight.bold),
```

```
            ),
            Text(
              "2 Orders",
              style: TextStyle(fontSize: 20.0, fontWeight: FontWeight.bold),
            )
          ],
        ),
        padding: EdgeInsets.all(20.0)));
    return new Scaffold(
      appBar: new AppBar(
        title: new Text("Customers"),
      ),
      body: new Center(
        child: new ListView(
          children: widgetList,
        ),
      ));
  }
}

class OrderWidget extends StatelessWidget {
  OrderWidget();

  @override
  Widget build(BuildContext context) {
    return new Scaffold(
      appBar: new AppBar(
        title: new Text("Order Info"),
      ),
      body: new Padding(
        padding: EdgeInsets.all(20.0),
        child: new ListView(
          children: <Widget>[
            Text("BikeCorp",
              style: TextStyle(
                fontSize: 30.0,
                fontWeight: FontWeight.bold,
              ),
              textAlign: TextAlign.center),
            Text("Atlanta",
              style: TextStyle(fontSize: 24.0, fontWeight: FontWeight.bold),
              textAlign: TextAlign.center),
            Text(""),
            Text("Bicycle Parts",
              style: TextStyle(fontSize: 18.0, fontWeight: FontWeight.bold),
              textAlign: TextAlign.center),
            Text("12/1/2019 \$123.23",
              style: TextStyle(fontSize: 18.0, fontWeight: FontWeight.bold),
              textAlign: TextAlign.center)
          ],
        ),
      ));
  }
}
```

Invoking Navigation with Named Routes #2

The approach #1 doesn't work really work when you have parameters and you need to pass data to a route though parameters.

Here is another way of routing with named routes, only this time it works with parameters.

Attach Route Handler to MaterialApp

This time we don't define routes in the Material App.
Instead we pass in a route handler to the MaterialApp at the top of the Widget tree (in this case 'handleRoute'):

```
class MyApp extends StatelessWidget {
  // This widget is the root of your application.
  @override
  Widget build(BuildContext context) {
    return new MaterialApp(
         … [other constructor arguments] …
onGenerateRoute: handleRoute,
    );
  }
}
```

Code Route Handler

We write a route handler that interprets the route info (parsing out the parameters) and returns a MaterialPageRoute containing a builder to create the correct Widget. This will work to generate the Widgets for all the routing.

Example

In the example below we convert the route info into a MaterialPageRoute for a Customer Widget or an Order Widget. Both receive the id as the constructor argument.

```
Route<dynamic> handleRoute(RouteSettings routeSettings) {
  // One route handler to handle them all.
  List<String> nameParm = routeSettings.name.split(":");
  assert(nameParm.length == 2);
  String name = nameParm[0];
  assert(name != null);
  int id = int.tryParse(nameParm[1]);
  assert(id != null);
  Widget childWidget;
  if (name == "/customer/") {
    childWidget = CustomerWidget(id);
  } else {
    childWidget = OrderWidget(id);
  }
  return MaterialPageRoute(
      builder: (context) => DataContainerWidget(child: childWidget));
}
```

Navigating Forward

Now we have a route handler that can interpret routes with data, we can route by name and id.

```
void navigateToCustomer(BuildContext context, Customer customer) {
  Navigator.pushNamed(context, '/customer/:${customer.id}');
}
```

Example – 'routes_named_with_parms'

This app looks and feels the same as the previous example but this time it passes the customer and order identifiers to the Customer and Order Widgets.

I added a DataContainerWidget to store Customer and Order state data in one place (more on InheritedWidgets later in their own chapter) and enable them to be queried by the identifier. Each widget is constructed (passing in the Customer or Order identifier) then calls code in the DataContainerWidget to get the data to display in the UI.

Source Code

```
import 'package:flutter/material.dart';

void main() => runApp(new MyApp());

class Order {
  int _id;
  DateTime _dt;
  String _description;
  double _total;

  Order(this._id, this._dt, this._description, this._total);
  Order.empty() : this(0, DateTime.now(), "", 0.0);

  int get id => _id;
  double get total => _total;
  String get description => _description;
  DateTime get dt => _dt;
}

class Customer {
  int _id;
  String _name;
  String _location;
  List<Order> _orders;

  Customer(this._id, this._name, this._location, this._orders);
  Customer.empty() : this(0, "", "", []);

  int get id => _id;
  List<Order> get orders => _orders;
  String get location => _location;
  String get name => _name;
}

class MyApp extends StatelessWidget {
  // This widget is the root of your application.
```

```
@override
Widget build(BuildContext context) {
  return new MaterialApp(
    title: 'Flutter Demo',
    theme: new ThemeData(
      primarySwatch: Colors.blue,
    ),
    home: new DataContainerWidget(child: HomeWidget()),
    onGenerateRoute: handleRoute);
}

Route<dynamic> handleRoute(RouteSettings routeSettings) {
  // One route handler to handle them all.
  List<String> nameParm = routeSettings.name.split(":");
  assert(nameParm.length == 2);
  String name = nameParm[0];
  assert(name != null);
  int id = int.tryParse(nameParm[1]);
  assert(id != null);
  Widget childWidget;
  if (name == "/customer/") {
    childWidget = CustomerWidget(id);
  } else {
    childWidget = OrderWidget(id);
  }
  return MaterialPageRoute(
    builder: (context) => DataContainerWidget(child: childWidget));
}
}

class DataContainerWidget extends InheritedWidget {
  DataContainerWidget({
    Key key,
    @required Widget child,
  }) : assert(child != null),
       super(key: key, child: child);

  List<Customer> _customerList = [
    Customer(1, "Bike Corp", "Atlanta", [
      Order(11, DateTime(2018, 11, 17), "Bicycle parts", 197.02),
      Order(12, DateTime(2018, 12, 1), "Bicycle parts", 107.45),
    ]),
    Customer(2, "Trust Corp", "Atlanta", [
      Order(13, DateTime(2017, 1, 3), "Shredder parts", 97.02),
      Order(14, DateTime(2018, 3, 13), "Shredder blade", 7.45),
      Order(15, DateTime(2018, 5, 2), "Shredder blade", 7.45),
    ]),
    Customer(3, "Jilly Boutique", "Birmingham", [
      Order(16, DateTime(2018, 1, 3), "Display unit", 97.01),
      Order(17, DateTime(2018, 3, 3), "Desk unit", 12.25),
      Order(18, DateTime(2018, 3, 21), "Clothes rack", 97.15),
    ]),
  ];

  List<Customer> get customerList => _customerList;

  Customer getCustomer(int id) {
    return _customerList.firstWhere((customer) => customer.id == id,
```

```
      orElse: () => Customer.empty());
  }

  Customer getCustomerForOrderId(int id) {
    return customerList.firstWhere(
      (customer) => customerHasOrderId(customer, id),
      orElse: () => Customer.empty());
  }

  Order getOrder(int id) {
    Customer customerThatOwnsOrder = getCustomerForOrderId(id);
    return customerThatOwnsOrder.orders
      .firstWhere((order) => order.id == id, orElse: () => Order.empty());
  }

  bool customerHasOrderId(Customer customer, int id) {
    Order order = customer.orders
      .firstWhere((order) => order.id == id, orElse: () => Order.empty());
    return order.id != 0;
  }

  static DataContainerWidget of(BuildContext context) {
    return context.inheritFromWidgetOfExactType(DataContainerWidget)
      as DataContainerWidget;
  }

  @override
  bool updateShouldNotify(covariant InheritedWidget oldWidget) {
    return false;
  }
}

class HomeWidget extends StatelessWidget {
  HomeWidget({Key key}) : super(key: key);

  void navigateToCustomer(BuildContext context, Customer customer) {
    Navigator.pushNamed(context, '/customer/:${customer.id}');
  }

  ListTile createCustomerWidget(BuildContext context, Customer customer) {
    return new ListTile(
      title: Text(customer.name),
      subtitle: Text(customer.location),
      trailing: Icon(Icons.arrow_right),
      onTap: () => navigateToCustomer(context, customer));
  }

  @override
  Widget build(BuildContext context) {
    DataContainerWidget data = DataContainerWidget.of(context);
    List<Widget> customerList = List.from(data.customerList
      .map((Customer customer) => createCustomerWidget(context, customer)));
    return new Scaffold(
      appBar: new AppBar(
        title: new Text("Customers"),
      ),
      body: new Center(
        child: new ListView(
```

```
          children: customerList,
        ),
      ));
  }
}

class CustomerWidget extends StatelessWidget {
  int _id;

  CustomerWidget(this._id);

  void navigateToOrder(BuildContext context, Order order) {
    Navigator.pushNamed(context, '/order/:${order.id}');
  }

  ListTile createOrderListWidget(BuildContext context, Order order) {
    return new ListTile(
        title: Text(order.description),
        subtitle: Text("${order.dt.month}/${order.dt.day}/${order.dt.year}: "
          "\$${order.total}"),
        trailing: Icon(Icons.arrow_right),
        onTap: () => navigateToOrder(context, order));
  }

  @override
  Widget build(BuildContext context) {
    DataContainerWidget data = DataContainerWidget.of(context);
    Customer customer = data.getCustomer(_id);
    List<Widget> orderListWidgets = List.from(customer.orders
        .map((Order order) => createOrderListWidget(context, order)));
    orderListWidgets.insert(
        0,
        Container(
          child: Column(
            children: <Widget>[
              Text(
                customer.name,
                style: TextStyle(fontSize: 30.0, fontWeight: FontWeight.bold),
              ),
              Text(
                customer.location,
                style: TextStyle(fontSize: 24.0, fontWeight: FontWeight.bold),
              ),
              Text(
                "${customer.orders.length} Orders",
                style: TextStyle(fontSize: 20.0, fontWeight: FontWeight.bold),
              )
            ],
          ),
          padding: EdgeInsets.all(20.0)));
    return new Scaffold(
        appBar: new AppBar(
          title: new Text("Customer Info"),
        ),
        body: new Center(
          child: new ListView(
            children: orderListWidgets,
          ),
```

```dart
      ));
    }
  }

class OrderWidget extends StatelessWidget {
  int _id;

  OrderWidget(this._id);

  @override
  Widget build(BuildContext context) {
    DataContainerWidget data =
      context.inheritFromWidgetOfExactType(DataContainerWidget);
    Customer customer = data.getCustomerForOrderId(_id);
    Order order = data.getOrder(_id);
    return new Scaffold(
      appBar: new AppBar(
        title: new Text("Order Info"),
      ),
      body: new Padding(
        padding: EdgeInsets.all(20.0),
        child: new ListView(
          children: <Widget>[
            Text(customer.name,
              style: TextStyle(
                fontSize: 30.0,
                fontWeight: FontWeight.bold,
              ),
              textAlign: TextAlign.center),
            Text(customer.location,
              style: TextStyle(fontSize: 24.0, fontWeight: FontWeight.bold),
              textAlign: TextAlign.center),
            Text(""),
            Text(order.description,
              style: TextStyle(fontSize: 18.0, fontWeight: FontWeight.bold),
              textAlign: TextAlign.center),
            Text(
              "${order.dt.month}/${order.dt.day}/${order.dt.year} \$$${order.total}",
              style: TextStyle(fontSize: 18.0, fontWeight: FontWeight.bold),
              textAlign: TextAlign.center)
          ],
        ),
      ));
  }
}
```

PageView

Introduction

You can navigate with PageViews as well. PageViews are useful for when you have a list of Widgets that each take up all the screen space and you want to swipe through them, either horizontally or vertically. The 'scrollDirection' constructor argument enables you to set the scrolling / swiping axis to be horizontal or vertical.

Child Widgets

PageViews can work with a list of child Widgets or you can them with a builder that creates child Widgets when they are required. If you want to use a builder then use the 'PageView.builder' named constructor. That is probably much better if you planning on giving the user many pages to swipe through. This Widget uses the 'Page' terminology to refer to a child Widget that takes up all of the available screen space.

Controller

PageViews also work with a controller, which you can specify as an argument in the PageView contructor. You can use the controller to move between the childWidgets. To move between childWidgets with animation, use 'animateToPage'. To jump to a page without animation, use 'jumpToPage'. You can also go to the previous and next pages.

Example – 'page_view_navigation'

This app is similar to the previous apps in this chapter. On the home page, you see a list of customers. You can tap on a customer to move to that Customer's page, or you can swipe through the Customers. There is a Home button on the toolbar to take you back to the home page.

Source Code

```
import 'package:flutter/material.dart';

void main() => runApp(new MyApp());

class Order {
  DateTime _dt;
  String _description;
  double _total;

  Order(this._dt, this._description, this._total);

  double get total => _total;
  String get description => _description;
  DateTime get dt => _dt;
}

class Customer {
  String _name;
  String _location;
  List<Order> _orders;

  Customer(this._name, this._location, this._orders);

  List<Order> get orders => _orders;
  String get location => _location;
  String get name => _name;
}

class MyApp extends StatelessWidget {
  // This widget is the root of your application.
  @override
  Widget build(BuildContext context) {
    return new MaterialApp(
      title: 'PageView Navigation',
      theme: new ThemeData(
        primarySwatch: Colors.blue,
      ),
      home: new MyHomePage(),
    );
  }
}

class MyHomePage extends StatelessWidget {
  final PageController _pageController = PageController(initialPage: 0);
  final Duration _duration = Duration(seconds: 1);
  final Curve _curve = Curves.ease;

  final List<Customer> _customerList = [
    Customer("Bike Corp", "Atlanta", [
      Order(DateTime(2018, 11, 17), "Bicycle parts", 197.02),
      Order(DateTime(2018, 12, 1), "Bicycle parts", 107.45),
    ]),
    Customer("Trust Corp", "Atlanta", [
      Order(DateTime(2017, 1, 3), "Shredder parts", 97.02),
      Order(DateTime(2018, 3, 13), "Shredder blade", 7.45),
      Order(DateTime(2018, 5, 2), "Shredder blade", 7.45),
```

```
    ]),
    Customer("Jilly Boutique", "Birmingham", [
      Order(DateTime(2018, 1, 3), "Display unit", 97.01),
      Order(DateTime(2018, 3, 3), "Desk unit", 12.25),
      Order(DateTime(2018, 3, 21), "Clothes rack", 97.15),
    ]),
  ];

  MyHomePage({Key key}) : super(key: key);

  Widget pageViewItemBuilder(BuildContext context, int index) {
    if (index == 0) {
      return createHomePage(context);
    } else {
      return createDetailPage(context, index);
    }
  }

  Widget createHomePage(BuildContext context) {
    List<Widget> widgetList = [];
    widgetList.add(Padding(
        padding: EdgeInsets.all(20.0),
        child: Text(
          "Customer List",
          style: TextStyle(fontSize: 30.0, fontWeight: FontWeight.bold),
          textAlign: TextAlign.center,
        )));
    for (int i = 0, ii = _customerList.length; i < ii; i++) {
      Customer customer = _customerList[i];
      widgetList.add(createHomePageListItem(context, customer, i));
    }
    return ListView(children: widgetList);
  }

  ListTile createHomePageListItem(
      BuildContext context, Customer customer, int index) {
    return new ListTile(
        title: Text(customer.name),
        subtitle: Text(customer.location),
        trailing: Icon(Icons.arrow_right),
        onTap: () => _pageController.animateToPage(index + 1,
            duration: _duration, curve: _curve));
  }

  Widget createDetailPage(BuildContext context, int index) {
    Customer customer = _customerList[index - 1];
    List<Widget> widgetList = List.from(customer.orders
        .map((Order order) => createOrderListWidget(context, customer, order)));
    widgetList.insert(
        0,
        Container(
          child: Column(
            children: <Widget>[
              Text(
                customer.name,
                style: TextStyle(fontSize: 30.0, fontWeight: FontWeight.bold),
              ),
              Text(
```

```
          customer.location,
          style: TextStyle(fontSize: 24.0, fontWeight: FontWeight.bold),
        ),
        Text(
          "${customer.orders.length} Orders",
          style: TextStyle(fontSize: 20.0, fontWeight: FontWeight.bold),
        ),
        Padding(padding: EdgeInsets.all(20.0)),
      ],
    ),
    padding: EdgeInsets.all(20.0)));
  return ListView(children: widgetList);
}

ListTile createOrderListWidget(
    BuildContext context, Customer customer, Order order) {
  return new ListTile(
    title: Text(order.description),
    subtitle: Text("${order.dt.month}/${order.dt.day}/${order.dt.year}: "
      "\$${order.total}"));
}

@override
Widget build(BuildContext context) {
  return new Scaffold(
    appBar: new AppBar(title: new Text("PageView Navigation"), actions: [
      IconButton(
        icon: Icon(Icons.home),
        onPressed: () => _pageController.animateToPage(0,
          duration: _duration, curve: _curve))
    ]),
    body: new Center(
      child: new PageView.builder(
        controller: _pageController,
        itemBuilder: pageViewItemBuilder,
        itemCount: _customerList.length + 1)),
  );
}
}
```

25.Forms

Introduction

We need to give the users the ability to enter information into forms, fields, validate it and show validation messages to the user if necessary.

The purpose of this chapter is to learn how get Flutter apps working with fields, forms and validations.

Flutter provides objects to help you with the process of building forms, validation and input fields. It provides a Form object, Form Field objects (indirectly) and all the input types below:

- Checkbox
- DropdownButton
- Radio
- Switch
- TextFormField / TextField

Form

This is a Widget that is designed to wrap form Widgets and provides control over validation.

The Form object gives you the following constructor arguments:
- 'autovalidate' to enable or disable automatic validation.
- 'onChanged' callback fired when one of the fields are changed.

The Form object gives you the following methods:
- 'reset' to reset fields.
- 'save' to save fields.
- 'validate' to validate, returning a true if the form fields are valid, false if one or more are invalid.

Form State

The Form object stores input state data from child TextFormFields but not other field types like Checkboxes, DropdownButtons, Radios, Switches.

So, if you want your form to work with those other types of fields, you need to store the state of those items. If you take a look a look at the example you will see that these fields are stored as state in the Stateful Widget.

Form Validation

As mentioned earlier, the Form class has a 'autovalidate' constructor argument.
- If this argument is set to true, the framework invokes validation as data is input.
- If this argument is set to false, the framework will not invoke validation until the 'validate' method is invoked.

Form / Field Integration

The FormField is a Widget used as a base class by field Widgets (such as TextFormField) to integrate the field with the parent Form Widget and provide services such as validation.

Form Fields

Checkbox

☐ Been at address 5 years?

This Widget that allows the user to select a yes / no.

It does not store state for you, you have to manage it yourself.
Use the following constructor arguments for state management.

	Description
value	Sets the value represented by the radio. Provide this from state.
onChanged	Method fired when the checkbox is selected or deselected. Add method to set state here.

DropdownButton

This is a material design button that allows the user to select an item from a list of items that implemented as a popup menu.

It does not store state for you, you have to manage it yourself.
Use the following constructor arguments for state management.

	Description
items	Sets the items in the list.
value	Sets the currently selected item. Provide this from state.
onChanged	Method fired when an item is selected or deselected. Add method to set state here.

Radio

This Widget does not store state for you, you have to manage it yourself.
Use the following constructor arguments for state management.

	Description
value	Sets the value represented by the radio.
groupValue	Sets the radio button's value. Provide this from state.
onChanged	Method fired when the radio button is selected. Add method to set state here.

TextFormField, TextField

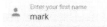

A TextField is a widget for a basic text field.
A TextFormField is a TextField with form integration.

Keyboard Types

The TextFormField object has a constructor argument 'keyboardType'. This lets you change the keyboard type to suit the field:

	Description
TextInputType.text	Default keyboard.
TextInputType.multiline	Default keyboard optimized for multiline entry.
TextInputType.number	Numeric keyboard.
TextInputType.phone	Phone keyboard.

InputFormatters

The TextFormField object has a constructor argument 'inputFormatters'. This lets you change the behavior of the field – what characters this input field will accept.

	Description
LengthLimitingTextInputFormatter	Limits the length of input fields.
WhitelistingTextInputFormatter.digitsOnly	Takes in digits [0–9] only.
BlacklistingTextInputFormatter.singleLineFormatter	Forces input to be a single line.

WhitelistingTextInputFormatter	For whitelisting input (regular expression).
BlacklistingTextInputFormatter	For blacklisting input (regular expression)

TextEditingController

A TextEditingController is a class that listens to its assigned TextField, and updates its own internal state every time the text in the TextField changes. Listeners can then read the text and selection properties to learn what the user has typed or how the selection has been updated. If you look at the example code you will see a TextEditingController for each TextFormField. These TextEditingControllers are used to get and set the values for these fields.

Validator

The TextFormField object has a constructor argument 'validator'. This lets you add a validation method to the field. If there is an error with the information the user has provided, the validator method must return a String containing an error message. If there are no errors, the method should not return anything.

Example

```
TextFormField(
  // The validator receives the text the user has typed in
  validator: (value) {
    if (value.isEmpty) {
      return 'Please enter some text';
    }
  },
);
```

Focus

TextFormFields also have a constructor argument that called 'autofocus' that sets up the text field to automatically be the first one with the focus. The other fields like Checkboxes, DropdownButtons, Radios don't have this.

InputDecorator

Input Decorators are widgets are used to decorate our fields, to give them things like:
- Icon
- Hint
- Label

Example – 'form_details'

This example attempts to use all the input field types: text, radio buttons, checkboxes, selection lists and dates.

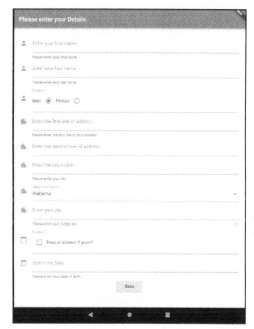

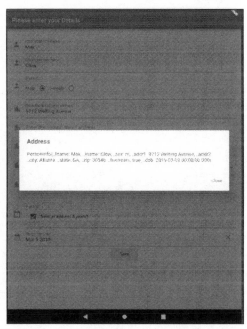

Dependencies

Add the following dependencies to your 'pubspec.yaml' file. After that you will need to do a 'flutter packages get' on the command line in the root of your project to download the dependencies.

```yaml
dependencies:
  flutter:
    sdk: flutter

  # The following adds the Cupertino Icons font to your application.
  # Use with the CupertinoIcons class for iOS style icons.
  cupertino_icons: ^0.1.2
  datetime_picker_formfield: ^0.1.3
```

Source Code

```dart
import 'package:flutter/material.dart';
import 'package:flutter/services.dart';
import 'package:datetime_picker_formfield/datetime_picker_formfield.dart';
import 'package:intl/intl.dart';

void main() => runApp(new MyApp());

class PersonInfo {
  String _fname = "";
  String _lname = "";
  String _sex = "m";
  String _addr1 = "";
  String _addr2 = "";
  String _city = "";
  String _state = "";
  String _zip = "";
  bool _fiveYears = false;
  DateTime _dob;

  PersonInfo(this._fname, this._lname, this._sex, this._addr1, this._addr2,
      this._city, this._state, this._zip, this._fiveYears, this._dob);

  PersonInfo.empty();

  String get fname => _fname;
  String get lname => _lname;
  String get sex => _sex;
  String get addr1 => _addr1;
  String get addr2 => _addr2;
  String get city => _city;
  String get state => _state;
  String get zip => _zip;
  bool get fiveYears => _fiveYears;
  DateTime get dob => _dob;

  @override
  String toString() {
    return 'PersonInfo{_fname: $_fname, _lname: $_lname, _sex: $_sex, _addr1: $_addr1, _addr2: $_addr2,
_city: $_city, _state: $_state, _zip: $_zip, _fiveYears: $_fiveYears, _dob: $_dob}';
```

```
  }
}

class MyApp extends StatelessWidget {
  @override
  Widget build(BuildContext context) {
    return new MaterialApp(
      title: 'Flutter Demo',
      theme: new ThemeData(
        primarySwatch: Colors.blue,
      ),
      home: new HomePage(),
    );
  }
}

class HomePage extends StatefulWidget {
  PersonInfo _address = PersonInfo.empty();

  HomePage({Key key}) : super(key: key);

  @override
  _HomePageState createState() => new _HomePageState(_address);
}

class _HomePageState extends State<HomePage> {
  PersonInfo _address;

  _HomePageState(this._address);

  @override
  Widget build(BuildContext context) {
    return new Scaffold(
      appBar: new AppBar(
        title: new Text("Please enter your Details"),
      ),
      body: new Center(
        child: new ListView(children: [
        Padding(
          padding: EdgeInsets.all(20.0),
          child: AddressWidget(address: _address, onSaved: _onSaved))
      ])));
  }

  _onSaved(PersonInfo address) {
    showDialog<bool>(
      context: context,
      builder: (BuildContext context) {
        return AlertDialog(
          title: const Text('Address'),
          content: Text(address.toString()),
          actions: <Widget>[
            FlatButton(
              onPressed: () {
                Navigator.pop(context, true);
              },
              child: const Text('Close'),
            )
```

```
      ],
    );
  });
  }
}

class AddressWidget extends StatefulWidget {
  PersonInfo _address;
  ValueChanged<PersonInfo> _onSaved;

  AddressWidget(
    {Key key,
    @required PersonInfo address,
    @required ValueChanged<PersonInfo> onSaved})
    : super(key: key) {
    this._address = address;
    this._onSaved = onSaved;
  }

  @override
  _AddressWidgetState createState() => new _AddressWidgetState(_address);
}

class _AddressWidgetState extends State<AddressWidget> {
  static const STATE_DROPDOWN_MENU_ITEMS = [
    DropdownMenuItem(value: "AL", child: const Text("Alabama")),
    DropdownMenuItem(value: "AK", child: const Text("Alaska")),
    DropdownMenuItem(value: "AZ", child: const Text("Arizona")),
    DropdownMenuItem(value: "AR", child: const Text("Arkansas")),
    DropdownMenuItem(value: "CA", child: const Text("California")),
    DropdownMenuItem(value: "CO", child: const Text("Colorado")),
    DropdownMenuItem(value: "CT", child: const Text("Connecticut")),
    DropdownMenuItem(value: "DE", child: const Text("Delaware")),
    DropdownMenuItem(value: "DC", child: const Text("District Of Columbia")),
    DropdownMenuItem(value: "FL", child: const Text("Florida")),
    DropdownMenuItem(value: "GA", child: const Text("Georgia")),
    DropdownMenuItem(value: "HI", child: const Text("Hawaii")),
    DropdownMenuItem(value: "ID", child: const Text("Idaho")),
    DropdownMenuItem(value: "IL", child: const Text("Illinois")),
    DropdownMenuItem(value: "IN", child: const Text("Indiana")),
    DropdownMenuItem(value: "IA", child: const Text("Iowa")),
    DropdownMenuItem(value: "KS", child: const Text("Kansas")),
    DropdownMenuItem(value: "KY", child: const Text("Kentucky")),
    DropdownMenuItem(value: "LA", child: const Text("Louisiana")),
    DropdownMenuItem(value: "ME", child: const Text("Maine")),
    DropdownMenuItem(value: "MD", child: const Text("Maryland")),
    DropdownMenuItem(value: "MA", child: const Text("Massachusetts")),
    DropdownMenuItem(value: "MI", child: const Text("Michigan")),
    DropdownMenuItem(value: "MN", child: const Text("Minnesota")),
    DropdownMenuItem(value: "MS", child: const Text("Mississippi")),
    DropdownMenuItem(value: "MO", child: const Text("Missouri")),
    DropdownMenuItem(value: "MT", child: const Text("Montana")),
    DropdownMenuItem(value: "NE", child: const Text("Nebraska")),
    DropdownMenuItem(value: "NV", child: const Text("Nevada")),
    DropdownMenuItem(value: "NH", child: const Text("New Hampshire")),
    DropdownMenuItem(value: "NJ", child: const Text("New Jersey")),
    DropdownMenuItem(value: "NM", child: const Text("New Mexico")),
    DropdownMenuItem(value: "NY", child: const Text("New York")),
```

```
DropdownMenuItem(value: "NC", child: const Text("North Carolina")),
DropdownMenuItem(value: "ND", child: const Text("North Dakota")),
DropdownMenuItem(value: "OH", child: const Text("Ohio")),
DropdownMenuItem(value: "OK", child: const Text("Oklahoma")),
DropdownMenuItem(value: "OR", child: const Text("Oregon")),
DropdownMenuItem(value: "PA", child: const Text("Pennsylvania")),
DropdownMenuItem(value: "RI", child: const Text("Rhode Island")),
DropdownMenuItem(value: "SC", child: const Text("South Carolina")),
DropdownMenuItem(value: "SD", child: const Text("South Dakota")),
DropdownMenuItem(value: "TN", child: const Text("Tennessee")),
DropdownMenuItem(value: "TX", child: const Text("Texas")),
DropdownMenuItem(value: "UT", child: const Text("Utah")),
DropdownMenuItem(value: "VT", child: const Text("Vermont")),
DropdownMenuItem(value: "VA", child: const Text("Virginia")),
DropdownMenuItem(value: "WA", child: const Text("Washington")),
DropdownMenuItem(value: "WV", child: const Text("West Virginia")),
DropdownMenuItem(value: "WI", child: const Text("Wisconsin")),
DropdownMenuItem(value: "WY", child: const Text("Wyoming"))
];

final _formKey = GlobalKey<FormState>();
String _state = STATE_DROPDOWN_MENU_ITEMS[0].value;
TextEditingController _fnameTextController;
TextEditingController _lnameTextController;
String _sex = "m";
TextEditingController _addr1TextController;
TextEditingController _addr2TextController;
TextEditingController _cityTextController;
TextEditingController _zipTextController;
bool _fiveYears = false;
DateFormat _dateFormat = DateFormat("MMM d yyyy");
TextEditingController _dobTextController;

_AddressWidgetState(final PersonInfo address) {
  _fnameTextController = TextEditingController(text: address.fname);
  _lnameTextController = TextEditingController(text: address.lname);
  _sex = address.sex;
  _addr1TextController = TextEditingController(text: address.addr1);
  _addr2TextController = TextEditingController(text: address.addr2);
  _cityTextController = TextEditingController(text: address.city);
  _zipTextController = TextEditingController(text: address.state);
  _fiveYears = address.fiveYears;
  _dobTextController = TextEditingController(
    text: address.dob != null ? _dateFormat.format(address.dob) : "");
}

@override
Widget build(BuildContext context) {
  List<Widget> formWidgetList = new List();
  formWidgetList.add(createFNameWidget());
  formWidgetList.add(createLNameWidget());
  formWidgetList.add(createSexWidget());
  formWidgetList.add(createAddr1Widget());
  formWidgetList.add(createAddr2Widget());
  formWidgetList.add(createCityWidget());
  formWidgetList.add(createStateWidget());
  formWidgetList.add(createZipWidget());
  formWidgetList.add(createFiveYearsWidget());
```

```
  formWidgetList.add(createDobWidget());
  formWidgetList.add(RaisedButton(
    onPressed: () {
      if (_formKey.currentState.validate()) {
        PersonInfo address = createDataObjectFromFormData();
        widget._onSaved(address);
      }
    },
    child: new Text('Save'),
  ));

  return Form(key: _formKey, child: Column(children: formWidgetList));
}

TextFormField createFNameWidget() {
  return new TextFormField(
    validator: (value) {
      if (value.isEmpty) {
        return 'Please enter your first name.';
      }
    },
    decoration: InputDecoration(
      icon: const Icon(Icons.person),
      hintText: 'First name',
      labelText: 'Enter your first name'),
    onSaved: (String value) {},
    controller: _fnameTextController,
    autofocus: true);
}

TextFormField createLNameWidget() {
  return new TextFormField(
    validator: (value) {
      if (value.isEmpty) {
        return 'Please enter your last name.';
      }
    },
    decoration: InputDecoration(
      icon: const Icon(Icons.person),
      hintText: 'Last name',
      labelText: 'Enter your last name'),
    onSaved: (String value) {},
    controller: _lnameTextController);
}

void _handleSexRadioChanged(String value) {
  setState(() {
    _sex = value;
  });
}

InputDecorator createSexWidget() {
  List<Widget> radioWidgets = [
    Text("Male"),
    Radio(
      value: "m",
      groupValue: _sex,
      onChanged: (s) => _handleSexRadioChanged(s)),
```

```
    Text("Female"),
    Radio(
      value: "f",
      groupValue: _sex,
      onChanged: (s) => _handleSexRadioChanged(s)),
  ];
  return InputDecorator(
    decoration: const InputDecoration(
      icon: const Icon(Icons.person),
      hintText: 'Been at address 5 years?',
      labelText: '5 years?',
    ),
    child: new DropdownButtonHideUnderline(
      child: Row(children: radioWidgets)));
}

TextFormField createAddr1Widget() {
  return new TextFormField(
    validator: (value) {
      if (value.isEmpty) {
        return 'Please enter the first line of your address.';
      }
    },
    decoration: InputDecoration(
      icon: const Icon(Icons.location_city),
      hintText: 'Address 1',
      labelText: 'Enter the first line of address'),
    onSaved: (String value) {},
    controller: _addr1TextController);
}

TextFormField createAddr2Widget() {
  return new TextFormField(
    decoration: InputDecoration(
      icon: const Icon(Icons.location_city),
      hintText: 'Address 2',
      labelText: 'Enter the second line of address'),
    onSaved: (String value) {},
    controller: _addr2TextController);
}

TextFormField createCityWidget() {
  return new TextFormField(
    validator: (value) {
      if (value.isEmpty) {
        return 'Please enter your city.';
      }
    },
    decoration: InputDecoration(
      icon: const Icon(Icons.location_city),
      hintText: 'City',
      labelText: 'Enter the city name'),
    onSaved: (String value) {},
    controller: _cityTextController);
}

InputDecorator createStateWidget() {
  DropdownButton<String> stateDropdownButton = DropdownButton<String>(
```

```
    items: STATE_DROPDOWN_MENU_ITEMS,
    value: _state,
    isDense: true,
    onChanged: (String value) {
     setState(() {
      this._state = value;
     });
    });
  return InputDecorator(
    decoration: const InputDecoration(
     icon: const Icon(Icons.location_city),
     hintText: 'Select the State',
     labelText: 'Select the State',
    ),
    child: new DropdownButtonHideUnderline(child: stateDropdownButton));
}

TextFormField createZipWidget() {
 return new TextFormField(
    validator: (value) {
     if ((value.isEmpty) || (value.length < 5)) {
      return 'Please enter your 5 digit zip.';
     }
    },
    maxLength: 5,
    maxLengthEnforced: true,
    keyboardType: TextInputType.phone,
    inputFormatters: [WhitelistingTextInputFormatter.digitsOnly],
    decoration: InputDecoration(
      icon: const Icon(Icons.location_city),
      hintText: 'Zip',
      labelText: 'Enter your zip'),
    onSaved: (String value) {},
    controller: _zipTextController);
}

InputDecorator createFiveYearsWidget() {
 Checkbox fiveYearsCheckbox = Checkbox(
    value: this._fiveYears,
    onChanged: (value) {
     setState(() {
      this._fiveYears = value;
     });
    });
  return InputDecorator(
    decoration: const InputDecoration(
     icon: const Icon(Icons.calendar_today),
     hintText: 'Been at address 5 years?',
     labelText: '5 years?',
    ),
    child: new DropdownButtonHideUnderline(
       child: Row(children: [
     fiveYearsCheckbox,
     Text("Been at address 5 years?")
    ])));
}

DateTimePickerFormField createDobWidget() {
```

```
   return new DateTimePickerFormField(
      validator: (value) {
       if ((value == null)) {
         return 'Please enter your date of birth.';
        }
      },
      dateOnly: true,
      format: _dateFormat,
      decoration: InputDecoration(
        icon: const Icon(Icons.date_range),
        hintText: 'Date',
        labelText: 'Select the Date'),
      controller: _dobTextController);
  }

  PersonInfo createDataObjectFromFormData() {
   return new PersonInfo(
      _fnameTextController.text,
      _lnameTextController.text,
      _sex,
      _addr1TextController.text,
      _addr2TextController.text,
      _cityTextController.text,
      _state,
      _zipTextController.text,
      _fiveYears,
      _dateFormat.parse(_dobTextController.text));
  }
}
```

Other Information

Input Decoration Themes

If you don't like the way the forms look or if you feel they don't highlight the field states well enough, you can change them in the theme.

Example - 'input_decoration_themes'

This app shows how your theme can change the appearance of input fields.

Source Code

```dart
import 'package:flutter/material.dart';

void main() => runApp(new MyApp());

class MyApp extends StatelessWidget {
  // This widget is the root of your application.
  @override
  Widget build(BuildContext context) {
    return new MaterialApp(
      title: 'Flutter Demo',
      theme: new ThemeData(
        primarySwatch: Colors.blue,
        inputDecorationTheme: InputDecorationTheme(
          border: const OutlineInputBorder(
            borderSide: BorderSide(color: Colors.blueGrey),
          ),
          enabledBorder: OutlineInputBorder(
            borderSide: BorderSide(color: Colors.green),
          ),
          focusedBorder: const OutlineInputBorder(
            borderSide: BorderSide(color: Colors.deepPurple),
          ),
          labelStyle: const TextStyle(
            color: Colors.blueGrey,
          ),
        ),
      ),
      home: new HomeWidget(),
    );
  }
}

class HomeWidget extends StatelessWidget {
```

```
final _formKey = GlobalKey<FormState>();
List<TextEditingController> _textEditingControllers = [];
List<Widget> _widgets = [];

HomeWidget({Key key}) : super(key: key) {
 List<String> fieldNames = [
  "First Name",
  "Last Name",
  "Address 1",
  "Address 2",
  "City",
  "State",
  "Zip"
 ];
 for (int i = 0, ii = fieldNames.length; i < ii; i++) {
  String fieldName = fieldNames[i];
  TextEditingController textEditingController =
    new TextEditingController(text: "");
  _textEditingControllers.add(textEditingController);
  _widgets.add(Padding(
   child: _createTextFormField(fieldName, i > 1, textEditingController),
   padding: EdgeInsets.all(10.0),
  ));
 }
 _widgets.add(RaisedButton(
  onPressed: () {
   _formKey.currentState.validate();
  },
  child: new Text('Save'),
 ));
}

TextFormField _createTextFormField(
  String fieldName, bool enabled, TextEditingController controller) {
 return new TextFormField(
   enabled: enabled,
   validator: (value) {
    if (value.isEmpty) {
     return 'Please enter ${fieldName}.';
    }
   },
   decoration: InputDecoration(
    icon: const Icon(Icons.person),
    hintText: fieldName,
    labelText: 'Enter ${fieldName}'),
   controller: controller);
}

@override
Widget build(BuildContext context) {
 return new Scaffold(
   appBar: new AppBar(
    title: new Text("Input Decoration Themes"),
   ),
   body: Padding(
     padding: EdgeInsets.all(20.0),
     child: Form(
       key: _formKey,
```

```
        child: ListView(
          children: _widgets,
        ))));
  }
}
```

Enabling / Disabling Form Buttons

When dealing with forms, remember that you can enable or disable buttons using the 'onPressed' constructor argument:
- If this argument is non-null, then the button is enabled.
- If this argument is null then the button is disabked.

Example – 'button_enablement'

This app only enables the register button when the user checks the checkbox to agree to the agreement.

Source Code

```
import 'package:flutter/material.dart';

void main() => runApp(new MyApp());

class MyApp extends StatelessWidget {
  @override
  Widget build(BuildContext context) {
    return new MaterialApp(
      title: 'Flutter Demo',
      theme: new ThemeData(
        primarySwatch: Colors.blue,
```

```
      },
      home: new HomeWidget(title: 'Button Enablement'),
    );
  }
}

class HomeWidget extends StatefulWidget {
  HomeWidget({Key key, this.title}) : super(key: key);

  final String title;

  @override
  _HomeWidgetState createState() => new _HomeWidgetState();
}

class _HomeWidgetState extends State<HomeWidget> {
  bool _checked = false;

  void _onCheck(val) {
    setState(() {
      _checked = val;
    });
  }

  void _onSubmit() {
    debugPrint("_onSubmit");
  }

  @override
  Widget build(BuildContext context) {
    return new Scaffold(
      appBar: new AppBar(
        title: new Text(widget.title),
      ),
      body: new Center(
        child: new Column(
          mainAxisAlignment: MainAxisAlignment.spaceEvenly,
          children: <Widget>[
            new Text('Please check below to agree to the terms.',
                style: const TextStyle(fontStyle: FontStyle.italic)),
            Row(mainAxisAlignment: MainAxisAlignment.center, children: [
              Checkbox(value: _checked, onChanged: (val) => _onCheck(val)),
              Text("I agree")
            ]),
            OutlineButton(
              onPressed: _checked ? () => _onSubmit() : null,
              child: const Text('Register'),
            )
          ],
        ),
      ));
  }
}
```

26.HTTP, APIs, REST & JSON

Introduction

Most Flutter projects involve HTTP communication between your app and some API on some server. Most of the time these server APIs are built to the REST design guidelines and the data will be transferred in the JSON format.

The purpose of this chapter is to learn about HTTP, APIs, REST and JSON before we hit the keyboard.

Asynchronous Communication

When your app communicates to and from a remote server using HTTP, it is doing so asynchronously. The app does not suddenly stop completely after it sends a request to the server. As mentioned in the chapter 'More Advanced Dart', the Dart language fully supports asynchronous programming, including Futures. The Flutter HTTP package (which we will cover soon) uses Futures to enable developers to communicate through HTTP asynchronously. Every time we communicate with the server using HTTP we don't stop doing things in the app but we process the success or error response when it comes back to us.

HTTP

Introduction

The Hypertext Transfer Protocol (HTTP) is designed to enable communications between clients and servers. HTTP works as a request-response protocol between a client and server.

A protocol describes how machines communicate with each other using messages. A protocol defines the format of these messages.

Tools

Introduction

One you are adept with Flutter you will end up spending considerable time writing code that communicates with servers using the HTTP. You may want to investigate these tools in advance, they will make your life easier.

Web Browser

You obviously already have one of these. If you want to see the HTTP protocol at work, open your browser, go to a website then use the hamburger menu to access the developer tools. Select the 'network' option to see the network traffic inspector. In the image below you can see the network traffic inspector on the right side, with one request selected and viewed in more detail.

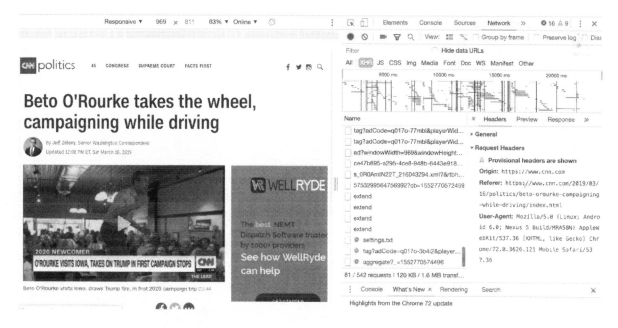

Postman

This tool will let you test HTTP requests to a server before you code them in Flutter. You can view the raw data and see what's going on.
Https://www.getpostman.com/

JSON Formatter

JSON is the data format you will be working with. You may also want to find a good online JSON formatter to make the JSON more readable.
Https://jsonformatter.curiousconcept.com/

Request

This is what your app will send to the server.

method   URI   http version

```
POST /create-user HTTP/1.1

Host: localhost:3000
Connection: keep-alive
Content-type: application/json

{ "name": "John", "age: 35 }
```

} header

} body

Response

This is what your app will receive back from the server.

http ver.   status

```
HTTP/1.1 200 OK

Date: 2017-01-10 12:28:53 GMT
Server: Apache/2.2.14
Content-type: text/html

<h1>Hello World</h1>
```

} header

} body

Methods

HTTP methods have been around for a long time. The most-commonly-used HTTP methods are POST, GET, PUT, PATCH, and DELETE. GET is used most of all because you tend to access data more often than you change it.

GET request 'method'. The 'method' describes what the app wants the server to do, what is the intent of the request. The most commonly used methods are 'get' and 'post'. The 'get' method is used to request data from the server. The 'post' method is used to send data to the server, to save it or update it. The 'put' method is used to update data on the server. The 'delete' method is used to delete data on the server.

URI

This is the address of where the request is going to. A specific path on a specific server. Example:
https://www.cnn.com/2019/03/16/politics/beto-orourke-campaigning-while-driving/index.html

Query Parameters

HTTP allows you to pass information to the server in the URL using query parameters. Example:
http://localhost:4200/sockjs-node/info?t=1498649243238

Matrix Parameters

HTTP allows you to pass information to the server in the URL using matrix parameters. For Example:
http://localhost:4200/sockjs-node/info;t=1498649243238

Matrix parameters are similar to query strings but use a different pattern. They also act differently because (not having a '?') they can be cached.

Path Parameters

HTTP allows you to pass information to the server in the URL using path parameters. For Example:
http://localhost:4200/api/badges/9243238

URI Encoding

Some characters cannot be part of a URL (for example spaces) and some other characters have a special meaning in a URL. To get around this, the URL syntax allows for encoding on parameters to ensure a valid URL.

Example:

The 'space' character between 'Atlantic' and 'City' is encoded to '%20'.

https://trailapi-trailapi.p.mashape.com/?q[city_cont]=Atlantic%20City

Status

This is part of the response. It indicates whether the request was successfully processed or not. Here are some of the HTTP status code values:

Code		Name	Description
1xx		Informational	
2xx		Success	
	200	Ok	
3xx		Redirect	
	301	Moved permanently	
	302	Moved temporarily	
4xx		Request error	
	400	Bad request	The request could not be understood by the server.
	403	Forbidden	User not authorized to perform the requested operation.
	404	Not found	The requested resource could not be found at the given URI.
	405	Method not allowed	The request method is not allowed on the specified resource.
5xx		Server error	
	500	Internal server error	The server encountered an unexpected condition, preventing it to fulfill the request.
	503	Service unavailable	The server is temporarily unavailable, usually due to overloading or maintenance.

Header

HTTP headers allow the client and the server to pass additional information with the request or the response. A request header consists of key value pairs - a case-insensitive key followed by a colon ':', then by its value (without line breaks).

```
Host: localhost:3000
Connection: keep-alive
Content-type: application/json
```

Body

Introduction

The HTTP body allows the client and the server to pass additional information with the request or the response after the header.

Request

In the Request, HTTP bodies are not always required because a body of information is not always needed. GET and DELETE HTTP requests usually don't need a body. POST, PUT and PATCH HTTP requests do - this is where the information to be created or modified is sent.

```
{ "name": "John", "age: 35 }
```

Response

The body is used to return information in the Response and it can get very large, with a considerable amount of data.

Example:
In this chapter's example HTTP code, we receive a response with a body containing the data for over 1000 employees.

APIs

When someone makes their API available to the world, they write the code for the api and they publish it to their HTTP web server. APIs are also known as web services.

Most APIs use the REST architectural style, which is a pattern of how you will communicate with the server over HTTP. APIs that conform to the REST architectural style mostly work in the same manner, with similar web addresses (URIs) and HTTP methods.

These similarities really help when going from one API to another.

REST

REST stands for Representational State Transfer. REST gives us high level design guidelines and leave you to think of your own implementation.

REST APIs should be stateless.

In the past, web applications used to store session data for the user. For example, the user would login and this would start a session and information could be kept in this session until the user logged out. This session data could include who the user is, what access they have and any other required information.

Now, with more modern APIs and REST, access to servers is controlled through tokens or api keys. Also, every API call is stateless - every single request from the client to server is self-contained and contains all of the data to identify who made the request and all of the request data itself to perform the operation. Such a request cannot take advantage of any pre-existing session data on the server.

Determining the User - Who Made the Request to the API?

Tokens

In most apps with a login, when a user login occurs, he or she is returned a temporary token for access. This token is encrypted and contains information about the user and the token itself (such as when it expires). This token can be refreshed every predetermined period of time (for example every 15 minutes). Whenever an API call is made from some device to the server, the token must be included in every single outgoing request header to the server. If the token is not present or invalid (they can expire) then the server returns an error code (usually a 401 or 403 HTTP code). If the token is good then the server knows that a valid logged-in user is using the app, the server has info about the user from the token and the API can perform its operation.

API Keys

If the user doesn't really need to login every time the app is used, an API key enables a registered user (for example a CAT API user) to be identified in the HTTP header as a valid user on every single outgoing request to the server. Like a token, this is validated and the server returns an error code if there is a problem with it.

No User Identification

Sometimes people publish APIs which don't need information about the user. For example, in this chapter we are going to use the dummy rest api here: http://dummy.restapiexample.com/

How REST Uses URLs

In REST, the URL is used to determine what resource you are doing it to. For example: employees, orders etc.

Base URL

The base URL is the first part of the API, without the REST part. The REST part comes after the base URL. The base URL is usually the following:
- The domain. E.g. www.example.com.
- Optionally a suffix 'api' to indicate that the path is for API use only.
- Optionally a suffix for the name of the app the API was written for.
- Optionally it also has the API version.

- For example, for the dummy REST API it is http://dummy.restapiexample.com/api/v1

URL & Paths

The URL of the REST API can be composed of several parts, of paths. Think of it the URL as a path to the resource (the data).

- Example:
  - http://www.example.com/customers/33245/orders/8769/lineitems/1
- Should be thought as:
  - Go to customer 33245.
  - Then go to order 8769 for <u>that</u> customer.
  - Then 'go to line item 1' for <u>that</u> order.

How REST Uses HTTP Method

In REST, the HTTP method is used to describe what you are doing. Getting data, posting new data (creating it), putting data (updating it), deleting it.

Accessing Data with a REST API

- URI
  - Identifies what data you are accessing.
  - A list of items.
    - This would be [base url] + the resource name. For example: http://www.example.com/products. This would usually return multiple projects.
    - The list of items could belong to another entity. Examples:
      - http://www.example.com/customers/33245/orders would return the list of orders for customer 33245.
      - http://www.example.com/customers/33245/orders/123/lineItems would return the line items for order 123 for customer 33245.
  - A searched list of items.
    - The URL would be similar to the list of items above, plus some additional info on the end to specify the search.
    - Additional info.
      - You could add query strings or matrix / path parameters to the end of the url. For example: http://www.example.com/products?name=mark . This is the preferred way to do this but REST URLs are often open to interpretation.
      - You could add '/search' then the search criteria to the end of the URL (or something similar). For example: http://www.example.com/products/search/name/mark would search for products by the name mark.

- o A single item.
  - ▪ The URL would be similar to the list of items plus a slash then an identifier to identify the item. For example: http://www.example.com/products/66432 would return product 66432.
  - ▪ The single item could belong to another entity. For example: http://www.example.com/customers/33245/orders/8769 would return a single item, order 8769 for customer 33245.
- HTTP Method
  - o You should use an HTTP 'get' method to access data through a REST API.
- HTTP Body
  - o Not used.

Inserting Data with a REST API

- URI
  - o Identifies what type of data you are inserting.
  - o This would be the same as the URL to the list of items. Examples:
    - ▪ http://www.example.com/products
    - ▪ http://www.example.com/customers/33245/orders or http://www.example.com/orders (implementation is open to interpretation).
- HTTP Method
  - o You should use an HTTP 'put' method to insert (or create) data through a REST Api.
- HTTP Body
  - o You normally put the data required for the insert in the request body.

Updating Data with a REST API

- URI
  - o Identifies what data you are updating.
  - o This would be the same as the URL for accessing a single item. Examples:
    - ▪ http://www.example.com/products/66432
    - ▪ http://www.example.com/customers/33245/orders/8769
- HTTP Method
  - o You use an HTTP 'put' method to update data through a REST Api.
- HTTP Body
  - o You normally put the data required for the update in the request body.

Deleting Data with a REST API

- URI
  - o Identifies what data you are deleting.
  - o This would be the same as the URL for accessing a single item. Examples:
    - ▪ http://www.example.com/products/66432

- http://www.example.com/customers/33245/orders/8769
- HTTP Method
  - You should use an HTTP 'delete' method to delete data through a REST Api.
- HTTP Body
  - Not used.

JSON

JSON stands for JavaScript Object Notation. It is a data format used to pass data between the client and the server (in both directions). It is the same data format used by the JavaScript language. It uses a comma to separate items and a colon to separate the name of a property with the data for that property. It uses different types of brackets to denote objects and arrays.

JSON For Passing an Object Containing Data.

The '{' and '}' brackets are used to denote the start and end of an object.

```
{ "name":"John", "age":31, "city":"New York" }
```

JSON For Passing an Array

The '[' and ']' brackets are used to denote the start and end of an array.

```
[ "Ford", "BMW", "Fiat"]
```

JSON For Passing an Array of Objects

The brackets are combined to create a cars object, which has two properties 'Nissan' and 'Ford'. Each property has an array of models.

```
{
  "cars": {
    "Nissan": [
      {"model":"Sentra", "doors":4},
      {"model":"Maxima", "doors":4}
    ],
    "Ford": [
      {"model":"Taurus", "doors":4},
      {"model":"Escort", "doors":4}
    ]
  }
}
```

27.Flutter with HTTP, APIs, REST & JSON

Introduction

In the previous chapter we learnt about HTTP, APIs, REST and JSON.

The purpose of this chapter is to write Flutter code that communicates with APIs over HTTP using REST with JSON as the data format.

Flutter & JSON

Introduction

So, we know that we communicate with servers using the HTTP protocol, using JSON as the data format.

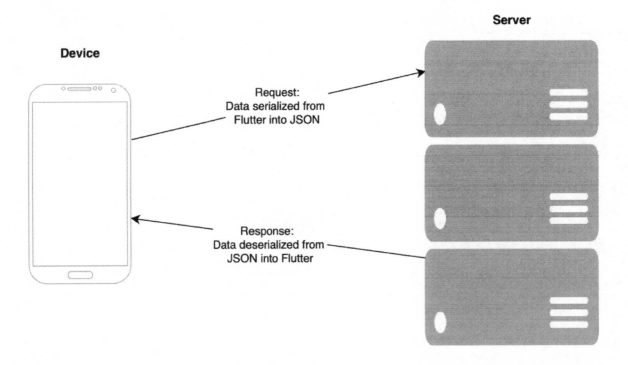

Request

When the app makes an outgoing request to an API on a server, it often needs to convert Flutter data (for example data in a form) into JSON. This conversion from Flutter data into JSON data is called serializing.

Response

When the server responds back, the app needs to convert JSON data into Flutter data. This conversion from JSON data back to Flutter data is called deserializing.

Serializing & Deserializing JSON.

So, we know we have to convert data between the JSON and Flutter.
- By JSON we mean a string of JSON.
- By Flutter we mean 'data in a Dart class in our Flutter app'.

Two Ways of Serializing & Deserializing JSON

These are the two main ways of serializing & deserializing JSON in a Flutter App:

1. Generating code for Serializing & Deserializing
   - Pluses.
     - You don't have to write the code.
     - Its generated code, it doesn't make mistakes.
   - Minuses.
     - It's not super-simple to setup, you need to know how it works.
     - It doesn't work with complicated cases as well as coding them.
2. Manually writing code for Serializing & Deserializing
   - Pluses.
     - You have to write the code.
     - You can code the more complex Serialization & Deserialization scenarios.
   - Minuses.
     - There will be bugs.
     - It's not super-simple to code, you need to know how it works.

Remember that You Can Combine the Two!

You can follow the 80 - 20 rule.
Do 80% the simple easiest way, generating the code for the serialization & deserialization of simple objects.
When you get to the more difficult 20% you can handcraft your own code to serialize and deserialize more complex objects.

The code examples follow this rule. We do the easy stuff using the code generator (simple serialization & deserialization) and the hard stuff (recursive serialization & deserialization) in the handwritten code.

Generating Code for Serializing & Deserializing

Introduction

This approach uses two packages:

- The 'json_serializable' package to generate the serialization & deserialization code for us.
- The 'build_runner' package to work with the 'json_serializable' package generate the code files.

Step 1 – Add Dependencies to Projects

Modify the project dependency file 'pubspec.yaml' to include two additional developer dependencies - build_runner and json_serializable:

```
dev_dependencies:
  flutter_test:
    sdk: flutter

  build_runner:
  json_serializable: ^0.5.0
```

Then you need to command Flutter to go get the dependencies:

```
flutter packages get
```

Step 2 – Amend the classes to be Serialized & Deserialized

Annotate the classes to be serialized & deserialized to include the import and annotations. In the example, this class is contained in the 'main.dart' file.

- Import the annotation.
- Add a @JsonSerializable() annotation just before the class declaration.
- Add field annotations just before the field declarations.
    - These aren't necessary if the JSON field name stays the same as the Dart field name.
    - The @JsonKey annotation declares the JSON name for the field if you want it to be different from the field name.

```
import 'package:json_annotation/json_annotation.dart';

...

@JsonSerializable()
class Person {
  final String name;
  @JsonKey(name: "addr1")
  final String addressLine1;
  @JsonKey(name: "city")
  final String addressCity;
  @JsonKey(name: "state")
  final String addressState;

  Person(this.name, this.addressLine1, this.addressCity, this.addressState);
```

```
@override
String toString() {
  return 'Person{name: $name, addressLine1: $addressLine1, addressCity: $addressCity, addressState:
$addressState}';
  }
}
```

Step 3 – Generate the Serialization & Deserialization Code '.g.dart' Files

Run the following command line in the project root:

```
flutter packages pub run build_runner build
```

This should generate a '.g.dart' file in the project for each file that you modified in Step 2. Note that these files contain 'Mixins', Dart classes that contain code that can be incorporated into other classes without the use of inheritance. Please take a look at the Mixins chapter.

In the example, this generates a file 'main.g.dart' to match the 'main.dart' file:

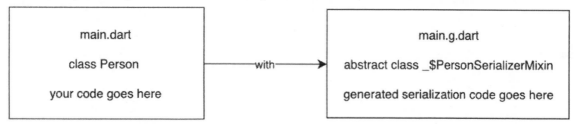

Step 4 – Amend the classes to be Serialized & Deserialized

Now we need to go back to the classes that we modified in step 2 and we need to modify them to utilize the generated code. We do this by first using a 'part' annotation to import the generated code. Then we use a mixin to combine the existing class and the generated class together.

- We insert a 'part' annotation for each file generated in Step 3. The 'part' annotation is used to inject content from another file. In the example file 'main.dart', we use this annotation to inject the content from the 'main.g.dart' file.

```
part 'main.g.dart';
```

- We modify the class declarations to extend the Object class with the Mixin (the abstract class) from the generated code (you may need to look in the '.g.dart' files to get the mixin names). In the example, we change the class declaration to the following (changes in bold):

```
class Person extends Object with _$PersonSerializerMixin {
```

Done

That's it, you should be done.
Make sure that you re-run the following command in your project root everytime you change something:

```
flutter packages pub run build_runner build
```

Example – 'serialize_with_generated_code'

This app creates a Person object for a person and displays a 'toString()' of the object below in black. It also serializes that object and displays the JSON in underneath in red. There is a 'Copy' button to copy the JSON to the clipboard so you can paste it into an online JSON formatter.

Remember that this should won't work recursively, unlike the example with the manually-written code.

Source Code

```
import 'dart:convert';

import 'package:flutter/material.dart';
import 'package:flutter/services.dart';
import 'package:json_annotation/json_annotation.dart';

part 'main.g.dart';

void main() => runApp(MyApp());

@JsonSerializable()
class Person extends Object with _$PersonSerializerMixin {
  final String name;
  @JsonKey(name: "addr1")
  final String addressLine1;
  @JsonKey(name: "city")
  final String addressCity;
  @JsonKey(name: "state")
  final String addressState;

  const Person(
```

```
      this.name, this.addressLine1, this.addressCity, this.addressState);

  @override
  String toString() {
    return 'Person{name: $name, addressLine1: $addressLine1, addressCity: $addressCity, addressState:
$addressState}';
  }
}

class MyApp extends StatelessWidget {
  // This widget is the root of your application.
  @override
  Widget build(BuildContext context) {
    return MaterialApp(
      title: 'Flutter Demo',
      theme: ThemeData(
        primarySwatch: Colors.blue,
      ),
      home: HomeWidget(),
    );
  }
}

class HomeWidget extends StatelessWidget {
  static const Person _person =
      Person("John Brown", "9621 Roberts Avenue", "Birmingham", "AL");

  @override
  Widget build(BuildContext context) {
    return Scaffold(
      appBar: AppBar(
        title: Text("Serialization"),
      ),
      body: Center(
        child: Padding(
          child: ListView(
            children: <Widget>[
              Padding(
                child: Text("Grandfather:\n${_person}"),
                padding: EdgeInsets.only(top: 0.0)),
              Padding(
                child: Text("Json Encoded:\n${json.encode(_person)}",
                    style: TextStyle(color: Colors.red)),
                padding: EdgeInsets.only(top: 10.0)),
              FlatButton(
                child: Text("Copy"),
                onPressed: (() {
                  Clipboard.setData(
                    ClipboardData(text: "${json.encode(_person)}"));
                })),
            ],
          ),
          padding: EdgeInsets.all(10.0),
        ),
      ));
  }
}
```

Example – 'deserialize_with_generated_code'

This app lets you enter the JSON for a person then hit the floating button to deserialize it.
- If successful, a 'toString()' of the Person object is displayed underneath (in black).
- If an error occurs (maybe you input bad JSON?), it is displayed underneath (in red).

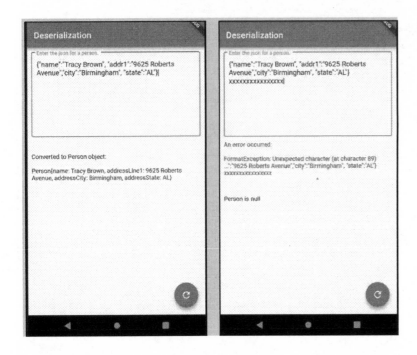

Remember that this should won't work recursively, unlike the example with the manually-written code.

Source Code

```dart
import 'package:flutter/material.dart';
import 'dart:convert';
import 'package:json_annotation/json_annotation.dart';

part 'main.g.dart';

void main() => runApp(MyApp());

@JsonSerializable()
class Person extends Object with _$PersonSerializerMixin {
  final String name;
  @JsonKey(name: "addr1")
  final String addressLine1;
  @JsonKey(name: "city")
  final String addressCity;
  @JsonKey(name: "state")
  final String addressState;

  Person(this.name, this.addressLine1, this.addressCity, this.addressState);

  @override
```

```dart
  String toString() {
    return 'Person{name: $name, addressLine1: $addressLine1, addressCity: $addressCity, addressState:
$addressState}';
  }
}

class MyApp extends StatelessWidget {
  // This widget is the root of your application.
  @override
  Widget build(BuildContext context) {
    return MaterialApp(
      title: 'Flutter Demo',
      theme: ThemeData(
        primarySwatch: Colors.blue,
      ),
      home: HomeWidget(),
    );
  }
}

class HomeWidget extends StatefulWidget {
  HomeWidget({Key key}) : super(key: key);

  @override
  _HomeWidgetState createState() => _HomeWidgetState();
}

class _HomeWidgetState extends State<HomeWidget> {
  final _jsonTextController = TextEditingController();
  Person _person;
  String _error;

  _HomeWidgetState() {
    final String person =
      "{\"name\":\"Tracy Brown\", \"addr1\":\"9625 Roberts Avenue\"," +
        "\"city\":\"Birmingham\", \"state\":\"AL\"}";

    _jsonTextController.text = person;
  }

  TextFormField _createJsonTextFormField() {
    return new TextFormField(
      validator: (value) {
        if (value.isEmpty) {
          return 'Please enter the json.';
        }
      },
      decoration: InputDecoration(
        border: OutlineInputBorder(),
        hintText: 'Json',
        labelText: 'Enter the json for a person.'),
      controller: _jsonTextController,
      autofocus: true,
      maxLines: 8,
      keyboardType: TextInputType.multiline);
  }

  _convertJsonToPerson() {
```

```
   _error = null;
   _person = null;
   setState(() {
     try {
       final String jsonText = _jsonTextController.text;
       debugPrint("JSON TEXT: ${jsonText}");
       var decoded = json.decode(jsonText); // text to map
       debugPrint("DECODED: type: ${decoded.runtimeType} value: ${decoded}");
       _person = _$PersonFromJson(decoded); // map to object
       debugPrint("PERSON OBJECT: type: ${_person.runtimeType} value: "
         "${_person}");
     } catch (e) {
       debugPrint("ERROR: ${e}");
       _error = e.toString();
     }
   });
 }

 @override
 Widget build(BuildContext context) {
   return Scaffold(
     appBar: AppBar(
       title: Text("Deserialization"),
     ),
     body: Center(
       child: Padding(
         child: ListView(
           children: <Widget>[
             _createJsonTextFormField(),
             Padding(
               padding: EdgeInsets.only(top: 10.0),
               child: Text(
                 _error == null ? '' : 'An error occurred:\n\n${_error}',
                 style: TextStyle(color: Colors.red))),
             Padding(
               padding: EdgeInsets.only(top: 10.0),
               child: Text(_person == null
                 ? 'Person is null'
                 : 'Converted to Person object:\n\n${_person}'))
           ],
         ),
         padding: EdgeInsets.all(10.0),
       ),
     ),
     floatingActionButton: FloatingActionButton(
       onPressed: _convertJsonToPerson,
       tooltip: 'Increment',
       child: Icon(Icons.refresh),
     ), // This trailing comma makes auto-formatting nicer for build methods.
   );
 }
}
```

Manually Writing Code for Serialization & Deserialization

Introduction

This approach uses the 'json' class in the core 'dart.convert' package to convert between maps and JSON strings.

When serializing an Object, we write code to convert the data in our class into a map so that the 'json' class can then convert it to a JSON string.

When deserializing an JSON string, we write code to convert the map into the data in our class.

Step 1 - Write Data Class Including 'toJson' & 'fromJson' Methods

- First of all, you need to write a Dart data class that will contain the data to be serialized and will contain the data after it has been deserialized.
- If serializing:
  - Write a 'toJson' method that returns a map from the data in that class (see 'Person' class for example).
- If deserializing:
  - Write a 'fromJson' factory method that creates an instance of the data class from a single map argument.

```dart
class Person {
  final String name;
  final String addressLine1;
  final String addressCity;
  final String addressState;
  final List<Person> children;

  const Person(this.name, this.addressLine1, this.addressCity,
    this.addressState, this.children);

  Map<String, dynamic> toJson() {
    var map = {
      'name': name,
      'addr': addressLine1,
      'city': addressCity,
      'state': addressState,
      'children': children
    };
    return map;
  }

  factory Person.fromJson(Map<String, dynamic> json) {
    if (json == null) {
      throw FormatException("Null JSON.");
    }

    // Recursion. Convert children into list of Person objects.
    List<dynamic> decodedChildren = json['children'];
    List<Person> children = [];
    decodedChildren.forEach((decodedChild) {
```

```
    children.add(Person.fromJson(decodedChild));
  });

  return Person(
    json['name'], json['addr1'], json['city'], json['state'], children);
  }

}
```

Step 2 - Add Code to Invoke Serialization / Deserialization of the Data Class

- If serializing:
    - Invoke 'json.encode' in the 'json' class in the core 'dart.convert' package.
        - The 'json' class invokes the 'toJson' method in your data class to create a map.
        - The 'json' class then converts the map to a JSON string.
- If deserializing:
    - Invoke 'json.decode' in the 'json' class in the core 'dart.convert' package to return a map.
        - The 'json' class will convert the JSON string into a map.
    - Invoke the factory '.fromJson' method in the data class to convert the map into an instance of the data class.

Examples – 'serialize_manually' & 'deserialize_manually'

Both the examples below demonstrate something more complex: recursive manual serialization / deserialization. I tried to do this with the generated code but could not get it to work.

We demonstrate serializing & deserializing a Person object recursively. These Person objects can have children, which in turn can have children etc. In this example, we can have children and grandchildren.

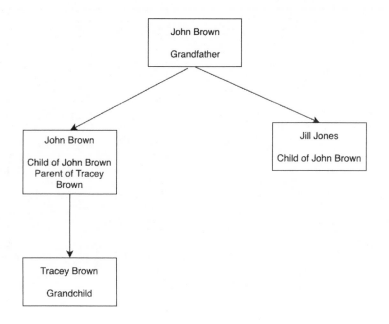

Example – 'serialize_manually'

This app creates Person objects for all the people in the family and displays a 'toString()' of each one (in black). It also deserializes each one, displaying the JSON in underneath (in red). There is a 'Copy' button to copy the JSON to the clipboard so you can paste it into an online JSON formatter.

Source Code

```dart
import 'dart:convert';

import 'package:flutter/material.dart';
import 'package:flutter/services.dart';

void main() => runApp(MyApp());

class Person {
  final String name;
  final String addressLine1;
  final String addressCity;
  final String addressState;
  final List<Person> children;

  const Person(this.name, this.addressLine1, this.addressCity,
    this.addressState, this.children);

  // You write this serialization code.
  Map<String, dynamic> toJson() {
    var map = {
      'name': name,
      'addr': addressLine1,
      'city': addressCity,
      'state': addressState,
      'children': children
    };
    return map;
  }
  // You write this serialization code.

  @override
  String toString() {
    return 'Person{name: $name, addressLine1: $addressLine1, addressCity: $addressCity, addressState:
$addressState, children: $children}';
  }
}

class MyApp extends StatelessWidget {
  // This widget is the root of your application.
  @override
  Widget build(BuildContext context) {
    return MaterialApp(
      title: 'Flutter Demo',
      theme: ThemeData(
        primarySwatch: Colors.blue,
      ),
      home: HomeWidget(),
    );
  }
}

class HomeWidget extends StatelessWidget {
  static const Person _grandchild =
    Person("Tracy Brown", "9625 Roberts Avenue", "Birmingham", "AL", []);
  static const Person _adultFather = const Person(
    "John Brown", "9625 Roberts Avenue", "Birmingham", "AL", [_grandchild]);
  static const Person _adultNoChildren =
```

```
     const Person("Jill Jones", "100 East Road", "Ocala", "FL", []);
static const Person _grandfather = Person("John Brown", "9621 Roberts Avenue",
  "Birmingham", "AL", [_adultFather, _adultNoChildren]);

@override
Widget build(BuildContext context) {
  return Scaffold(
    appBar: AppBar(
      title: Text("Recursive Serialization"),
    ),
    body: Center(
      child: Padding(
        child: ListView(
          children: <Widget>[
            Padding(
              child: Text("Grandfather:\n${_grandfather}"),
              padding: EdgeInsets.only(top: 0.0)),
            Padding(
              child: Text("Json Encoded:\n${json.encode(_grandfather)}",
                style: TextStyle(color: Colors.red)),
              padding: EdgeInsets.only(top: 10.0)),
            FlatButton(
              child: Text("Copy"),
              onPressed: (() {
               Clipboard.setData(
                  ClipboardData(text: "${json.encode(_grandfather)}"));
              })),
            Padding(
              child: Text("Adult Father:\n${_adultFather}"),
              padding: EdgeInsets.only(top: 30.0)),
            Padding(
              child: Text("Json Encoded:\n${json.encode(_adultFather)}",
                style: TextStyle(color: Colors.red)),
              padding: EdgeInsets.only(top: 10.0)),
            FlatButton(
              child: Text("Copy"),
              onPressed: (() {
               Clipboard.setData(
                  ClipboardData(text: "${json.encode(_adultFather)}"));
              })),
            Padding(
              child: Text("Adult No Children:\n${_adultNoChildren}"),
              padding: EdgeInsets.only(top: 30.0)),
            Padding(
              child: Text(
                "Json Encoded:\n${json.encode(_adultNoChildren)}",
                style: TextStyle(color: Colors.red)),
              padding: EdgeInsets.only(top: 10.0)),
            FlatButton(
              child: Text("Copy"),
              onPressed: (() {
               Clipboard.setData(ClipboardData(
                  text: "${json.encode(_adultNoChildren)}"));
              })),
            Padding(
              child: Text("Grandchild:\n${_grandchild}"),
              padding: EdgeInsets.only(top: 30.0)),
            Padding(
```

```
            child: Text("Json Encoded:\n${json.encode(_grandchild)}",
              style: TextStyle(color: Colors.red)),
            padding: EdgeInsets.only(top: 10.0)),
        FlatButton(
          child: Text("Copy"),
          onPressed: (() {
            Clipboard.setData(
              ClipboardData(text: "${json.encode(_grandchild)}"));
          })),
      ],
    ),
    padding: EdgeInsets.all(10.0),
  ),
 ));
 }
}
```

Example – 'deserialize_manually'

This app lets you enter the JSON for a person then hit the floating button to deserialize it.

- If successful, a 'toString()' of the Person object is displayed underneath (in black).
- If an error occurs (maybe you input bad JSON?), it is displayed underneath (in red).

Remember that this should work recursively - the Person JSON can have children, which will create a Person object with children (and so on). This app defaults your initial JSON input to the grandparent John Brown so that you can see this recursion working.

This app also writes to the console so you can follow whats happening.

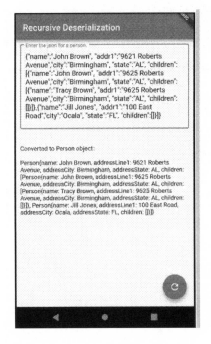
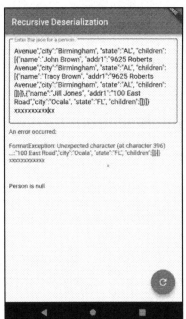

Source Code

```dart
import 'package:flutter/material.dart';
import 'dart:convert';

void main() => runApp(MyApp());

class Person {
  final String name;
  final String addressLine1;
  final String addressCity;
  final String addressState;
  final List<Person> children;

  const Person(this.name, this.addressLine1, this.addressCity,
    this.addressState, this.children);

  // You write this deserialization code.
  factory Person.fromJson(Map<String, dynamic> json) {
    if (json == null) {
      throw FormatException("Null JSON.");
    }

    // Recursion. Convert children into list of Person objects.
    List<dynamic> decodedChildren = json['children'];
    List<Person> children = [];
    decodedChildren.forEach((decodedChild) {
      children.add(Person.fromJson(decodedChild));
    });

    return Person(
      json['name'], json['addr1'], json['city'], json['state'], children);
  }
  // You write this deserialization code.

  @override
  String toString() {
    return 'Person{name: $name, addressLine1: $addressLine1, addressCity: $addressCity, addressState:
$addressState, children: $children}';
  }
}

class MyApp extends StatelessWidget {
  // This widget is the root of your application.
  @override
  Widget build(BuildContext context) {
    return MaterialApp(
      title: 'Flutter Demo',
      theme: ThemeData(
        primarySwatch: Colors.blue,
      ),
      home: HomeWidget(),
    );
  }
}

class HomeWidget extends StatefulWidget {
  HomeWidget({Key key}) : super(key: key);
```

```
  @override
  _HomeWidgetState createState() => _HomeWidgetState();
}

class _HomeWidgetState extends State<HomeWidget> {
  final _jsonTextController = TextEditingController();
  Person _person;
  String _error;

  _HomeWidgetState() {
    final String grandchild =
        "{\"name\":\"Tracy Brown\", \"addr1\":\"9625 Roberts Avenue\"," +
          "\"city\":\"Birmingham\", \"state\":\"AL\", \"children\":[" +
          "]}";
    final String adultFather =
        "{\"name\":\"John Brown\", \"addr1\":\"9625 Roberts Avenue\"," +
          "\"city\":\"Birmingham\", \"state\":\"AL\", \"children\":[" +
          grandchild +
          "]}";
    final String adultNoChildren =
        "{\"name\":\"Jill Jones\", \"addr1\":\"100 East Road\"," +
          "\"city\":\"Ocala\", \"state\":\"FL\", \"children\":[" +
          "]}";
    final String grandfather =
        "{\"name\":\"John Brown\", \"addr1\":\"9621 Roberts Avenue\"," +
          "\"city\":\"Birmingham\", \"state\":\"AL\", \"children\":[" +
          adultFather +
          "," +
          adultNoChildren +
          "]}";

    _jsonTextController.text = grandfather;
  }

  TextFormField _createJsonTextFormField() {
    return new TextFormField(
      validator: (value) {
       if (value.isEmpty) {
         return 'Please enter the json.';
       }
      },
      decoration: InputDecoration(
         border: OutlineInputBorder(),
         hintText: 'Json',
         labelText: 'Enter the json for a person.'),
      controller: _jsonTextController,
      autofocus: true,
      maxLines: 8,
      keyboardType: TextInputType.multiline);
  }

  _convertJsonToPerson() {
    _error = null;
    _person = null;
    setState(() {
      try {
       final String jsonText = _jsonTextController.text;
       debugPrint("JSON TEXT: ${jsonText}");
```

```
    var decoded = json.decode(jsonText); // text to map
    debugPrint("DECODED:  type: ${decoded.runtimeType} value: ${decoded}");
    _person = Person.fromJson(decoded); // map to object
    debugPrint("PERSON OBJECT: type: ${_person.runtimeType} value: "
       "${_person}");
  } catch (e) {
    debugPrint("ERROR: ${e}");
    _error = e.toString();
  }
  });
}

@override
Widget build(BuildContext context) {
 return Scaffold(
   appBar: AppBar(
    title: Text("Recursive Deserialization"),
   ),
   body: Center(
    child: Padding(
      child: ListView(
       children: <Widget>[
        _createJsonTextFormField(),
        Padding(
          padding: EdgeInsets.only(top: 10.0),
          child: Text(
            _error == null ? '' : 'An error occurred:\n\n${_error}',
            style: TextStyle(color: Colors.red))),
        Padding(
          padding: EdgeInsets.only(top: 10.0),
          child: Text(_person == null
            ? 'Person is null'
            : 'Converted to Person object:\n\n${_person}'))
      ],
     ),
     padding: EdgeInsets.all(10.0),
    ),
   ),
   floatingActionButton: FloatingActionButton(
    onPressed: _convertJsonToPerson,
    tooltip: 'Increment',
    child: Icon(Icons.refresh),
   ), // This trailing comma makes auto-formatting nicer for build methods.
  );
 }
}
```

Flutter & HTTP

Introduction

Now we know how to convert the data from Flutter to JSON and back again, we need to write code that communicates with APIs on servers, using the HTTP protocol.

Flutter HTTP Package

To do this we will use the Flutter HTTP Package. It is not a core package so we will have to add a dependency for it.

Dependency

To use it, you have to add the dependency to your project in the 'pubspec.yaml' file:

```
dependencies:
  HTTP: ^0.12.0+1
```

Remember to do a 'flutter packages get' afterwards.

More info here: https://pub.dartlang.org/packages/http

Dummy API

We are going to use someone's API for these exercises and for the example code.
In this case we are going to use the dummy rest api here: http://dummy.restapiexample.com/,
because it covers all of the following: get data, add data, update data and delete data. It also
doesn't require a key or registration.

Exercise - Get Data Using Postman

In this exercise, we will use the API to get information about employees.
- Open Postman
- Copy and paste 'http://dummy.restapiexample.com/api/v1/employees' into the Request URL at top.
- Hit the 'Send' button.
- Data should show up at the bottom.

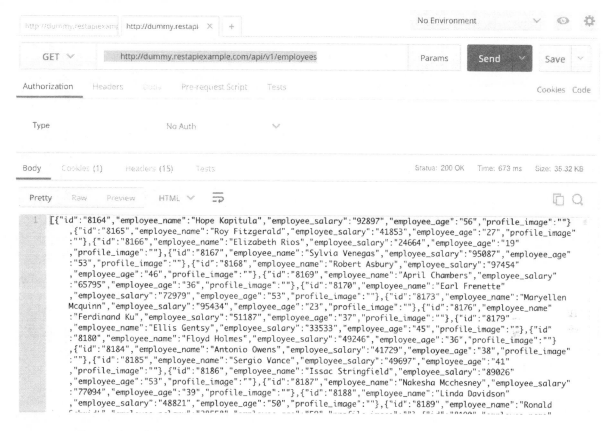

Exercise – Format Data

- Click on the data near the bottom, then select all and copy.
- Go to https://jsonformatter.curiousconcept.com/ in your browser.
- Paste the data into the box 'JSON Data/URL' (see below).

- Hit the 'Process' button. You should be taken to a formatted view of the data (see below).

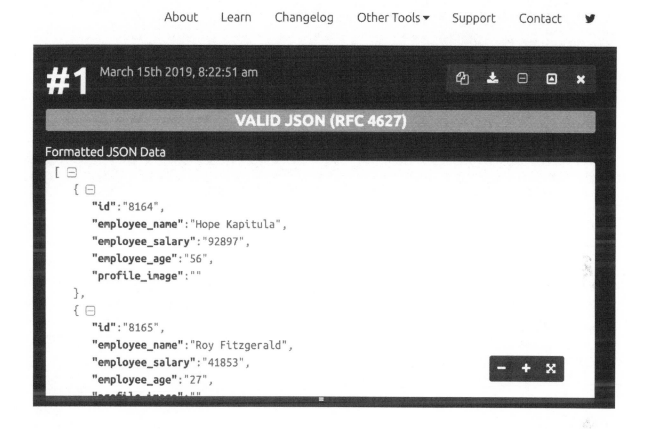

Error Handling

As mentioned in the chapter before, the Flutter HTTP package enables us to communicate with APIs asynchronously using HTTP and this makes error handling a little more complex:

- You need to add an error handler in case an error occurs when you first make the request.
- You need to add an error handler incase the future terminates with an error.
- You need to check the HTTP code of the response from the server incase anything was incorrect or went wrong on that end.

Please refer to the error handling in the example code below.

Example 'http_employees'

In preparing this example, I had to find an API that was public to work with that would work with all of the HTTP verbs, so you could see getting data, adding data, updating data and deleting data. I ended up using http://dummy.restapiexample.com/ . It is a REST Api that enables people to maintain a list of employees. Like many such Apis, does not exactly subscribe to the REST pattern prescribed in this chapter. Some of the url patterns have been interpreted differently to how I expected them to. However, it is good to use for an example and I am grateful to them for putting it out there.

This example app connects to dummy Api and enables you to add employees, update employees and delete them. It starts with a list of employees and you can tap on one to view and make changes. You can also delete employees but tapping longer on an employee in the list of employees.

This example app should also demonstrate how you may sometimes encounter errors when communicating with Apis. For example, the dummy Api doesn't allow the same employee name twice. If you enter the same employee name twice and attempt to save, then the dummy Api will return an error and this is displayed to the user. This could be handled more gracefully but at least it catches it and shows some information at the bottom.

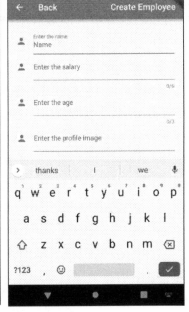

This example app may be useful because it combines multiple Flutter topics together:

- Communicating with a REST Api on an HTTP server.
- Forms and validation.
- Modal dialogs.
- State management using inherited widget and stateful widgets.
- Error handling.

Source Code

Dependencies

Add the following dependencies into the 'pubspec.yaml' file. After that you will need to do a 'flutter packages get' on the command line in the root of your project to download the dependencies.

```
dependencies:
 flutter:
  sdk: flutter
 rxdart: 0.18.1
 HTTP: ^0.11.0
 cupertino_icons: ^0.1.2
```

Source Code

```
import 'dart:async';
import 'dart:convert';

import 'package:flutter/material.dart';
import 'package:flutter/services.dart';
```

```dart
import 'package:HTTP/HTTP.dart' as HTTP;
import 'package:HTTP/HTTP.dart';

void main() => runApp(new MyApp());

class Employee {
  String id;
  String employeeName;
  String employeeSalary;
  String employeeAge;
  String profileImage;

  Employee(this.id, this.employeeName, this.employeeSalary, this.employeeAge,
    this.profileImage);

  Employee.empty() {
    id = "";
    employeeName = "";
    employeeSalary = "";
    employeeAge = "";
    profileImage = "";
  }

  factory Employee.fromJson(Map<String, dynamic> json) {
    if (json == null) {
      throw FormatException("Null JSON.");
    }
    return Employee(json['id'], json['employee_name'], json['employee_salary'],
      json['employee_age'], json['profile_image']);
  }

  Map<String, dynamic> toJson() {
    var map = {
      'name': employeeName,
      'salary': employeeSalary,
      'age': employeeAge
    };
    if (id.isNotEmpty) {
      map['id'] = id;
    }
    if (profileImage.isNotEmpty) {
      map['profileImage'] = profileImage;
    }
    return map;
  }

  get hasEmptyId {
    return id.isEmpty;
  }
}

class PleaseWaitWidget extends StatelessWidget {
  PleaseWaitWidget({
    Key key,
  }) : super(key: key);

  // This widget is the root of your application.
  @override
```

```
Widget build(BuildContext context) {
  return Container(
    child: Center(
      child: CircularProgressIndicator(),
    ),
    color: Colors.white.withOpacity(0.8));
  }
}

class ApiWidget extends InheritedWidget {
  static final String _BASE_URL = "http://dummy.restapiexample.com/api/v1";
  static const _TIMEOUT = Duration(seconds: 10);

  ApiWidget({
    Key key,
    @required Widget child,
  }) : assert(child != null),
       super(key: key, child: child);

  static ApiWidget of(BuildContext context) {
    return context.inheritFromWidgetOfExactType(ApiWidget) as ApiWidget;
  }

  @override
  bool updateShouldNotify(covariant InheritedWidget oldWidget) {
    return false;
  }

  Future<List<Employee>> loadAndParseEmployees() async {
    var url = '${_BASE_URL}/employees';
    final response = await HTTP.get(url).timeout(_TIMEOUT);
    if (response.statusCode == 200) {
      final parsed = json.decode(response.body).cast<Map<String, dynamic>>();
      var list =
        parsed.map<Employee>((json) => Employee.fromJson(json)).toList();
      return list;
    } else {
      badStatusCode(response);
    }
  }

  Future<Employee> loadEmployee(String id) async {
    var url = '${_BASE_URL}/employee/${id}';
    final response = await HTTP.get(url).timeout(_TIMEOUT);
    if (response.statusCode == 200) {
      final parsed = json.decode(response.body);
      return Employee.fromJson(parsed);
    } else {
      badStatusCode(response);
    }
  }

  Future<dynamic> saveEmployee(Employee employee) async {
    bool isUpdate = employee.id.isNotEmpty;
    final uri = _BASE_URL + (isUpdate ? '/update/${employee.id}' : '/create');
    // profile image does not seem to update
    final response = isUpdate
      ? await HTTP.put(uri, body: json.encode(employee)).timeout(_TIMEOUT)
```

```
      : await HTTP.post(uri, body: json.encode(employee)).timeout(_TIMEOUT);
    if (response.statusCode == 200) {
      return json.decode(response.body);
    } else {
      // If that response was not OK, throw an error.
      badStatusCode(response);
    }
  }

  Future<dynamic> deleteEmployee(String id) async {
    final uri = '${_BASE_URL}/delete/${id}';
    final response = await HTTP.delete(uri).timeout(_TIMEOUT);
    if (response.statusCode == 200) {
      return json.decode(response.body);
    } else {
      // If that response was not OK, throw an error.
      badStatusCode(response);
    }
  }

  badStatusCode(Response response) {
    debugPrint("Bad status code ${response.statusCode} returned from server.");
    debugPrint("Response body ${response.body} returned from server.");
    throw Exception(
        'Bad status code ${response.statusCode} returned from server.');
  }
}

class MyApp extends StatelessWidget {
  @override
  Widget build(BuildContext context) {
    return new ApiWidget(
        child: MaterialApp(
          title: 'Flutter Demo',
          theme: new ThemeData(
            primarySwatch: Colors.blue,
          ),
          home: new EmployeeListWidget()));
  }
}

class EmployeeListWidget extends StatefulWidget {
  @override
  _EmployeeListWidgetState createState() => new _EmployeeListWidgetState();
}

class _EmployeeListWidgetState extends State<EmployeeListWidget> {
  final GlobalKey<ScaffoldState> _scaffoldKey = GlobalKey<ScaffoldState>();
  final PleaseWaitWidget _pleaseWaitWidget =
      PleaseWaitWidget(key: ObjectKey("pleaseWaitWidget"));

  bool _refresh = true;
  List<Employee> _employees;
  bool _pleaseWait = false;

  _showSnackBar(String content, {bool error = false}) {
    _scaffoldKey.currentState.showSnackBar(SnackBar(
      content:
```

```
      Text('${error ? "An unexpected error occurred: " : ""}${content}'),
    ));
  }

  _showPleaseWait(bool b) {
    setState(() {
      _pleaseWait = b;
    });
  }

  _navigateToEmployee(BuildContext context, String employeeId) {
    Navigator.push(
      context,
      MaterialPageRoute(builder: (context) => EmployeeDetailWidget(employeeId)),
    ).then((result) {
      if ((result != null) && (result is bool) && (result == true)) {
        _showSnackBar('Employee saved.');
        _refreshEmployees();
      }
    });
  }

  _deleteEmployee(BuildContext context, Employee employee) async {
    _showDeleteConfirmDialog(employee).then((result) {
      if ((result != null) && (result is bool) && (result == true)) {
        _showPleaseWait(true);
        try {
          ApiWidget.of(context).deleteEmployee(employee.id).then((employee) {
            _showPleaseWait(false);
            _showSnackBar('Employee deleted.');
            _refreshEmployees();
          }).catchError((error) {
            _showPleaseWait(false);
            _showSnackBar(error.toString(), error: true);
          });
        } catch (e) {
          _showPleaseWait(false);
          _showSnackBar(e.toString(), error: true);
        }
      }
    });
  }

  Future<bool> _showDeleteConfirmDialog(Employee employee) async {
    return await showDialog<bool>(
      context: context,
      builder: (BuildContext context) {
        return AlertDialog(
          title: const Text('Delete Employee'),
          content: Text(
            'Are you sure you want to delete ${employee.employeeName}?'),
          actions: <Widget>[
            FlatButton(
              onPressed: () {
                Navigator.pop(context, true);
              },
              child: const Text('Yes'),
            ),
```

```
      FlatButton(
        onPressed: () {
          Navigator.pop(context, false);
        },
        child: const Text('No'),
      )
    ],
  );
});
}

_refreshEmployees() {
 setState(() {
  _refresh = true;
 });
}

_loadEmployees(BuildContext context) {
 _showPleaseWait(true);
 try {
  ApiWidget.of(context).loadAndParseEmployees().then((employees) {
   // Sort first.
   employees.sort((a, b) => a.employeeName
     .toLowerCase()
     .compareTo(b.employeeName.toLowerCase()));
   setState(() {
    _employees = employees;
   });
   _showPleaseWait(false);
  }).catchError((error) {
   _showPleaseWait(false);
   _showSnackBar(error.toString(), error: true);
  });
 } catch (e) {
  _showPleaseWait(false);
  _showSnackBar(e.toString(), error: true);
 }
}

@override
Widget build(BuildContext context) {
 if (_refresh) {
  _refresh = false;
  _loadEmployees(context);
 }

 ListView builder = ListView.builder(
   itemCount: _employees != null ? _employees.length : 0,
   itemBuilder: (context, index) {
    Employee employee = _employees[index];
    return ListTile(
      title: Text('${employee.employeeName}'),
      subtitle: Text('Age: ${employee.employeeAge}'),
      trailing: Icon(Icons.arrow_right),
      onTap: () => _navigateToEmployee(context, employee.id),
      onLongPress: () => _deleteEmployee(context, employee));
   });
```

```
    Widget bodyWidget = _pleaseWait
      ? Stack(key: ObjectKey("stack"), children: [_pleaseWaitWidget, builder])
      : Stack(key: ObjectKey("stack"), children: [builder]);

  return new Scaffold(
    key: _scaffoldKey,
    appBar: new AppBar(
     title: new Text("Employees"),
     actions: <Widget>[
       IconButton(
         icon: Icon(Icons.add),
         tooltip: 'Add',
         onPressed: () {
           _navigateToEmployee(context, null);
         }),
       IconButton(
         icon: Icon(Icons.refresh),
         tooltip: 'Refresh',
         onPressed: () {
           _refreshEmployees();
         })
     ],
    ),
    body: new Center(
     child: bodyWidget,
    ));
  }
}

class EmployeeDetailWidget extends StatefulWidget {
 String _employeeId;

 EmployeeDetailWidget(this._employeeId);

 @override
 _EmployeeDetailState createState() => _EmployeeDetailState(this._employeeId);
}

class _EmployeeDetailState extends State<EmployeeDetailWidget> {
 final GlobalKey<ScaffoldState> _scaffoldKey = GlobalKey<ScaffoldState>();
 final _formKey = GlobalKey<FormState>();
 final PleaseWaitWidget _pleaseWaitWidget =
   PleaseWaitWidget(key: ObjectKey("pleaseWaitWidget"));

 String _employeeId;
 bool _loaded = false;
 bool _pleaseWait = false;
 Employee _employee;
 TextEditingController _nameTextController = TextEditingController();
 TextEditingController _salaryTextController = TextEditingController();
 TextEditingController _ageTextController = TextEditingController();
 TextEditingController _profileImageTextController = TextEditingController();

 _EmployeeDetailState(this._employeeId);

 _showSnackBar(String content, {bool error = false}) {
  _scaffoldKey.currentState.showSnackBar(SnackBar(
   content:
```

```
      Text('${error ? "An unexpected error occurred: " : ""}${content}'),
   ));
 }

_showPleaseWait(bool b) {
  setState(() {
    _pleaseWait = b;
  });
}

TextFormField _createNameWidget() {
  return new TextFormField(
    validator: (value) {
      if (value.isEmpty) {
        return 'Please enter the name.';
      }
    },
    decoration: InputDecoration(
        icon: const Icon(Icons.person),
        hintText: 'Name',
        labelText: 'Enter the name'),
    onSaved: (String value) {
      this._employee.employeeName = value;
    },
    controller: _nameTextController,
    autofocus: true,
  );
}

TextFormField _createSalaryWidget() {
  return new TextFormField(
    validator: (value) {
      if (value.isEmpty) {
        return 'Please enter the salary.';
      }
      int salary = int.parse(value);
      if (salary == null) {
        return 'Please enter the salary as a number.';
      }
      if ((salary < 10000) || (salary > 500000)) {
        return 'Please enter an age between 10000 and 50000.';
      }
    },
    maxLength: 6,
    maxLengthEnforced: true,
    keyboardType: TextInputType.phone,
    inputFormatters: [WhitelistingTextInputFormatter.digitsOnly],
    decoration: InputDecoration(
        icon: const Icon(Icons.person),
        hintText: 'Salary',
        labelText: 'Enter the salary'),
    onSaved: (String value) {
      this._employee.employeeSalary = value;
    },
    controller: _salaryTextController,
  );
}
```

```
TextFormField _createAgeWidget() {
 return new TextFormField(
  validator: (value) {
   if (value.isEmpty) {
    return 'Please enter the age.';
   }
   int age = int.parse(value);
   if (age == null) {
    return 'Please enter the age as a number.';
   }
   if ((age < 1) || (age > 114)) {
    return 'Please enter an age between 1 and 114.';
   }
  },
  maxLength: 3,
  maxLengthEnforced: true,
  keyboardType: TextInputType.phone,
  inputFormatters: [WhitelistingTextInputFormatter.digitsOnly],
  decoration: InputDecoration(
   icon: const Icon(Icons.person),
   hintText: 'Age',
   labelText: 'Enter the age'),
  onSaved: (String value) {
   this._employee.employeeAge = value;
  },
  controller: _ageTextController,
 );
}

TextFormField _createProfileImageWidget() {
 return new TextFormField(
  decoration: InputDecoration(
   icon: const Icon(Icons.person),
   hintText: 'Profile image',
   labelText: 'Enter the profile image'),
  onSaved: (String value) {
   this._employee.profileImage = value;
  },
  controller: _profileImageTextController,
 );
}

_loadEmployee(BuildContext context) {
 _showPleaseWait(true);
 try {
  ApiWidget.of(context).loadEmployee(_employeeId).then((employee) {
   setState(() {
    _employee = employee;
    _nameTextController.text = employee.employeeName;
    _salaryTextController.text = employee.employeeSalary;
    _ageTextController.text = employee.employeeAge;
    _profileImageTextController.text = employee.profileImage;
   });
   _showPleaseWait(false);
  }).catchError((error) {
   _showPleaseWait(false);
   _showSnackBar(error.toString(), error: true);
  });
```

```
  } catch (e) {
   _showPleaseWait(false);
   _showSnackBar(e.toString(), error: true);
  }
 }

 _saveEmployee(BuildContext context) {
  _showPleaseWait(true);
  try {
   ApiWidget.of(context).saveEmployee(_employee).then((employee) {
    _showPleaseWait(false);
    Navigator.pop(context, true);
   }).catchError((error) {
    _showPleaseWait(false);
    _showSnackBar(error.toString(), error: true);
   });
  } catch (e) {
   _showPleaseWait(false);
   _showSnackBar(e.toString(), error: true);
  }
 }

 @override
 Widget build(BuildContext context) {
  if (!_loaded) {
   _loaded = true;
   if (_employeeId == null) {
    _employee = Employee.empty();
   } else {
    _loadEmployee(context);
   }
  }

  List<Widget> formWidgetList = [
   _createNameWidget(),
   _createSalaryWidget(),
   _createAgeWidget(),
   _createProfileImageWidget(),
   RaisedButton(
    onPressed: () {
     if (_formKey.currentState.validate()) {
      _formKey.currentState.save();
      _saveEmployee(context);
     }
    },
    child: new Text('Save'),
   )
  ];
  Form form = Form(key: _formKey, child: ListView(children: formWidgetList));

  Widget bodyWidget = _pleaseWait
    ? Stack(key: ObjectKey("stack"), children: [_pleaseWaitWidget, form])
    : Stack(key: ObjectKey("stack"), children: [form]);

  return new Scaffold(
    key: _scaffoldKey,
    appBar: new AppBar(
     title: new Row(children: [
```

```
        Text("Back"),
        Spacer(),
        Text(_employeeId == null ? "Create Employee" : "Edit Employee")
      ]),
    ),
    body: new Padding(padding: EdgeInsets.all(20.0), child: bodyWidget));
  }
}
```

Other Information

Alice

One of the useful things about doing web development is that your web browser has a 'developer tools' console that lets you inspect the HTTP traffic. Unfortunately, your app does not have this built in.

Alice is a package that can use to inspect the HTTP traffic going between your app and HTTP servers. It has turned out to be both easy to use and useful to me.

Further Reading

Https://medium.com/flutter-community/inspecting-HTTP-requests-in-flutter-9deeddfe8d1

HAL / HATEOS

To talk to the server, apps need to know the URLs that the server resources are available on. Most of the time this information is hardcoded, which is not ideal.

It is much better if the server tells incudes information about available resources (and their URLs) when it returns information in the response back to the app. There are various standards as to the format of sending this information back to the client, including HATEOS & HAL.

For example, if you have an app which sends a request to the server to retrieve a list of customers, the information could should include the URLs for the API calls to access the data for each customer. This avoids hardcoding the customer AJAX request URL.

Further Reading

Https://martinfowler.com/articles/richardsonMaturityModel.html
Https://en.wikipedia.org/wiki/HATEOAS

28.State

Introduction

So now we know the basics about Widgets, composition and how we can get data from servers, we need to start writing interactive apps. However, to write interactive apps you first need to consider state and events.

The purpose of this chapter is to introduce state and events.

State & Events

State is the data in the app, often displayed in the UI.
Events are what may happen in the app.
You want Events to affect State, that's an Interactive User Interface is all about.

Storing State

Say we have an application structured like this:
- The user logs into the app using their username and password in a Login Widget, which talks to a server.
- The server gets the username and password info from the Login Widget and returns info about the user.
- The user enters data in a Data Entry Widget. This widget needs info about the user, i.e. what kinds of data entry can be performed by the user.
- The user views reports in a Report Widget. This widget needs info about the user, i.e. what reports can be viewed by the user.

Note the locations of the state in the diagram below (white text with grey background).

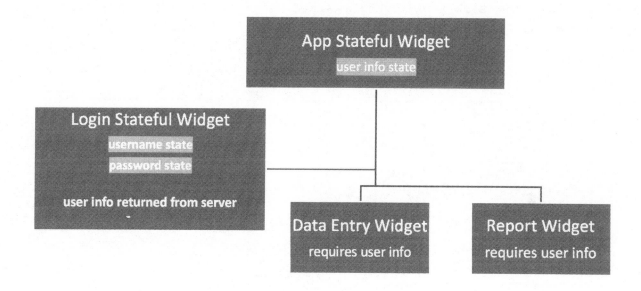

Kinds of State

In this example, there are 2 kinds of state.

- Local State – this is state info which is just needed in one place.
  - For example, the username and password are needed in the Login Widget but in no other widgets.

- Global State – this is state info which is needed almost everywhere.
  - For example, the user info is needed in multiple widgets, to know what kinds of data entry the user can do and/or what reports he or she can view.

How to Determine Where to Store State

These points are just a guideline:

1. Remember the golden rule - keep things simple.

2. Don't store state unnecessarily. Store what you absolutely need to store as state and no more.

3. Don't repeat state. Don't store the same item multiple times in state.
See that the user info state is stored up in the App Stateful Widget, above the Data Entry and Report Widgets? It was moved up a level in the object hierarchy so that it's not repeated. The child widgets can get that state info from their parent widget.

4. Place the state as close to where it is needed.

State

See that the username and password state are stored in the Login Stateful Widget. That is because user username and password state is local as its not needed anywhere else.

Responding to Events

Introduction

A modern user interface reacts to Events:
- User clicking on buttons.
- Data coming in from a server.
- Time passing.
- etc

Events Can Affect State

When Events occur, they tend to affect State at a ***similar or higher*** level up in the Object hierarchy.

For Example:

Say we have an application structured like this:
- The app displays a list of customers.
- Each customer in the list has a delete button.
- The user clicks on the delete button and the customer disappears.

If you have a list of customers in a home page and you delete the customer, then the Event may be triggered from a button in a lower-level widget but affect the customer list state, which is held in a higher-level home page widget.

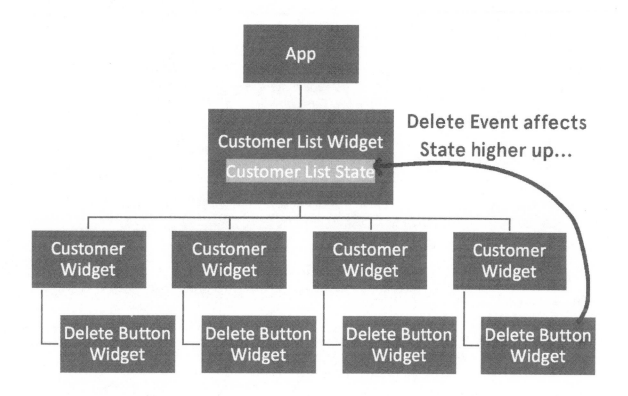

State & Events – Problems

So, after reading about State and Events, we realize we have two problems:

- We need to store State in higher-level objects in the Widget tree but we need to pass that state data down to lower-level objects so it can be rendered (i.e. so its data can be put into Widgets).
    - Example.
        - Store Customer List state in higher-level Customer List Widget.
        - Pass Customer information down from Customer List Widget to Customer Widgets.

- We need to process Events and change state in higher-level objects when events occur in lower-level objects in the Widget tree.
    - Example.
        - Have Delete button events flow up from Delete Button Widgets up to Customer List Widget, affecting state in Customer List Widget.

State & Events – Different Approaches

There have been several different approaches to the problems above and we are about to cover them in more detail. Bear in mind these approaches are evolving and that there will probably be new ones by the time this book is released.

Mixing Approaches

It's all about finding out what approach you understand and like, or rolling your own. Remember you can mix these approaches. You could have an app that uses multiple InheritedWidgets, uses Streams and StreamBuilders but also uses Stateful Widgets.

How I Decide Where to Put State

When I write apps, I usually do the following:

- I put the global state (or other state shared by multiple Widgets) in one or more BLoC's.
  - I use Streams & StreamBuilders to update the UI when state changes.

- I put local state in StatefulWidgets.
  - Stateful Widgets were designed for storing local state.

State & Events – Commonly-Used Approaches

Stateful Widget Approach

- Store state in Stateful Widgets at a high-enough level in the Widget tree to ensure that the data is not repeated.
- Pass state from parent Widgets to child Widgets through the constructor.
- Pass event handler method (that modifies state) from parent Widget methods to child Widgets through the constructor. Child Widgets can then invoke method to change state in Parent Widget.

Example:

To see an example of this, see State & Stateful Widget Approach

Pros/Cons

- It works well for smaller apps.
- It doesn't work well for bigger apps.

- o   It can get messy, especially if you need to pass state / event handlers though multiple levels of the Widget tree.

InheritedWidget Approach

- This approach removes most of the requirements to use Stateful Widgets, enabling the user to use Stateless Widgets instead in many cases.
- You create a 'state holder' class that acts as a Widget in the Widget hierarchy. This class extends InheritedWidget, stores the state data and has a single child widget.
- All the Widgets below this class can then be Stateless Widgets and they can use the BuildContext to access this InheritedWidget and its state data.

Example

To see an example of this, see State & InheritedWidget Approach

Pros/Cons

- It works well for smaller apps.
- It doesn't work well for bigger apps

Scoped Model Approach

- This approach removes most of the requirements to use Stateful Widgets, enabling the user to use Stateless Widgets instead in many cases.
- Use a 3rd party package called ScopedModel to store a state model in your Widget Tree. You can write code in your 'build' method of your widget and there use the Context to get a reference to this Scoped Model so that you can read and write its state.
- This works well for simple apps but is not structured enough for larger apps.

Example

To see an example of this, see State & ScopedModel Approach

Pros/Cons

- It works well for smaller apps.

BLoC w/Streams Approach

- BLoC stands for 'Business Logic Components'.
- It's a pattern for state management recommended by Google developers.
- It about storing the app State in a central place (a business logic object stored in a Stateful Widget) and it communicates with the rest of the app's (mostly) Stateless Widgets using streams.

Example

To see an example of this, see Chapter State & BLoCs w/Streams Approach

Pros/Cons

- It is overkill for smaller apps.

29. State & Stateful Widget Approach

Introduction

This is the most obvious approach and uses Flutter Widgets in the most obvious manner possible.

The purpose of this chapter is to learn this approach and its shortcomings.

Approach

- Store state in Stateful Widgets at a high-enough level in the Widget tree to ensure that the data is not repeated.
- Pass state from parent Widgets to child Widgets through the constructor.
- Pass event handler method (that modifies state) from parent Widget methods to child Widgets through the constructor. Child Widgets can then invoke method to change state in Parent Widget.

Exercise – 'state_and_stateful_widget'

Introduction

We start off by creating a create basic app with Stateful and Stateless Widgets.
Later on, we add some state & event handling so that the user can select a car and see it highlighted.
- The car selection comes from a tap event in the lower-level CarWidget.
- It changes the selected car state in the higher-level MyHomePageWidget.

Step 1 – Create Default Flutter App

Follow the instructions in <u>Generate Your First App</u>
Leave project open.

Step 2 – Replace Application Code

Replace contents of file 'main.dart' in folder 'lib' with the following:

```
import 'package:flutter/material.dart';

void main() => runApp(new MyApp());
```

```
class MyApp extends StatelessWidget {
 @override
 Widget build(BuildContext context) {
  return new MaterialApp(
    title: 'Flutter Demo',
    theme: new ThemeData(
      primarySwatch: Colors.blue,
    ),
    home: new MyHomePage(),
  );
 }
}

class Car {
 String _make;
 String _model;
 String _imageSrc;

 Car(this._make, this._model, this._imageSrc);

 operator ==(other) =>
    (other is Car) && (_make == other._make) && (_model == other._model);

 int get hashCode => _make.hashCode ^ _model.hashCode ^ _imageSrc.hashCode;

}

class MyHomePage extends StatefulWidget {
 @override
 _HomePageState createState() => _HomePageState("Cars");
}

class _HomePageState extends State<MyHomePage> {
 String _title;
 List<Car> _cars;

 _HomePageState(this._title) {
  _cars = [
    Car(
      "Bmw",
      "M3",
      "Https://media.ed.edmunds-
media.com/bmw/m3/2018/oem/2018_bmw_m3_sedan_base_fq_oem_4_150.jpg
Https://media.ed.edmunds-
media.com/bmw/m3/2018/oem/2018_bmw_m3_sedan_base_fq_oem_4_150.jpg
",
    ),
    Car(
      "Nissan",
      "GTR",
      "Https://media.ed.edmunds-media.com/nissan/gt-r/2018/oem/2018_nissan_gt-
r_coupe_nismo_fq_oem_1_150.jpg
Https://media.ed.edmunds-media.com/nissan/gt-r/2018/oem/2018_nissan_gt-
r_coupe_nismo_fq_oem_1_150.jpg
",
    ),
    Car(
```

```
        "Nissan",
        "Sentra",
        "Https://media.ed.edmunds-media.com/nissan/sentra/2017/oem/2017_nissan_sentra_sedan_sr-
turbo_fq_oem_4_150.jpg
Https://media.ed.edmunds-media.com/nissan/sentra/2017/oem/2017_nissan_sentra_sedan_sr-
turbo_fq_oem_4_150.jpg
",
      }
    ];
  }

  @override
  Widget build(BuildContext context) {
    List<CarWidget> carWidgets = _cars.map((Car car) {
      return CarWidget(car);
    }).toList();
    return new Scaffold(
        appBar: new AppBar(
          title: new Text(_title),
        ),
        body: new ListView(children: carWidgets));
  }
}

class CarWidget extends StatelessWidget {
  CarWidget(this._car) : super();

  final Car _car;

  @override
  Widget build(BuildContext context) {
    return Padding(
        padding: EdgeInsets.all(20.0),
        child: Container(
          decoration: BoxDecoration(border: Border.all()),
          padding: EdgeInsets.all(20.0),
          child: Center(
            child: Column(children: <Widget>[
          Text('${_car._make} ${_car._model}',
              style: TextStyle(fontSize: 24.0)),
          Padding(
              padding: EdgeInsets.only(top: 20.0),
              child: Image.network(_car._imageSrc))
        ]))));
  }
}
```

Step 3 – Open Emulator & Run

Follow the instructions in <u>Open Android Emulator & Run Your First App</u>

You should get something like the following as it is somewhat similar to the previous example:

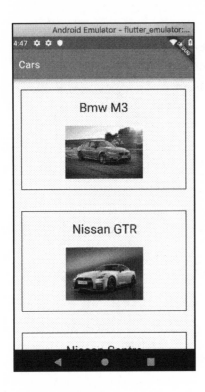

Summary

- The MyApp & Material App Widgets are unchanged.
- We declare a new class called Car.
  - This will store information about each car: its make, model and image.
  - Note that the '==' operator is overloaded so it considers two Cars equal if they have the same make and model.
- The MyHomePage Stateless Widget has become two different widgets instead:
  - MyHomePage StatefulWidget
  - MyHomePageState State Object
    - This holds the App Bar title and the list of Car objects. These are initiated in the constructor.
    - The State object contains the 'build' method that converts the list of Car objects into a list of CarWidgets. Then it returns a Scaffold containing the AppBar and a ListView containing the list of CarWidgets.
  - CarWidget
    - This displays a car's make, model and image.
    - Notice that it now accepts a Car object in the constructor. This gives it all the info to display a car's make, model and image.

Step 4– Add Car Selection

This is going to be achieved by holding state in the MyHomePage state object.

This state is going to be set by a method. This method is going to be passed to each Car Widget so it can be invoked by the Car Widget when the user taps on it.

Modify MyHomePageState

- We add variable '_selectedCar' to store which car is selected.
- We add a method '_selectionHandler' to handle car selection.
    - This provides an inline JavaScript function that sets the variables '_title' and '_selectedCar'.
    - This inline JavaScript function is passed to setState. Using 'setState' tells Flutter that the state of this object has changed and that this Widget will need to be re-rendered.
- We change the code that constructs the CarWidgets to include 2 additional constructor arguments:
    - A boolean indicating if the car is the selected car.
    - The selection handler method that handles the car selection in this class.

```
class MyHomePageState extends State<MyHomePage> {
 String _title;
 List<Car> _cars;
 Car _selectedCar;

 MyHomePageState(this._title) {
  _cars = [
   Car(
    "Bmw",
    "M3",
    "Https://media.ed.edmunds-
media.com/bmw/m3/2018/oem/2018_bmw_m3_sedan_base_fq_oem_4_150.jpg",
    ),
    Car(
    "Nissan",
    "GTR",
    "Https://media.ed.edmunds-media.com/nissan/gt-r/2018/oem/2018_nissan_gt-
r_coupe_nismo_fq_oem_1_150.jpg",
    ),
    Car(
    "Nissan",
    "Sentra",
    "Https://media.ed.edmunds-media.com/nissan/sentra/2017/oem/2017_nissan_sentra_sedan_sr-
turbo_fq_oem_4_150.jpg",
    )
  ];
 }

 void _selectionHandler(Car selectedCar) {
  setState(() {
   _title = 'Selected ${selectedCar._make} ${selectedCar._model}';
   _selectedCar = selectedCar;
  });
 }

 @override
 Widget build(BuildContext context) {
```

```
  List<CarWidget> carWidgets = _cars.map((Car car) {
    return CarWidget(car, car == _selectedCar, _selectionHandler);
  }).toList();
  return new Scaffold(
    appBar: new AppBar(
      title: new Text(_title),
    ),
      body: new ListView(children: carWidgets));
 }
}
```

Modify CarWidget

- We add instance variable '_isSelected' to store if this car is selected or not.
- We add instance variable '_parentSelectionHandler' to store the selection handler method from the parent MyHomePageState class.
- We modify the constructor to accept & set these two instance variables.
- We add a new method '_handleTap' to handle the 'onTap' event from the GestureDetector. This method invokes the '_parentSelectionHandler' from the parent MyHomePageState class.
- We modify the 'build' method.
    o We wrap the Container with a GestureDetector. This is so we can listen for the 'onTap' event.
    o We modify the 'BoxDecoration' to set the background color according to if the instance variable 'isSelected' is set to true or false. If true the background color is set to blue, otherwise white.

```
class CarWidget extends StatelessWidget {
 CarWidget(this._car, this._isSelected, this._parentSelectionHandler)
   : super();

 final Car _car;
 final bool _isSelected;
 final ValueChanged<Car> _parentSelectionHandler;

 void _handleTap() {
   _parentSelectionHandler(_car);
 }

 @override
 Widget build(BuildContext context) {
  return Padding(
     padding: EdgeInsets.all(20.0),
     child: GestureDetector(
      onTap: _handleTap,
       child: Container(
         decoration: BoxDecoration(
           color: _isSelected ? Colors.blue : Colors.white,
           border: Border.all()),
         padding: EdgeInsets.all(20.0),
         child: Center(
           child: Column(children: <Widget>[
          Text('${_car._make} ${_car._model}',
            style: TextStyle(fontSize: 24.0)),
```

```
    Padding(
      padding: EdgeInsets.only(top: 20.0),
      child: Image.network(_car._imageSrc))
  ])))));
}
}
```

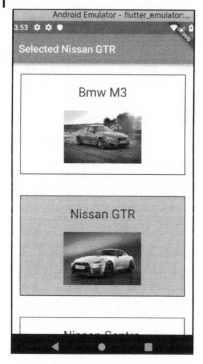

Further Reading

- Adding Interactivity to Your Flutter App: Https://flutter.io/docs/development/ui/interactive

- Pete Hunt at Facebook wrote a superb article here.
The article may be about React but many of the same rules apply.
Https://facebook.github.io/react/docs/thinking-in-react.html.

30. State & InheritedWidget Approach

Introduction

This is a way to access State that is stored in a higher-level Widget (called an InheritedWidget) from a lower-level Widget. Think of it like this: "Reach Up the Tree and Get Data". Flutter uses InheritedWidgets itself. The Theme Widget is in an InheritedWidget.

The purpose of this chapter is to learn what InheritedWidgets are and how to use them.

Approach

- This approach removes many of the requirements to use Stateful Widgets, often enabling the user to use Stateless Widgets instead.
- You create a 'state holder' class that acts as a Widget in the Widget hierarchy. This class extends InheritedWidget, stores the state data and has a single child widget.
- All the Widgets below this class can then be Stateless Widgets and they can use the BuildContext to access this InheritedWidget and its state data.
- To see an example of this, see Chapter 'State & InheritedWidget Approach'.

Exercise – 'state_and_inherited_widget_add'

In this exercise, I put the state for the car list into CarsInheritedWidget and I access it in CarWidget. I add a toolbar button to add another car to the list.

Please read the summary before starting this exercise. This exercise shows how using a state and an inherited Widget <u>won't</u> work as expected.

Step 1 – Create Default Flutter App

Follow the instructions in <u>Generate Your First App</u>
Leave project open.

Step 2 – Replace Application Code

Replace contents of file 'main.dart' in folder 'lib' with the following:

```
import 'package:collection/collection.dart';
import 'package:flutter/material.dart';

void main() => runApp(new MyApp());
```

```
class Car {
 String _make;
 String _model;
 String _imageSrc;

 Car(this._make, this._model, this._imageSrc);

 operator ==(other) =>
    (other is Car) && (_make == other._make) && (_model == other._model);

 int get hashCode => _make.hashCode ^ _model.hashCode ^ _imageSrc.hashCode;
}

class CarsInheritedWidget extends InheritedWidget {
 List<Car> _cars = [
  Car(
    "Bmw",
    "M3",
    "Https://media.ed.edmunds-
media.com/bmw/m3/2018/oem/2018_bmw_m3_sedan_base_fq_oem_4_150.jpg
Https://media.ed.edmunds-
media.com/bmw/m3/2018/oem/2018_bmw_m3_sedan_base_fq_oem_4_150.jpg
",
  ),
  Car(
    "Nissan",
    "GTR",
    "Https://media.ed.edmunds-media.com/nissan/gt-r/2018/oem/2018_nissan_gt-
r_coupe_nismo_fq_oem_1_150.jpg
Https://media.ed.edmunds-media.com/nissan/gt-r/2018/oem/2018_nissan_gt-
r_coupe_nismo_fq_oem_1_150.jpg
",
  ),
  Car(
    "Nissan",
    "Sentra",
    "Https://media.ed.edmunds-media.com/nissan/sentra/2017/oem/2017_nissan_sentra_sedan_sr-
turbo_fq_oem_4_150.jpg
Https://media.ed.edmunds-media.com/nissan/sentra/2017/oem/2017_nissan_sentra_sedan_sr-
turbo_fq_oem_4_150.jpg
",
  )
 ];

 CarsInheritedWidget(child) : super(child: child);

 List<Car> get cars {
  return _cars;
 }

 void addNissanSentra() {
  _cars.add(Car(
    "Nissan",
    "Sentra",
    "Https://media.ed.edmunds-media.com/nissan/sentra/2017/oem/2017_nissan_sentra_sedan_sr-
turbo_fq_oem_4_150.jpg
```

```
Https://media.ed.edmunds-media.com/nissan/sentra/2017/oem/2017_nissan_sentra_sedan_sr-
turbo_fq_oem_4_150.jpg
",
  ));
}

@override
bool updateShouldNotify(CarsInheritedWidget old) => true;

static CarsInheritedWidget of(BuildContext context) {
  return (context.inheritFromWidgetOfExactType(CarsInheritedWidget));
}
}

class MyApp extends StatelessWidget {
// This widget is the root of your application.
@override
Widget build(BuildContext context) {
  return new MaterialApp(
    title: 'Flutter Demo',
    theme: new ThemeData(
      // This is the theme of your application.
      //
      // Try running your application with "flutter run". You'll see the
      // application has a blue toolbar. Then, without quitting the app, try
      // changing the primarySwatch below to Colors.green and then invoke
      // "hot reload" (press "r" in the console where you ran "flutter run",
      // or press Run > Flutter Hot Reload in IntelliJ). Notice that the
      // counter didn't reset back to zero; the application is not restarted.
      primarySwatch: Colors.blue,
    ),
    home: CarsInheritedWidget(MyHomePage(title: 'Flutter Demo Home Page')),
  );
}
}

class MyHomePage extends StatelessWidget {
MyHomePage({Key key, this.title}) : super(key: key);

final String title;

@override
Widget build(BuildContext context) {
  List<CarWidget> carWidgets =
    CarsInheritedWidget.of(context).cars.map((Car car) {
    return CarWidget(car);
  }).toList();
  return new Scaffold(
    appBar: new AppBar(
      title: new Text("Cars"),
      actions: <Widget>[
        IconButton(
          icon: Icon(Icons.add),
          onPressed: () {
            CarsInheritedWidget.of(context).addNissanSentra();
          })
      ],
    ),
```

```
      body: new ListView(children: carWidgets));
 }
}

class CarWidget extends StatelessWidget {
 CarWidget(this._car) : super();

 final Car _car;

 @override
 Widget build(BuildContext context) {
  return Padding(
     padding: EdgeInsets.all(20.0),
     child: Container(
        decoration: BoxDecoration(border: Border.all()),
        padding: EdgeInsets.all(20.0),
        child: Center(
          child: Column(children: <Widget>[
         Text('${_car._make} ${_car._model}',
            style: TextStyle(fontSize: 24.0)),
         Padding(
            padding: EdgeInsets.only(top: 20.0),
            child: Image.network(_car._imageSrc))
       ]))));
 }
}
```

Step 3 – Open Emulator & Run

Follow the instructions in Open Android Emulator & Run Your First App
You should get something like the following as it is somewhat similar to the previous example:

State & InheritedWidget Approach

However, note that the Add button on the toolbar does not work!!!!!

Summary

We created a class CarsInheritedWidget that inherits from Inherited Object and we added into the Widget Tree, wrapping the HomePage Widget.
It seems we can access the state in that Widget, the list of Cars.
However, when we add a car it doesn't show up.

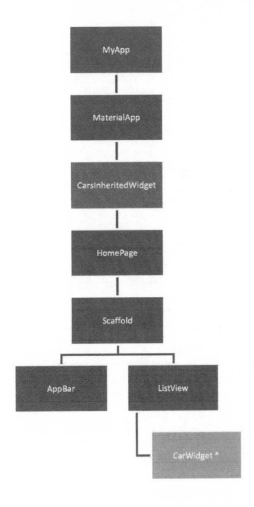

After reading some articles, it became obvious that to mutate the State of an InheritedWidget and have the UI re-render the state changes, **you need to wrap the InheritedWidget in a StatefulWidget.**

This example is based on the article below:
Https://medium.com/flutter-io/managing-flutter-application-state-with-inheritedwidgets-1140452befe1

Exercise – 'state_and_inherited_widget'

In this exercise, we get the State mutation to work on-screen and explain the changes.

Step 1 – Create Default Flutter App

Follow the instructions in Generate Your First App
Leave project open.

Step 2 – Replace Application Code

Replace contents of file 'main.dart' in folder 'lib' with the following:

```dart
import 'package:collection/collection.dart';
import 'package:flutter/material.dart';

void main() => runApp(new MyApp());

class Car {
  final String _make;
  final String _model;
  final String _imageSrc;

  const Car(this._make, this._model, this._imageSrc);

  operator ==(other) =>
    (other is Car) && (_make == other._make) && (_model == other._model);

  int get hashCode => _make.hashCode ^ _model.hashCode ^ _imageSrc.hashCode;
}

class CarModel {
  const CarModel(this.carList);

  final List<Car> carList;

  @override
  bool operator ==(Object other) {
    if (identical(this, other)) {
      return true;
    } else if (other.runtimeType != runtimeType) {
      return false;
    } else {
      final CarModel otherModel = other;
      return IterableEquality().equals(otherModel.carList, carList);
    }
  }

  int get hashCode => carList.hashCode;
}

class _ModelBindingScope<T> extends InheritedWidget {
  const _ModelBindingScope({Key key, this.modelBindingState, Widget child})
    : super(key: key, child: child);
```

```
 final _ModelBindingState<T> modelBindingState;

 @override
 bool updateShouldNotify(_ModelBindingScope oldWidget) => true;
}

class ModelBinding<T> extends StatefulWidget {
 ModelBinding({Key key, @required this.initialModel, this.child})
   : assert(initialModel != null),
     super(key: key);

 final T initialModel;
 final Widget child;

 _ModelBindingState<T> createState() => _ModelBindingState<T>();

 static Type _typeOf<T>() => T;

 static T of<T>(BuildContext context) {
  final Type scopeType = _typeOf<_ModelBindingScope<T>>();
  final _ModelBindingScope<T> scope =
    context.inheritFromWidgetOfExactType(scopeType);
  return scope.modelBindingState.currentModel;
 }

 static void update<T>(BuildContext context, T newModel) {
  final Type scopeType = _typeOf<_ModelBindingScope<T>>();
  final _ModelBindingScope<dynamic> scope =
    context.inheritFromWidgetOfExactType(scopeType);
  scope.modelBindingState.updateModel(newModel);
 }
}

class _ModelBindingState<T> extends State<ModelBinding<T>> {
 T currentModel;

 @override
 void initState() {
  super.initState();
  currentModel = widget.initialModel;
 }

 void updateModel(T newModel) {
  if (newModel != currentModel) {
   setState(() {
    currentModel = newModel;
   });
  }
 }

 @override
 Widget build(BuildContext context) {
  return _ModelBindingScope<T>(
   modelBindingState: this,
   child: widget.child,
  );
 }
```

```
}
class MyApp extends StatelessWidget {
  // This widget is the root of your application.
  @override
  Widget build(BuildContext context) {
    return new MaterialApp(
      title: 'Flutter Demo',
      theme: new ThemeData(
        primarySwatch: Colors.blue,
      ),
      home: ModelBinding<CarModel>(
        initialModel: const CarModel(const [
          Car(
            "Bmw",
            "M3",
            "Https://media.ed.edmunds-
media.com/bmw/m3/2018/oem/2018_bmw_m3_sedan_base_fq_oem_4_150.jpg",
          ),
          Car(
            "Nissan",
            "GTR",
            "Https://media.ed.edmunds-media.com/nissan/gt-r/2018/oem/2018_nissan_gt-
r_coupe_nismo_fq_oem_1_150.jpg",
          ),
          Car(
            "Nissan",
            "Sentra",
            "Https://media.ed.edmunds-media.com/nissan/sentra/2017/oem/2017_nissan_sentra_sedan_sr-
turbo_fq_oem_4_150.jpg",
          )
        ]),
        child: new MyHomePage(title: 'Flutter Demo Home Page')),
    );
  }
}

class MyHomePage extends StatelessWidget {
  MyHomePage({Key key, this.title}) : super(key: key);

  final String title;

  @override
  Widget build(BuildContext context) {
    CarModel model = ModelBinding.of(context);
    List<CarWidget> carWidgets = model.carList.map((Car car) {
      return CarWidget(car);
    }).toList();
    return new Scaffold(
      appBar: new AppBar(
        title: new Text("Cars"),
        actions: <Widget>[
          IconButton(
            icon: Icon(Icons.add),
            onPressed: () {
              List<Car> carList = List.from(model.carList);
              carList.add(Car(
                "Nissan",
```

```
               "Sentra",
               "Https://media.ed.edmunds-
media.com/nissan/sentra/2017/oem/2017_nissan_sentra_sedan_sr-turbo_fq_oem_4_150.jpg",
             ));
             ModelBinding.update(context, new CarModel(carList));
          })
      ],
      ),
      body: new ListView(children: carWidgets));
  }
}

class CarWidget extends StatelessWidget {
  CarWidget(this._car) : super();

  final Car _car;

  @override
  Widget build(BuildContext context) {
   return Padding(
      padding: EdgeInsets.all(20.0),
      child: Container(
         decoration: BoxDecoration(border: Border.all()),
         padding: EdgeInsets.all(20.0),
         child: Center(
           child: Column(children: <Widget>[
          Text('${_car._make} ${_car._model}',
            style: TextStyle(fontSize: 24.0)),
          Padding(
            padding: EdgeInsets.only(top: 20.0),
            child: Image.network(_car._imageSrc))
         ]))));
  }
}
```

Step 3 – Open Emulator & Run

Follow the instructions in <u>Open Android Emulator & Run Your First App</u>
This works much better; the user interface responds to the '+' button and adds another car to the list.

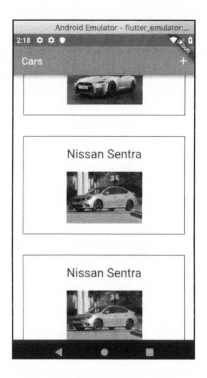

Summary

In this example, we to wrap the InheritedWidget in a StatefulWidget to enable it to re-render part of the Widget Tree.

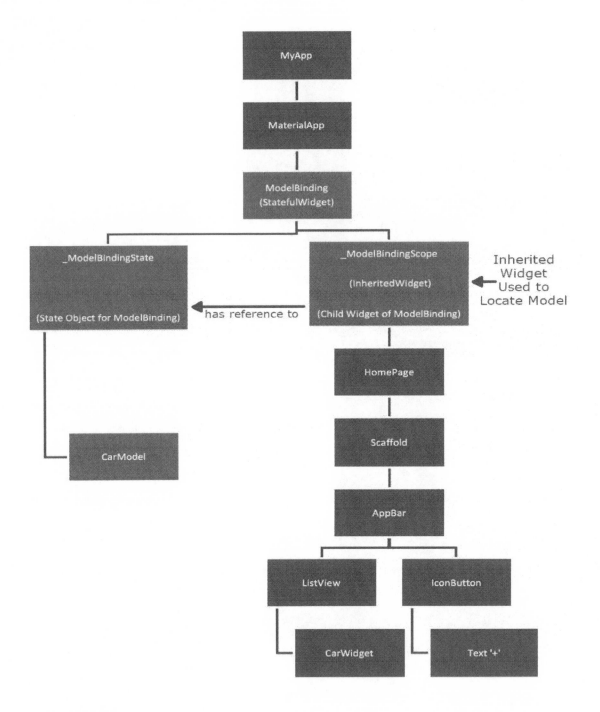

- ModelBinding.
  - o The ModelBinding class is a Stateful Widget. Remember, to mutate the State of an InheritedWidget and have the UI re-render the state changes, you need to wrap the InheritedWidget in a StatefulWidget. This is what the ModelBinding class does. The 'update' method is used to update the state (the CarModel) in this Stateful Widget.

- _ModelBindingState.
  - This is the State for the ModelBinding Stateful Widget. It contains the CarModel. The 'updateModel' method is used to replace the model (the CarModel) in this class with a new one, calling 'setState' to force the UI to re-render the state changes.

- _ModelBindingScope.
  - This is an InheritedWidget, used to locate items in the Widget Tree. Used by lower-level Widgets to locate and access the _ModelBindingState, which is the State Object for the ModelBinding StatefulWidget.

- CarModel
  - This represents the state for the app.
  - Currently it holds the list of Car objects.
  - The data in this class is immutable, it cannot be changed.
  - To change the state in the app (the Car list), the 'update' method in the ModelBinding class must be invoked, passing in a new CarModel.

Conclusion

At first, I thought that the InheritedWidget would make life easy. I thought that you could "Reach Up the Tree and Get Data": get data, update it and the UI would re-render itself. It doesn't.

You can use InheritedWidget in a simple manner to hold non-mutating state data and access it from lower-level widgets.

However, if you want to hold mutating state data, update it and have the UI re-render itself, you have to wrap the InheritedWidget within a StatefulWidget and force the StatefulWidget to re-render the State Tree by calling the 'setState' method. A lot more complicated.

Further Reading

I highly recommend the following articles:
https://www.didierboelens.com/2018/06/widget---state---context---inheritedwidget/
https://stackoverflow.com/questions/49491860/flutter-how-to-correctly-use-an-inherited-widget
https://medium.com/flutter-io/managing-flutter-application-state-with-inheritedwidgets-1140452befe1

31.State & ScopedModel Approach

Introduction

I don't think that the InheritedWidget approach turned out to be a good solution for our state issues. Once you added state / mutation and re-rendering of new state into account, it turned out a lot more complicated than expected.

The purpose of this chapter is to take a look at the ScopedModel approach.

Approach

This approach removes most of the requirements to use Stateful Widgets, enabling the user to use Stateless Widgets instead in many cases.

ScopedModel has been mentioned in many articles as an alternative to just using InheritedWidget. At first sight, it looks like the ScopedModel package is basically InheritedWidget, only made easier to use.

Package

ScopedModel is a Dart package and it is available here:
https://pub.dartlang.org/packages/scoped_model

As it is a package you will have to install it:
https://pub.dartlang.org/packages/scoped_model - -installing-tab-

Package Readme

The package README.md file includes the following text:
A set of utilities that allow you to easily pass a data Model from a parent Widget down to its descendants. In addition, it also rebuilds all of the children that use the model when the model is updated. This library was originally extracted from the Fuchsia codebase.
This package provides three main classes:
1. Model
   o You will extend this class to create your own Models, such as SearchModel or UserModel.
   o You can listen to Models for changes!

2. ScopedModel Widget.
   - o If you need to pass a Model deep down your Widget hierarchy, you can wrap your Model in a ScopedModel Widget.
   - o This will make the Model available to all descendant Widgets.
3. ScopedModelDescendant Widget.
   - o Use this Widget to find the appropriate ScopedModel in the Widget tree.
   - o It will automatically rebuild whenever the Model notifies that change has taken place.

Multiple Models

At first glance, it looks as if this package allows the user to use multiple State Models. This certainly makes it a better candidate for working with larger applications. You could have User data in one model, Transaction data in another etc.

Exercise – 'state_and_scoped_model'

The code below is not perfect by any means (you can add the same car twice and when you tap on it, it selects both) but it demonstrates how to get an app up and working with ScopedModel and how you can maintain separate states in separate models.

In this exercise, I use the ScopedModel to handle two separate state models:
1. a list of cars (to which we can add cars)
2. the currently selected car (which you can change by tapping on a car).

There is more code for you to copy and paste in this example. However, this app does more than some of the previous examples: it allows you to add cars and allows you to select cars.

Step 1 – Create Default Flutter App

Follow the instructions in Generate Your First App
Leave project open.

Step 2 – Replace Application Code

Replace contents of file 'main.dart' in folder 'lib' with the following:

```
import 'package:flutter/material.dart';
import 'package:scoped_model/scoped_model.dart';

void main() => runApp(new CarAppWidget());

class Car {
  String _make;
```

```dart
  String _model;
  String _imageSrc;

  Car(this._make, this._model, this._imageSrc);

  operator ==(other) =>
    (other is Car) && (_make == other._make) && (_model == other._model);

  int get hashCode => _make.hashCode ^ _model.hashCode ^ _imageSrc.hashCode;
}
class CarListModel extends Model {
  List<Car> _carList = [
    Car(
      "Bmw",
      "M3",
      "Https://media.ed.edmunds-
media.com/bmw/m3/2018/oem/2018_bmw_m3_sedan_base_fq_oem_4_150.jpg",
    ),
    Car(
      "Nissan",
      "GTR",
      "Https://media.ed.edmunds-media.com/nissan/gt-r/2018/oem/2018_nissan_gt-
r_coupe_nismo_fq_oem_1_150.jpg",
    ),
    Car(
      "Nissan",
      "Sentra",
      "Https://media.ed.edmunds-media.com/nissan/sentra/2017/oem/2017_nissan_sentra_sedan_sr-
turbo_fq_oem_4_150.jpg",
    )
  ];

  List<Car> get carList => _carList;

  void add(String make, String model, String imageSrc) {
    _carList.add(Car(make, model, imageSrc));
    notifyListeners();
  }
}

class CarSelectionModel extends Model {
  Car _selectedCar;

  Car get selectedCar => _selectedCar;

  void set selectedCar(Car selectedCar) {
    _selectedCar = selectedCar;
    notifyListeners();
  }

  bool isSelected(Car car) {
    if (_selectedCar == null) {
      return false;
    } else {
      return car == _selectedCar;
    }
  }
```

```
}
class CarAppWidget extends StatelessWidget {
  @override
  Widget build(BuildContext context) {
    return new MaterialApp(
      title: 'Car App',
      theme: new ThemeData(
        primarySwatch: Colors.blue,
      ),
      home: ScopedModel<CarListModel>(
        model: CarListModel(),
        child: ScopedModel<CarSelectionModel>(
          model: CarSelectionModel(),
          child: CarAppLayoutWidget(title: 'Cars'))));
  }
}

class CarAppLayoutWidget extends StatelessWidget {
  CarAppLayoutWidget({Key key, this.title}) : super(key: key);
  final String title;

  _addCar(BuildContext context) {
    ScopedModel.of<CarListModel>(context, rebuildOnChange: true).add(
      "Subaru",
      "WRX",
      "Https://media.ed.edmunds-media"
      ".com/subaru/wrx/2018/oem/2018_subaru_wrx_sedan_sti-limited_s_oem_1_150"
      ".jpg");
  }

  String _calculateSelectedCarName(BuildContext context) {
    Car selectedCar =
      ScopedModel.of<CarSelectionModel>(context, rebuildOnChange: true)
        .selectedCar;

    if (selectedCar == null) {
      return "No car selected.";
    } else {
      return "Selected: ${selectedCar._make} ${selectedCar._model}";
    }
  }

  @override
  Widget build(BuildContext context) {
    return new Scaffold(
      appBar: new AppBar(
        title: new Text(title),
      ),
      body: Center(child: CarListWidget()),
      persistentFooterButtons: <Widget>[
        Text(_calculateSelectedCarName(context)),
        IconButton(
          icon: Icon(Icons.add),
          onPressed: () {
            _addCar(context);
          }),
      ]);
```

```
  }
}

class CarListWidget extends StatelessWidget {
@override
 Widget build(BuildContext context) {
   final carList =
      ScopedModel.of<CarListModel>(context, rebuildOnChange: true).carList;
   List<CarWidget> carWidgets = carList.map((Car car) {
    return CarWidget(car);
   }).toList();
   return new ListView(children: carWidgets);
 }
}

class CarWidget extends StatelessWidget {
 CarWidget(this._car) : super();

 final Car _car;

 _buildCarWidget(context, child, CarSelectionModel selectionModel) {
  return GestureDetector(
     onTap: () => selectionModel.selectedCar = _car,
     child: Padding(
        padding: EdgeInsets.all(20.0),
        child: Container(
           decoration: BoxDecoration(
              border: Border.all(),
              color: selectionModel.isSelected(_car)
                 ? Colors.blue
                 : Colors.white),
           padding: EdgeInsets.all(20.0),
           child: Center(
              child: Column(children: <Widget>[
            Text('${_car._make} ${_car._model}',
               style: TextStyle(fontSize: 24.0)),
            Padding(
               padding: EdgeInsets.only(top: 20.0),
               child: Image.network(_car._imageSrc))
          ]))));
 }

 @override
 Widget build(BuildContext context) {
  return ScopedModelDescendant<CarSelectionModel>(
     builder: (context, child, selectionModel) =>
        _buildCarWidget(context, child, selectionModel));
 }
}
```

Step 3 – Open Emulator & Run

Follow the instructions in <u>Open Android Emulator & Run Your First App</u>
If you tap on the '+' button at the bottom it adds another car.
If you tap on a car it selects the car (adding a blue background) and sets the text of the selected car at the bottom.

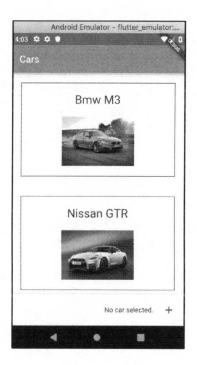

Summary

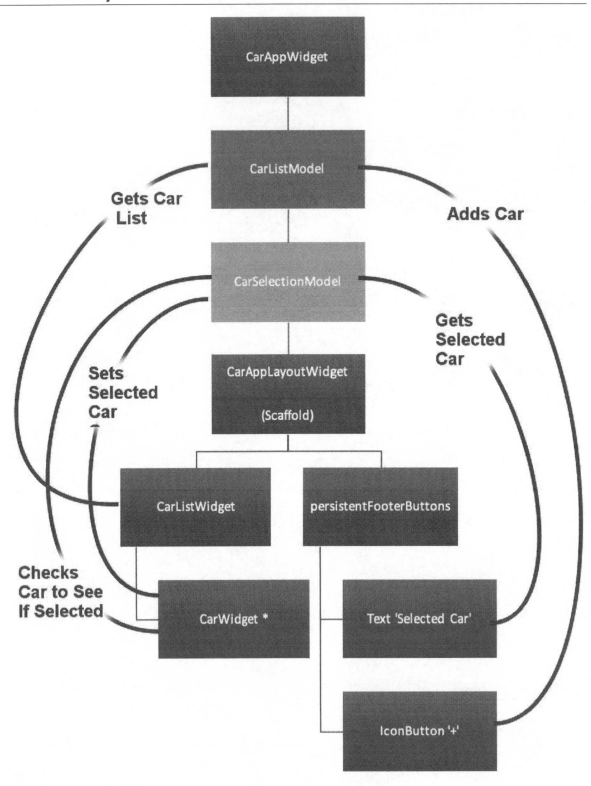

- CarListModel holds state for car list.
  - Note that the 'add' method add a car and that it calls 'notifyListeners' to ensure the children in the Widget Tree are updated.
- CarSelectionModel holds state for selected car.
  - Note that the 'set' method for the 'selectedCar' calls 'notifyListeners' to ensure the children in the Widget Tree are updated.
- CarListWidget is used to render car list. It gets its state from the CarListModel.
- CarWidget uses a ScopedModelDescendant from this package to use a builder to build the car widget. It gets the data for the car from the constructor. The ScopedModelDescendant enables the builder to get the selection state from the CarSelectionModel.
- CarAppLayoutWidget lays out the Widgets in a Scaffold.
  - PersistentFooterButtons is used to show Text and a Button at the bottom, even if the user scrolls.
    - The Text for the selected car name is calculated by calling 'ScopedModel.of' to get to the CarSelectionModel and calling a method there to get the text.
    - The '+' Button calls 'ScopedModel.of' to get to the CarListModel and calls a method there to add a car to the list of cars.

Conclusion

I was impressed by this package; how simple it was to get going and how well it worked with multiple models. I really think this is the way to go for small / medium sized projects. It was easy to get to the models using builders or using the 'ScopedModel.of' method. Nice and flexible.

32. State & BLoCs w/Streams Approach

Introduction

BLoC stands for 'Business Logic Components'.
It's a pattern for state management recommended by Google developers.

The purpose of this chapter is to learn this pattern for state management.

BLoC Pattern

This pattern is about storing the app main state in a central place (a business logic object stored in a Stateful Widget) and having it communicate with the rest of the app's Widgets using streams and RxDart.
Note that this pattern uses InheritedWidget to store the Business Logic Component within a widget in the hierarchy.

Reactive Programming

Reactive Programming is an asynchronous programming paradigm concerned with data streams and the propagation of change. It is all about asynchronously emitting data to these streams or listening to those streams and doing something with the data (perform operations on it). To oversimplify things, Observable objects write to these streams and Subscribers listen to these streams. Operators do something with the stream data, like create it, transform it, filter it, combine it etc. It sounds complicated but it can make your code much simpler when you get the hang of it.

One great thing about streams is that you can use them to commutate between software components. For example, rather than have 'Component 1' directly call a method in 'Component 2' when something happens, you could have Component 2 subscribe to an event stream in Component 1. When something happens in Component 1, it posts to the event stream and Component 2 is notified and does something.

RxDart

The BLoC pattern uses the RxDart package.
RxDart is a reactive functional programming library for Google Dart, based on ReactiveX. Google Dart comes with a very decent Streams API out-of-the-box; rather than attempting to provide

an alternative to this API, RxDart adds functionality on top of it. So basically, RxDart enhances the Dart support for Streams!

StreamBuilder

This approach uses the StreamBuilder class to build stateless child Widgets. StreamBuilder is a Widget that builds itself based on the latest update from a Stream.
StreamBuilders listen for changes in streams and build Widgets when the stream data changes. Thus, your Widgets can update when the state changes and the state change is pushed to a stream.

Exercise – 'state_and_block_with_streams'

In this exercise, we use a BLoC with states and streams to enable the user to re-order a list of customers.

Step 1 – Create Default Flutter App

Follow the instructions in Generate Your First App
Leave project open.

Step 2 – Add the RxDart Dependency

Add the following dependencies to your 'pubspec.yaml' file. After that you will need to do a 'flutter packages get' on the command line in the root of your project to download the dependencies.

```
dependencies:
  flutter:
    sdk: flutter

  # The following adds the Cupertino Icons font to your application.
  # Use with the CupertinoIcons class for iOS style icons.
  cupertino_icons: ^0.1.2
  rxdart: 0.18.1

dev_dependencies:
  flutter_test:
    sdk: flutter
```

Step 3 – Replace Application Code

Replace contents of file 'main.dart' in folder 'lib' with the following:

```
import 'dart:async';
```

```dart
import 'package:flutter/material.dart';
import 'package:rxdart/rxdart.dart';

class Customer {
  String _firstName;
  String _lastName;
  bool _upButton;
  bool _downButton;

  Customer(this._firstName, this._lastName) {
    _upButton = false;
    _downButton = false;
  }

  String get name => _firstName + " " + _lastName;

  bool get upButton => _upButton;

  set upButton(bool value) {
    _upButton = value;
  }

  bool get downButton => _downButton;

  set downButton(bool value) {
    _downButton = value;
  }

  operator ==(other) =>
      (other is Customer) &&
      (_firstName == other._firstName) &&
      (_lastName == other._lastName);

  int get hashCode => _firstName.hashCode ^ _lastName.hashCode;
}

class Bloc {
  // BLoC stands for Business Logic Component.
  List<Customer> _customerList = [];

  Bloc() {
    _upActionStreamController.stream.listen(_handleUp);
    _downActionStreamController.stream.listen(_handleDown);
  }

  List<Customer> initCustomerList() {
    _customerList = [
      new Customer("Fred", "Smith"),
      new Customer("Brian", "Johnson"),
      new Customer("James", "McGirt"),
      new Customer("John", "Brown")
    ];
    updateUpDownButtons();
    return _customerList;
  }

  void dispose() {
    _upActionStreamController.close();
```

```
    _downActionStreamController.close();
  }

  void _handleUp(Customer customer) {
    swap(customer, true);
    updateUpDownButtons();

    _customerListSubject.add(_customerList);
    _messageSubject.add(customer.name + " moved up");
  }

  void _handleDown(Customer customer) {
    swap(customer, false);
    updateUpDownButtons();

    _customerListSubject.add(_customerList);
    _messageSubject.add(customer.name + " moved down");
  }

  void swap(Customer customer, bool up) {
    int idx = _customerList.indexOf(customer);
    _customerList.remove(customer);
    _customerList.insert(up ? idx - 1 : idx + 1, customer);
  }

  void updateUpDownButtons() {
    //TODO We dont really need to update them all, but this is just an example.
    for (int idx = 0, lastIdx = _customerList.length - 1;
        idx <= lastIdx;
        idx++) {
      Customer customer = _customerList[idx];
      customer.upButton = (idx > 0);
      customer.downButton = (idx < lastIdx);
    }
  }

  // Streams for State Updates
  Stream<List<Customer>> get customerListStream => _customerListSubject.stream;
  final _customerListSubject = BehaviorSubject<List<Customer>>();

  Stream<String> get messageStream => _messageSubject.stream;
  final _messageSubject = BehaviorSubject<String>();

  // Sinks for Actions
  Sink<Customer> get upAction => _upActionStreamController.sink;
  final _upActionStreamController = StreamController<Customer>();

  Sink<Customer> get downAction => _downActionStreamController.sink;
  final _downActionStreamController = StreamController<Customer>();
}

class BlocProvider extends InheritedWidget {
  final Bloc bloc;

  BlocProvider({
    Key key,
    @required this.bloc,
    Widget child,
```

```
  }) : super(key: key, child: child);

  @override
  bool updateShouldNotify(InheritedWidget oldWidget) => true;

  static Bloc of(BuildContext context) =>
     (context.inheritFromWidgetOfExactType(BlocProvider) as BlocProvider).bloc;
}

class CustomerWidget extends StatelessWidget {
  final Customer _customer;

  CustomerWidget(this._customer);

  @override
  Widget build(BuildContext context) {
   final bloc = BlocProvider.of(context);
   Text text = Text(_customer.name,
      style: const TextStyle(fontSize: 15.0, fontWeight: FontWeight.bold));
   IconButton upButton = IconButton(
      icon: new Icon(Icons.arrow_drop_up, color: Colors.blue),
      onPressed: () {
       bloc.upAction.add(_customer);
      });
   IconButton downButton = IconButton(
      icon: new Icon(Icons.arrow_drop_down, color: Colors.blue),
      onPressed: () {
       bloc.downAction.add(_customer);
      });
   List<Widget> children = [];
   children.add(Expanded(
      child: Padding(padding: EdgeInsets.only(left: 20.0), child: text)));
   if (_customer.upButton) {
    children.add(upButton);
   }
   if (_customer.downButton) {
    children.add(downButton);
   }
   return Padding(
      padding: EdgeInsets.all(6.0),
      child: ClipRRect(
        borderRadius: BorderRadius.circular(8.0),
        child: Container(
          decoration: BoxDecoration(color: Colors.cyan[100]),
          child: Row(
            children: children,
            mainAxisAlignment: MainAxisAlignment.start))));
  }
}

void main() => runApp(new CustomerAppWidget());

class CustomerAppWidget extends StatelessWidget {
  // This widget is the root of your application.
  final Bloc _bloc = new Bloc();

  @override
  Widget build(BuildContext context) {
```

```
  return new MaterialApp(
    title: 'Flutter Demo',
    theme: new ThemeData(
      primarySwatch: Colors.blue,
    ),
    home: BlocProvider(
      bloc: _bloc,
      child: new CustomerListWidget(
        title: 'Flutter '
          'Demo Home Page',
        messageStream: _bloc.messageStream,
      ),
    ),
  );
  }
}

class CustomerListWidget extends StatelessWidget {
  CustomerListWidget({Key key, this.title, Stream<String> this.messageStream})
    : super(key: key) {
    this.messageStream.listen((message) {
      _scaffoldKey.currentState.showSnackBar(SnackBar(
        content: Text(message),
        duration: Duration(seconds: 1),
      ));
    });
  }

  final GlobalKey<ScaffoldState> _scaffoldKey = GlobalKey<ScaffoldState>();
  final String title;
  final Stream<String> messageStream;

  @override
  Widget build(BuildContext context) {
    final bloc = BlocProvider.of(context);
    return new Scaffold(
      key: _scaffoldKey,
      appBar: new AppBar(
        title: new Text(title),
      ),
      body: StreamBuilder<List<Customer>>(
        stream: bloc.customerListStream,
        initialData: bloc.initCustomerList(),
        builder: (context, snapshot) {
          List<Widget> customerWidgets =
            snapshot.data.map((Customer customer) {
            return CustomerWidget(customer);
          }).toList();
          return ListView(
            padding: const EdgeInsets.all(10.0),
            children: customerWidgets);
        }));
  }
}
```

Step 4 – Open Emulator & Run

Follow the instructions in <u>Open Android Emulator & Run Your First App</u>
You can move the customers up and down using the arrow icons.
Note that the user is also presented with a message at the bottom.

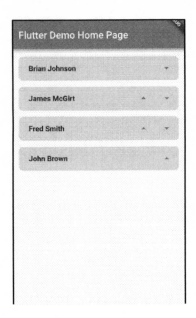

Summary

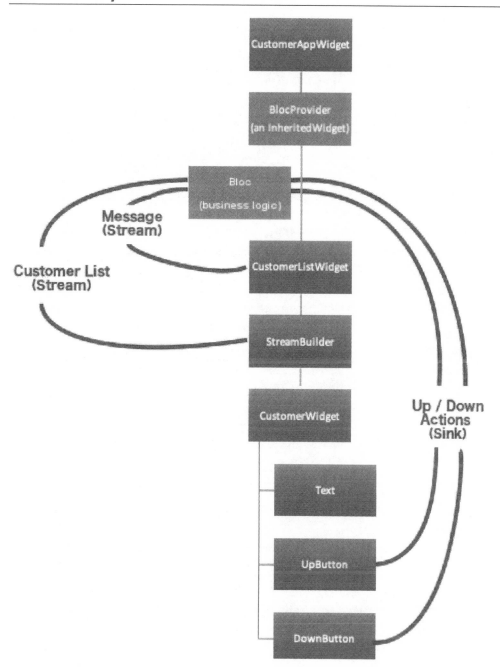

- CustomerAppWidget
  - Stateless Widget
  - Root of your application.
- BlocProvider

- o   InheritedWidget
- o   Wraps CustomerListWidget
- o   Contains instance of Bloc object.
  - ▪   Has 'of' method to return instance of 'Bloc' to Widgets at lower levels of Widget tree.
- Bloc
  - o   Plain Dart class.
  - o   Business Logic Component.
  - o   Contains state (list of customer objects).
  - o   Contains 2 behavior subjects with streams.
    - ▪   Subject are something that can be observed. A BehaviorSubject is a subject that always provides the last emitted value from the stream, even if the subscription is added after that value was omitted.
    - ▪   Streams may be used to get an observable for a subject.
    - ▪   BehaviorSubjects and Streams are used to provide observable state to Widgets in the tree below.
  - o   Contains 2 stream controllers with sinks.
    - ▪   StreamControllers give you streams and a way to add events to the stream at any point, and from anywhere.
    - ▪   Sinks are generic destinations for data that can have values written to.
    - ▪   StreamControllers and Sinks are used here to listen for incoming data from a Widget event (customer clicks on up or down button).
- CustomerListWidget
  - o   Stateless Widget.
  - o   Contains list of customer widgets.
  - o   Has 'message stream' argument in constructor.
    - ▪   This is to listen to message stream in BLoC, displaying a message to the user every time the stream changes.
  - o   Has child StreamBuilder which listens to customer list stream in BLoC, returning a ListView of CustomerWidget objects every time the stream changes.
- CustomerWidget
  - o   Stateless Widget that draws a Customer with the name and up / down buttons.

Conclusion

This is a pattern rather than a package - you will have to implement the code yourself.
This looks straightforward.

- You could use multiple BLoCs in a single app to simplify a larger app. For example, you could have a CustomerBLoC, an OrderBLoC etc., just an InheritedWidget for each BLoC.
- You use a InheritedWidget to get access to the BLoC (or BLoCs) from anywhere in the Widget tree.
- You put the dynamic UI inside StreamBuilders, which listen to streams in the BLoC.

- Your event handling will write values to the Sinks to update the state.

I have used this pattern before and I think it works well. The only downside I see is you're your build methods have to use StreamBuilders when rendering dynamic data and this can make the code slightly more complex.

Further Reading

https://www.didierboelens.com/2018/12/reactive-programming---streams---bloc---practical-use-cases/
https://medium.com/flutter-community/reactive-programming-streams-bloc-6f0d2bd2d248

33.Local Persistence

Introduction

In computer science, persistence refers to the characteristic of state that outlives the process that created it. This is achieved in practice by storing the state as data in computer data storage.

So, it means the storage of data for later use, even after the program that created it has been closed.

In the context of this book, there are two main types of persistence:

- Remote Persistence.
  - This would be achieved by communicating with a remote computer using a protocol like Http. We have already covered Http in another chapter.
- Local Persistence
  - Persisting data to the device running the Flutter app.

The purpose of this chapter is to cover Local Persistence.

Your Options

In regard to local persistence, you have the following options:

- Using a sql database
  - This is (obviously) the most powerful option, especially for querying data.
  - We will cover the SQLite database in this chapter. It is recommended for Flutter as it is an easy-to-use package for Flutter and it works on both Android & iOS.
- Using local files.
  - Not good for querying data.
  - Good for complicated objects and large amounts of data.
  - You have to write the code that reads the data from the files, as well as the code that writes the data to the files.
  - You have full control over the file format.
  - Easy to copy this data to another device as a file.
- Using shared preferences.
  - This is using the shared_preferences package.
  - This is great for simple data, it's very easy to use.
  - Probably not the best way to store complicated objects or large amounts of data.

SQLite Database

This Flutter package is available here: https://pub.dartlang.org/packages/sqflite

Introduction

This database runs amazingly fast. Note that there is no 'please wait' code in the example. It was just not required as all of the database operations were instantaneous.
It was also simple to setup and get working.
It also had versioning built-in out of the box. You could write code to the database object to handle initial database creation, when the database version changed etc.
It had the ability to use 'data objects' (in the example this is a Word object).
It had transaction handling.

Step 1 – Add Dependencies to Project

Add the following dependencies to your 'pubspec.yaml' file. After that you will need to do a 'flutter packages get' on the command line in the root of your project to download the dependencies.

- The sqflite package provides classes and functions that allow you to interact with a SQLite database.
- The path package provides functions that allow you to correctly define the location to store the database on disk.

```
dependencies:
 flutter:
  sdk: flutter
 sqflite:
 path:
```

Step 2 – Define the Data Model

At this point you should create the Dart classes that represent entities in your database. In my example, I create a 'Word' class. Note how I implemented the 'equals' and 'hashcode' so that the Word could be compared with other Words using an '=='.

```
class Word {
 final int _id;
 final String _english;
 final String _spanish;

 Word(this._id, this._english, this._spanish);

 Map<String, dynamic> toMap() {
  return {'id': _id, 'english': _english, 'spanish': _spanish};
 }

 String get spanish => _spanish;
```

```
  String get english => _english;

 int get id => _id;

 operator ==(other) =>
    (other != null) && (other is Word) && (_id == other._id);

 int get hashCode => _id.hashCode;
}
```

Step 3 – Open the Database

You should open the database when the app runs. It is two-step procedure and each step is asynchronous:

- Load database path.
- Open database.

Load Database Path

```
Future<bool> loadDatabasesPath() async {
   _databasesPath = await getDatabasesPath();
   return true;
 }
```

Open Database

Note how the 'openAndInitDatabase' method in the example code both initializes (only once) and returns the database. The database initialization is performed when it is fired by 'onCreate'.

```
Future<bool> openAndInitDatabase() async {
   _database = await openDatabase(
    join(_databasesPath, 'vocabulary.db'),
    onCreate: (db, version) {
      debugPrint("creating database...");
      db.execute("CREATE TABLE word(id INTEGER PRIMARY KEY, english TEXT, "
        "spanish TEXT, correct INTEGER, incorrect INTEGER)");
      db.execute("INSERT INTO word(english, spanish) "
        "VALUES ('uncle', 'tio')");
      db.execute("INSERT INTO word(english, spanish) "
        "VALUES ('reader', 'lector')");
      db.execute("INSERT INTO word(english, spanish) "
        "VALUES ('to keep vigil over', 'velar')");
      db.execute("INSERT INTO word(english, spanish) "
        "VALUES ('to remove', 'quitar')");
      db.execute("INSERT INTO word(english, spanish) "
        "VALUES ('to continue', 'reanudar')");
      db.execute("INSERT INTO word(english, spanish) "
        "VALUES ('until', 'hasta')");
      debugPrint("done");
    },
    version: 1,
   );
   return true;
 }
```

Retrieve Rows from Database

You use the 'query' method to retrieve data from the database.

```
final List<Map<String, dynamic>> words = await _database.query('word');
final List<Word> list = List.generate(words.length, (i) {
  return Word(words[i]['id'], words[i]['english'], words[i]['spanish']);
});
```

Executing SQL

The database object provides a 'execute' method in case you need to execute an SQL commands.

```
db.execute("INSERT INTO word(english, spanish) "
        "VALUES ('uncle', 'tio')");
```

Insert into Database

The database object provides an 'insert' method in case you need to insert rows into the database. Make sure that the primary key field is null if you want the SQLite to insert a new id for you.

```
Future<int> addWord(Word word) async {
  return await _database.insert(
    'word',
    word.toMap(),
    conflictAlgorithm: ConflictAlgorithm.replace,
  );
}
```

Update Row in Database

The database object provides an 'update' method in case you need to insert rows into the database.

```
Future<void> updateDog(Dog dog) async {
  // Get a reference to the database
  final db = await database;

  // Update the given Dog
  await db.update(
    'dogs',
    dog.toMap(),
    // Ensure we only update the Dog with a matching id
    where: "id = ?",
    // Pass the Dog's id through as a whereArg to prevent SQL injection
    whereArgs: [dog.id],
  );
}
```

Delete Row in Database

The database object provides an 'delete' method in case you need to delete rows into the database.

```
Future<void> deleteWord(Word word) async {
  return await _database.delete(
    'word',
    where: "id = ?",
    whereArgs: [word.id],
  );
}
```

Example – 'sqlite_vocabulary'

This app was written to help either an English-speaking person learn Spanish or a Spanish-speaking person learn English. The UI could definitely be improved but really the purpose of this app is to show how Flutter can work with a database.

It has three buttons at the top:
- Change mode from English -> Spanish to Spanish -> English (and back again).
- Add a new word.
- Delete the current word.

It has two floating buttons at the bottom:
- The button in the middle reveals the answer for the current word. For example, if you are asked 'Word in English is reader. What is the word in Spanish?' then it will reveal 'lector'.
- The button on the right moves onto the next word, randomly chosen.

 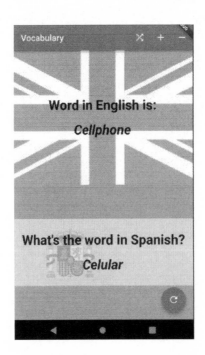

Dependencies

Add the following dependencies to your 'pubspec.yaml' file. After that you will need to do a 'flutter packages get' on the command line in the root of your project to download the dependencies.

```
dependencies:
  flutter:
    sdk: flutter

  # The following adds the Cupertino Icons font to your application.
  # Use with the CupertinoIcons class for iOS style icons.
  cupertino_icons: ^0.1.2

  sqflite:
  path:
```

Source Code

All of the words are stored in the database and all of the database code is contained in the 'DbWidget' inherited widget, at the top of the Widget tree so it can be accessed from any other Widget.

```dart
import 'dart:async';
import 'dart:math';

import 'package:flutter/material.dart';
import 'package:path/path.dart';
import 'package:sqflite/sqflite.dart';

void main() {
  runApp(MyApp());
}

enum Language { english, spanish }

class Word {
  final int _id;
  final String _english;
  final String _spanish;

  Word(this._id, this._english, this._spanish);

  Map<String, dynamic> toMap() {
    return {'id': _id, 'english': _english, 'spanish': _spanish};
  }

  String get spanish => _spanish;

  String get english => _english;

  int get id => _id;

  operator ==(other) =>
      (other != null) && (other is Word) && (_id == other._id);

  int get hashCode => _id.hashCode;
```

```
}
class MyApp extends StatelessWidget {
 // This widget is the root of your application.
 @override
 Widget build(BuildContext context) {
  return DbWidget(
     child: MaterialApp(
        title: 'Flutter Demo',
        theme: ThemeData(
          primarySwatch: Colors.blue,
        ),
        home: HomeWidget()));
 }
}

class DbWidget extends InheritedWidget {
 final _random = new Random();
 Database _database;
 String _databasesPath;

 DbWidget({Key key, @required Widget child})
    : assert(child != null),
      super(key: key, child: child);

 Future<bool> loadDatabasesPath() async {
  _databasesPath = await getDatabasesPath();
   return true;
 }

 Future<bool> openAndInitDatabase() async {
  _database = await openDatabase(
   join(_databasesPath, 'vocabulary.db'),
   onCreate: (db, version) {
    debugPrint("creating database...");
    db.execute("CREATE TABLE word(id INTEGER PRIMARY KEY, english TEXT, "
       "spanish TEXT, correct INTEGER, incorrect INTEGER)");
    db.execute("INSERT INTO word(english, spanish) "
       "VALUES ('uncle', 'tio')");
    db.execute("INSERT INTO word(english, spanish) "
       "VALUES ('reader', 'lector')");
    db.execute("INSERT INTO word(english, spanish) "
       "VALUES ('to keep vigil over', 'velar')");
    db.execute("INSERT INTO word(english, spanish) "
       "VALUES ('to remove', 'quitar')");
    db.execute("INSERT INTO word(english, spanish) "
       "VALUES ('to continue', 'reanudar')");
    db.execute("INSERT INTO word(english, spanish) "
       "VALUES ('until', 'hasta')");
    debugPrint("done");
   },
   version: 1,
  );
   return true;
 }

 Future<Word> loadNextWord(Word priorWord) async {
  final List<Map<String, dynamic>> words = await _database.query('word');
```

```
    final List<Word> list = List.generate(words.length, (i) {
      return Word(words[i]['id'], words[i]['english'], words[i]['spanish']);
    });

    Word nextWord = null;
    do {
     int nextWordIndex = _nextRandom(0, list.length);
     nextWord = list[nextWordIndex];
    } while (nextWord == priorWord);
    return nextWord;
  }

  Future<int> addWord(Word word) async {
    return await _database.insert(
     'word',
     word.toMap(),
     conflictAlgorithm: ConflictAlgorithm.replace,
    );
  }

  Future<void> deleteWord(Word word) async {
    return await _database.delete(
     'word',
     where: "id = ?",
     whereArgs: [word.id],
    );
  }

  static DbWidget of(BuildContext context) {
    return context.inheritFromWidgetOfExactType(DbWidget) as DbWidget;
  }

  @override
  bool updateShouldNotify(covariant InheritedWidget oldWidget) {
    return false;
  }

  int _nextRandom(int min, int max) => min + _random.nextInt(max - min);
}

class HomeWidget extends StatefulWidget {
  HomeWidget({Key key}) : super(key: key);

  @override
  _HomeWidgetState createState() => _HomeWidgetState();
}

class _HomeWidgetState extends State<HomeWidget> {
  final GlobalKey<ScaffoldState> _scaffoldKey = GlobalKey<ScaffoldState>();

  bool _loadedDatabasePath = false;
  bool _openedDatabase = false;
  Language _language = Language.spanish;
  Word _priorWord;
  Word _word;

  _showSnackBar(String content, {bool error = false}) {
    _scaffoldKey.currentState.showSnackBar(SnackBar(
```

```
      content:
        Text('${error ? "An unexpected error occurred: " : ""}${content}'),
  ));
}

_loadDatabasesPath(BuildContext context) {
  try {
    DbWidget.of(context).loadDatabasesPath().then((b) {
      setState(() {
        _loadedDatabasePath = true;
      });
    }).catchError((error) {
      _showSnackBar(error.toString(), error: true);
    });
  } catch (e) {
    _showSnackBar(e.toString(), error: true);
  }
}

_openAndInitDatabase(BuildContext context) {
  try {
    DbWidget.of(context).openAndInitDatabase().then((b) {
      setState(() {
        _openedDatabase = true;
      });
    }).catchError((error) {
      _showSnackBar(error.toString(), error: true);
    });
  } catch (e) {
    _showSnackBar(e.toString(), error: true);
  }
}

_loadWord(BuildContext context) {
  try {
    DbWidget.of(context).loadNextWord(_priorWord).then((word) {
      setState(() {
        _word = word;
      });
    }).catchError((error) {
      _showSnackBar(error.toString(), error: true);
    });
  } catch (e) {
    _showSnackBar(e.toString(), error: true);
  }
}

@override
Widget build(BuildContext context) {
  if (!_loadedDatabasePath) {
    _loadDatabasesPath(context);
  } else if (!_openedDatabase) {
    _openAndInitDatabase(context);
  } else if (_word == null) {
    _loadWord(context);
  }

  WordWidget englishWordWidget =
```

```
      WordWidget(Language.english, _language, _word);
    WordWidget spanishWordWidget =
      WordWidget(Language.spanish, _language, _word);

    Column wordWidgets = _language == Language.spanish
      ? Column(children: [englishWordWidget, spanishWordWidget])
      : Column(children: [spanishWordWidget, englishWordWidget]);

    AppBar appBar = AppBar(title: Text("Vocabulary"), actions: <Widget>[
      IconButton(icon: Icon(Icons.shuffle), onPressed: () => _switchLanguage()),
      IconButton(icon: Icon(Icons.add), onPressed: () => _addWord(context)),
      IconButton(
        icon: Icon(Icons.remove), onPressed: () => _deleteWord(context))
    ]);

    return Scaffold(
      key: _scaffoldKey,
      appBar: appBar,
      body: wordWidgets,
      floatingActionButton: FloatingActionButton(
        child: Icon(Icons.refresh), onPressed: () => _loadNextWord()));
  }

  _loadNextWord() {
   setState(() {
    _priorWord = _word;
    _word = null;
   });
  }

  _switchLanguage() {
   Language newLanguage =
     _language == Language.spanish ? Language.english : Language.spanish;
   setState(() => _language = newLanguage);
  }

  _addWord(BuildContext context) async {
   Word word = await showDialog<Word>(
     context: context,
     builder: (BuildContext context) {
      return Dialog(child: AddDialogWidget());
     });
   if (word != null) {
    try {
     DbWidget.of(context).addWord(word).then((_) {
      _loadNextWord();
      _showSnackBar("Added word.");
     }).catchError((e) => _showSnackBar(e.toString(), error: true));
    } catch (e) {
     _showSnackBar(e.toString(), error: true);
    }
   }
  }

  _deleteWord(BuildContext context) {
   _showConfirmDialog(context, _word).then((result) {
    if (result == true) {
     try {
```

```
      DbWidget.of(context).deleteWord(_word).then((_) {
        _loadNextWord();
        _showSnackBar("Deleted word.");
      }).catchError((e) => _showSnackBar(e.toString(), error: true));
    } catch (e) {
      _showSnackBar(e.toString(), error: true);
    }
  }
 });
 }
}

class WordWidget extends StatefulWidget {
 WordWidget(this._widgetLanguage, this._language, this._word) {}

 final Language _widgetLanguage;
 final Language _language;
 final Word _word;

 @override
 _WordWidgetState createState() => _WordWidgetState();
}

class _WordWidgetState extends State<WordWidget> {
 bool _revealed = false;

 _WordWidgetState() {}

 @override
 void didUpdateWidget(Widget oldWidget) {
  _revealed = false;
 }

 @override
 Widget build(BuildContext context) {
  bool isReveal = widget._widgetLanguage == widget._language;

  List<Widget> widgets = [];

  String titleText = isReveal
     ? "What's the word in ${getLanguageName(widget._widgetLanguage)}?"
     : "Word in ${getLanguageName(widget._widgetLanguage)} is:";

  widgets.add(Padding(
     padding: EdgeInsets.only(bottom: 20.0),
     child: Text(titleText,
        style: const TextStyle(fontSize: 30.0, fontWeight: FontWeight.bold),
        textAlign: TextAlign.center)));

  if ((isReveal) && (!_revealed)) {
    widgets.add(FloatingActionButton(
       child: Icon(Icons.remove_red_eye),
       onPressed: () => {setState(() => _revealed = true)}));
  } else {
    String word = widget._word == null
       ? ""
       : widget._widgetLanguage == Language.english
         ? widget._word._english
```

```
            : widget._word._spanish;
        widgets.add(Text(
          word,
          style: const TextStyle(
              fontSize: 30.0,
              fontWeight: FontWeight.bold,
              fontStyle: FontStyle.italic),
          textAlign: TextAlign.center,
        ));
      }

      return Expanded(
          child: Container(
          child: Column(
            mainAxisAlignment: MainAxisAlignment.center,
            crossAxisAlignment: CrossAxisAlignment.stretch,
            children: widgets),
          decoration: BoxDecoration(
            image: DecorationImage(
              colorFilter: new ColorFilter.mode(
                Colors.white.withOpacity(0.3), BlendMode.dstATop),
              image: NetworkImage(widget._widgetLanguage == Language.english
                ? "https://upload.wikimedia.org/wikipedia/en/thumb/a/ae/" +
                    "Flag_of_the_United_Kingdom.svg/" +
                    "510px-Flag_of_the_United_Kingdom.svg.png"
                : "https://upload.wikimedia.org/wikipedia/en/thumb/9/9a/" +
                    "Flag_of_Spain.svg/400px-Flag_of_Spain.svg.png"),
              fit: BoxFit.cover,
            ),
          ),
          padding: EdgeInsets.all(10.0),
        ));
    }

    String getLanguageName(Language language) {
      return widget._widgetLanguage == Language.spanish ? "Spanish" : "English";
    }
  }

  class AddDialogWidget extends StatelessWidget {
    static final _formKey = GlobalKey<FormState>();
    static final TextEditingController _englishTextController =
        new TextEditingController();
    static final TextEditingController _spanishTextController =
        new TextEditingController();

    AddDialogWidget() : super();

    @override
    Widget build(BuildContext context) {
      return Container(
        height: 260.0,
        width: 250.0,
        child: Padding(
          padding: EdgeInsets.all(10.0),
          child: Form(
            key: _formKey,
            child: Column(
```

```
                mainAxisAlignment: MainAxisAlignment.spaceAround,
                children: [
                  Text("Add Word",
                      style: TextStyle(
                          fontSize: 20.0, fontWeight: FontWeight.bold)),
                  TextFormField(
                      validator: (value) {
                        if (value.isEmpty) {
                          return 'Please enter the word in English.';
                        }
                      },
                      decoration: InputDecoration(
                          icon: const Icon(Icons.location_city),
                          hintText: 'English',
                          labelText: 'Enter the word in English'),
                      onSaved: (String value) {},
                      controller: _englishTextController),
                  TextFormField(
                      validator: (value) {
                        if (value.isEmpty) {
                          return 'Please enter the word in Spanish.';
                        }
                      },
                      decoration: InputDecoration(
                          icon: const Icon(Icons.location_city),
                          hintText: 'Spanish',
                          labelText: 'Enter the word in Spanish'),
                      onSaved: (String value) {},
                      controller: _spanishTextController),
                  FlatButton(
                      child: Text("Add"),
                      onPressed: () {
                        if (_formKey.currentState.validate()) {
                          _formKey.currentState.save();
                          Navigator.pop(
                            context,
                            Word(null, _englishTextController.text,
                                _spanishTextController.text));
                          _englishTextController.text = "";
                          _spanishTextController.text = "";
                        }
                      })
                ]))));
  }
}

Future<bool> _showConfirmDialog(BuildContext context, Word word) async {
  return await showDialog<bool>(
      context: context,
      builder: (BuildContext context) {
        return AlertDialog(
          title: const Text('Confirm'),
          content: Text(
              'Are you sure you want to delete the word "${word.english}?'),
          actions: <Widget>[
            FlatButton(
              onPressed: () {
                Navigator.pop(context, true);
```

```
      },
      child: const Text('Yes'),
     ),
     FlatButton(
      onPressed: () {
       Navigator.pop(context, false);
      },
      child: const Text('No'),
     )
    ],
   );
  });
}
```

Further Reading

https://medium.com/flutter-community/using-sqlite-in-flutter-187c1a82e8b
https://flutter.dev/docs/cookbook/persistence/sqlite
https://proandroiddev.com/flutter-bookshelf-app-part-3-managing-data-the-right-way-30569abf9487

Local Files

Introduction

If you don't need to query but you need to store possibly complex objects and lots of data with full-control then this is probably the best way to do it.

Flutter provides a core package 'dart.io' to help you with input and output at the device level. Remember that this may be different for different devices (platforms). For example, some of the file details may be different for an Android than iOS. That is why the Platform class is covered below.

The Flutter 'dart.io' core package includes Directory and File objects for the purpose of working with Directories and Files. These objects are excellent because they can work both synchronously and asynchronously, allowing you to maintain a responsive app even when dealing with large amounts of data.

However, this package does not tell you how to store the data in the files, what file format to use and how to serialize and deserialize objects into files. That is both good and bad but it requires some work on your part.

Platform

When you are coding with local files and directories, sometimes you need information about the device platform:

- Number of processors.
- Path separator.
- Operating System.
- Operating System version.
- Local hostname.
- Version.

The Platform class exists to provide this information to you.

Path Separator

Very useful when you want to separate elements from the path, such as the directory and the filename.

In the example below, I create a 'Directory' object and use it to query local files in the 'Application Documents' directory. When I do this, I get a list of files and each file has a path, which includes the filename at the end. I parse out the filename by finding the last path file separator (using Platform.pathSeparator) and calculating the filename as the rest of the path from there onward.

```
Directory(_path).listSync().forEach((FileSystemEntity fse) {
    String path = fse.path;
    if (path.endsWith(".themeColor")) {
      int startIndex = path.lastIndexOf(Platform.pathSeparator) + 1;
      int endIndex = path.lastIndexOf(".themeColor");
      filenameList.add(path.substring(startIndex, endIndex));
    }
  });
```

Path Provider Package

This is a package that (obviously) provides information about commonly used locations on the filesystem:

```
Directory tempDir = await getTemporaryDirectory();
Directory appDocDir = await getApplicationDocumentsDirectory();
```

It supports iOS and Android. More information here:
https://pub.dartlang.org/packages/path_provider

We use it in the example below, as it involves files in the Application Documents directory.

Application Documents Directory

This is a directory that your app has access to, as a place to store local files. Remember that you can create subdirectories within this directory as well as files. If you look at the constructor for the BLoC in the example code below, you will see that you get its value using an asynchronous method call to 'getApplicationDocumentsDirectory' in the path provider package (see above).

```
ThemeBLOC({Key key, @required Widget child})
  : assert(child != null),
    super(key: key, child: child) {
  getApplicationDocumentsDirectory()
    .then((directory) => _path = directory.path);
```

Directories

In order to work with Directories, the core Flutter package 'dart.io' provides a Directory object. You can create Directory objects from paths or uris. It provides methods for getting information about the directory, as well as methods for modifying it. It also has properties for providing more information.

Files

In order to work with Files, the core Flutter package 'dart.io' provides a File object. You can create File objects from paths or uris. It provides methods for getting information about the file, as well as methods for opening it, reading from it, writing to it and setting file information (such as when it was last accessed or modified). It also has properties for providing more information.

Note that you can open files in the following modes:

Mode	Description
READ	Mode for opening a file only for reading.
WRITE	Mode for opening a file for reading and writing.
APPEND	Mode for opening a file for reading and writing to the end of it.
WRITE ONLY	Mode for opening a file for writing only.
WRITE ONLY APPEND	Mode for opening a file for writing only to the end of it.

Directory & File Methods

Note that the Directory and File objects provide both synchronous and asynchronous methods. Obviously, you should consider asynchronous methods if you think these methods could take some time to complete.

Reading & Writing Data to a File

You need to decide the file format before you write code to read & write the data in the file. You can choose a text format or a binary file format.

Text & Binary Files

A text file stores data in the form of alphabets, digits and other special symbols by storing their ASCII values and are in a human readable format.

A binary file contains a sequence or a collection of bytes which are not in a human readable format.

A small error in a textual file can be recognized and eliminated when seen. Whereas, a small error in a binary file corrupts the file and is not easy to detect.

Text / JSON Format

When I wrote this example, I had just covered the working on the Flutter JSON example here: Serializing & Deserializing JSON. So JSON was fresh in my mind and I chose that format, working with the Flutter 'convert' package methods 'jsonEncode' and 'jsonDecode'.

Within the JSON encoding, the example uses two methods to serialize/deserialize the color: 'colorToJson' and 'jsonToColor'.

- 'colorToJson' works by matching the color from the list of colors using the color value, then returning the text.
- 'jsonToColor' works by matching the color from the list of colors using the text value, then returning the color.

Write Data to a File

Note that there are different ways to write data to a file:
- Write as bytes.
- Write as string.

Note that you can perform this operation synchronously or asynchronously.

Code from the example below:

```
saveAs(String filename) {
  String json = jsonEncode(_colorOptions.toJson());
  File("${_path}/${filename}.themeColor").writeAsString(json);
}
```

Read Data from a File

Note that there are different ways to read a file:
- Read as bytes.
- Read as lines.
- Read as strings.

Note that you can perform this operation synchronously or asynchronously.

Code from the example below:

```
File("${fse.path}").readAsString().then((str) {
    ColorOptions newColorOptions = ColorOptions.fromJson(jsonDecode(str));
    this.colorOptions = newColorOptions;
    });
```

Example 'persistence_files'

This app shows the grid of cat pictures but it also has toolbar options to configure the colors, open a color theme and save a color theme. It stores the color themes as local files (with the file extension '.themeColor').

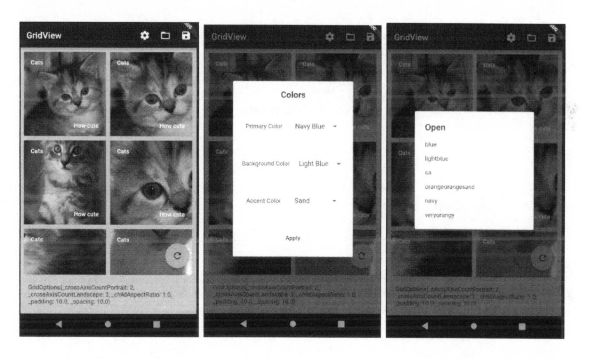

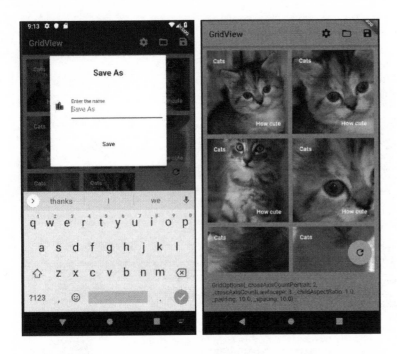

This example uses the BLoC pattern for the theme color state: <u>State & BLoCs w/Streams Approach</u> .

This example also has some useful keyboard code that only allows the user to enter names with letters a-z.

Dependencies

Add the following dependencies to your 'pubspec.yaml' file. After that you will need to do a 'flutter packages get' on the command line in the root of your project to download the dependencies.

```yaml
dependencies:
  flutter:
    sdk: flutter
  rxdart: 0.18.1
  # The following adds the Cupertino Icons font to your application.
  # Use with the CupertinoIcons class for iOS style icons.
  cupertino_icons: ^0.1.2
  path_provider: ^0.5.0+1
dev_dependencies:
  flutter_test:
    sdk: flutter
```

Source Code:

```dart
import 'dart:convert';
import 'dart:io';

import 'package:flutter/material.dart';
import 'package:flutter/services.dart';
import 'package:path_provider/path_provider.dart';
```

```
import 'package:rxdart/rxdart.dart';

void main() => runApp(ThemeBLOC(child: new GridViewApp()));

//TODO Fix horrible color choices. :)
const COLOR_COFFEE = Color.fromARGB(0xFF, 112, 80, 80);
const COLOR_DARK_BROWN = Color.fromARGB(0xFF, 59, 20, 18);
const COLOR_GREY = Color.fromARGB(0xFF, 68, 68, 68);
const COLOR_LIGHT_BLUE = Color.fromARGB(0xFF, 122, 207, 221);
const COLOR_MAROON = Color.fromARGB(0xFF, 86, 18, 16);
const COLOR_NAVY_BLUE = Color.fromARGB(0xFF, 15, 32, 67);
const COLOR_ORANGE = Color.fromARGB(0xFF, 240, 146, 34);
const COLOR_SAND = Color.fromARGB(0xFF, 213, 184, 88);
const COLOR_YELLOW = Color.fromARGB(0xFF, 246, 236, 32);

const COLOR_DROPDOWN_MENU_ITEMS = [
  DropdownMenuItem(value: COLOR_COFFEE, child: const Text("Coffee")),
  DropdownMenuItem(value: COLOR_DARK_BROWN, child: const Text("Dark Brown")),
  DropdownMenuItem(value: COLOR_GREY, child: const Text("Grey")),
  DropdownMenuItem(value: COLOR_LIGHT_BLUE, child: const Text("Light Blue")),
  DropdownMenuItem(value: COLOR_MAROON, child: const Text("Maroon")),
  DropdownMenuItem(value: COLOR_NAVY_BLUE, child: const Text("Navy Blue")),
  DropdownMenuItem(value: COLOR_ORANGE, child: const Text("Orange")),
  DropdownMenuItem(value: COLOR_SAND, child: const Text("Sand")),
  DropdownMenuItem(value: COLOR_YELLOW, child: const Text("Yellow")),
];

class ColorOptions {
  Color primaryColor;
  Color scaffoldBackgroundColor;
  Color accentColor;

  ColorOptions(
      {@required this.primaryColor,
      @required this.scaffoldBackgroundColor,
      @required this.accentColor});

  ColorOptions.copyOf(ColorOptions other) {
    this.primaryColor = other.primaryColor;
    this.scaffoldBackgroundColor = other.scaffoldBackgroundColor;
    this.accentColor = other.accentColor;
  }

  Map<String, dynamic> toJson() {
    Map<String, dynamic> map = {
      'primaryColor': '${colorToJson(primaryColor)}',
      'scaffoldBackgroundColor': '${colorToJson(scaffoldBackgroundColor)}',
      'accentColor': '${colorToJson(accentColor)}'
    };
    return map;
  }

  ColorOptions.fromJson(Map<String, dynamic> json)
      : primaryColor = jsonToColor(json['primaryColor']),
        scaffoldBackgroundColor = jsonToColor(json['scaffoldBackgroundColor']),
        accentColor = jsonToColor(json['accentColor']);

  static String colorToJson(Color color) {
```

```
    DropdownMenuItem menuItemForColor =
      COLOR_DROPDOWN_MENU_ITEMS.firstWhere((item) => item.value == color);
    return (menuItemForColor.child as Text).data;
  }

  static Color jsonToColor(String json) {
    DropdownMenuItem menuItemForColor = COLOR_DROPDOWN_MENU_ITEMS
      .firstWhere((item) => (item.child as Text).data == json);
    return menuItemForColor.value;
  }
}

class GridOptions {
  int crossAxisCountPortrait;
  int crossAxisCountLandscape;
  double childAspectRatio;
  double padding;
  double spacing;

  GridOptions(
    {@required this.crossAxisCountPortrait,
    @required this.crossAxisCountLandscape,
    @required this.childAspectRatio,
    @required this.padding,
    @required this.spacing});

  @override
  String toString() {
    return 'GridOptions{_crossAxisCountPortrait: $crossAxisCountPortrait, _crossAxisCountLandscape:
$crossAxisCountLandscape, _childAspectRatio: $childAspectRatio, _padding: $padding, _spacing:
$spacing}';
  }
}

class ThemeBLOC extends InheritedWidget {
  String _path;

  ThemeBLOC({Key key, @required Widget child})
    : assert(child != null),
      super(key: key, child: child) {
    getApplicationDocumentsDirectory()
      .then((directory) => _path = directory.path);
  }

  ColorOptions _colorOptions = ColorOptions(
    primaryColor: COLOR_NAVY_BLUE,
    scaffoldBackgroundColor: COLOR_LIGHT_BLUE,
    accentColor: COLOR_SAND);

  static ThemeBLOC of(BuildContext context) {
    return context.inheritFromWidgetOfExactType(ThemeBLOC) as ThemeBLOC;
  }

  ThemeData get startingThemeData {
    return createThemeDataFromColorOptions();
  }

  ThemeData createThemeDataFromColorOptions() {
```

```
  return ThemeData(
    primaryColor: _colorOptions.primaryColor,
    scaffoldBackgroundColor: _colorOptions.scaffoldBackgroundColor,
    accentColor: _colorOptions.accentColor);
}

@override
bool updateShouldNotify(covariant InheritedWidget oldWidget) {
  // We are going to use a stream for updating widget tree (see StreamBuilder).
  return false;
}

// Used to update widget tree (see StreamBuilder).
Stream<ThemeData> get themeStream => _themeSubject.stream;
final _themeSubject = BehaviorSubject<ThemeData>();

ColorOptions get colorOptions => _colorOptions;

set colorOptions(ColorOptions value) {
  _colorOptions = value;
  _themeSubject.add(createThemeDataFromColorOptions()); // update widget tree
}

List<String> get filenames {
  List<String> filenameList = [];
  Directory(_path).listSync().forEach((FileSystemEntity fse) {
    String path = fse.path;
    if (path.endsWith(".themeColor")) {
      int startIndex = path.lastIndexOf(Platform.pathSeparator) + 1;
      int endIndex = path.lastIndexOf(".themeColor");
      filenameList.add(path.substring(startIndex, endIndex));
    }
  });
  return filenameList;
}

open(String filename) {
  FileSystemEntity fse =
    Directory(_path).listSync().firstWhere((FileSystemEntity fse) {
    String path = fse.path;
    if (path.endsWith(".themeColor")) {
      int startIndex = path.lastIndexOf(Platform.pathSeparator) + 1;
      if (startIndex != -1) {
        int endIndex = path.lastIndexOf(".themeColor");
        if (endIndex != -1) {
          var pathFilename = path.substring(startIndex, endIndex);
          if (pathFilename == filename) {
            return true;
          }
        }
      }
    }
    return false;
  });
  if (fse != null) {
    File("${fse.path}").readAsString().then((str) {
      ColorOptions newColorOptions = ColorOptions.fromJson(jsonDecode(str));
      this.colorOptions = newColorOptions;
```

```
      });
    }
  }

  saveAs(String filename) {
    String json = jsonEncode(_colorOptions.toJson());
    File("${_path}/${filename}.themeColor").writeAsString(json);
  }
}

class GridViewApp extends StatelessWidget {
  // This widget is the root of your application.
  @override
  Widget build(BuildContext context) {
    ThemeBLOC bloc = ThemeBLOC.of(context);
    return StreamBuilder<ThemeData>(
        // listens to stream in ThemeBLOC to know when to update
        stream: bloc._themeSubject,
        initialData: bloc.startingThemeData,
        builder: (context, snapshot) {
          ThemeData themeData = snapshot.data;
          return MaterialApp(
            title: 'Flutter Demo',
            theme: themeData,
            home: HomeWidget(title: 'Flutter Demo Home Page'),
          );
        });
  }
}

class HomeWidget extends StatefulWidget {
  HomeWidget({Key key, this.title}) : super(key: key);

  final String title;

  @override
  _HomeWidgetState createState() => new _HomeWidgetState();
}

class _HomeWidgetState extends State<HomeWidget> {
  List<Widget> _kittenTiles = [];
  int _gridOptionsIndex = 0;
  List<GridOptions> _gridOptions = [
    GridOptions(
        crossAxisCountPortrait: 2,
        crossAxisCountLandscape: 3,
        childAspectRatio: 1.0,
        padding: 10.0,
        spacing: 10.0),
    GridOptions(
        crossAxisCountPortrait: 3,
        crossAxisCountLandscape: 4,
        childAspectRatio: 1.5,
        padding: 10.0,
        spacing: 10.0),
    GridOptions(
        crossAxisCountPortrait: 2,
        crossAxisCountLandscape: 3,
```

```
        childAspectRatio: 2.0,
        padding: 10.0,
        spacing: 30.0),
];

_HomeWidgetState() : super() {
 for (int i = 200; i < 1000; i += 100) {
  String imageUrl = "http://placekitten.com/200/${i}";
  _kittenTiles.add(GridTile(
      header: GridTileBar(
        title:
            Text("Cats", style: TextStyle(fontWeight: FontWeight.bold))),
      footer: GridTileBar(
        title: Text("How cute",
            textAlign: TextAlign.right,
            style: TextStyle(fontWeight: FontWeight.bold))),
      child: Image.network(imageUrl, fit: BoxFit.cover)));
 }
}

void _tryMoreGridOptions() {
 setState(() {
  _gridOptionsIndex++;
  if (_gridOptionsIndex >= (_gridOptions.length - 1)) {
   _gridOptionsIndex = 0;
  }
 });
}

@override
Widget build(BuildContext context) {
 GridOptions options = _gridOptions[_gridOptionsIndex];
 return Scaffold(
  appBar: AppBar(title: Text("GridView"), actions: [
   IconButton(
      icon: Icon(Icons.settings),
      tooltip: 'Color Options',
      onPressed: () => _showColorOptionsDialog()),
   IconButton(
      icon: Icon(Icons.folder_open),
      tooltip: 'Open',
      onPressed: () {
       List<String> names = ThemeBLOC.of(context).filenames;
       _showOpenDialog(context, names);
      }),
   IconButton(
      icon: Icon(Icons.save),
      tooltip: 'Save',
      onPressed: () => _showSaveAsDialog(context))
  ]),
  body: OrientationBuilder(builder: (context, orientation) {
   return GridView.count(
      crossAxisCount: (orientation == Orientation.portrait)
         ? options.crossAxisCountPortrait
         : options.crossAxisCountLandscape,
      childAspectRatio: options.childAspectRatio,
      padding: EdgeInsets.all(options.padding),
      mainAxisSpacing: options.spacing,
```

```
          crossAxisSpacing: options.spacing,
          children: _kittenTiles);
    }),
    bottomNavigationBar: Container(
      child: Text(options.toString()), padding: EdgeInsets.all(20.0)),
    floatingActionButton: new FloatingActionButton(
     onPressed: _tryMoreGridOptions,
     tooltip: 'Try more grid options',
     child: new Icon(Icons.refresh),
    ), // This trailing comma makes auto-formatting nicer for build methods.
  );
}

void _showColorOptionsDialog() async {
  ColorOptions colorOptions = await showDialog<ColorOptions>(
    context: context,
    builder: (BuildContext context) {
      return Dialog(
        child: ColorDialogWidget(ThemeBLOC.of(context).colorOptions));
    });
  if (colorOptions != null) {
    ThemeBLOC.of(context).colorOptions = colorOptions;
  }
}

void _showOpenDialog(BuildContext context, List<String> names) async {
  List<SimpleDialogOption> children = names.map((s) {
    return SimpleDialogOption(
      onPressed: () {
        Navigator.pop(context, s);
      },
      child: Text(s),
    );
  }).toList(growable: false);

  String name = await showDialog<String>(
    context: context,
    builder: (BuildContext context) {
      return SimpleDialog(title: const Text('Open'), children: children);
    });

  if (name != null) {
    setState(() {
     ThemeBLOC.of(context).open(name);
    });
  }
}

void _showSaveAsDialog(BuildContext context) async {
  String name = await showDialog<String>(
    context: context,
    builder: (BuildContext context) {
      return Dialog(child: SaveAsDialogWidget());
    });
  if (name != null) {
    ThemeBLOC.of(context).saveAs(name);
  }
}
```

```
}
class ColorDialogWidget extends StatefulWidget {
  ColorOptions _colorOptions;

  ColorDialogWidget(this._colorOptions) : super();

  @override
  _CustomDialogWidgetState createState() =>
    new _CustomDialogWidgetState(ColorOptions.copyOf(this._colorOptions));
}

class _CustomDialogWidgetState extends State<ColorDialogWidget> {
  ColorOptions _colorOptions;

  _CustomDialogWidgetState(this._colorOptions);

  @override
  Widget build(BuildContext context) {
   return Container(
      height: 400.0,
      width: 250.0,
      child:
        Column(mainAxisAlignment: MainAxisAlignment.spaceAround, children: <
          Widget>[
        Text("Colors",
          style: TextStyle(fontSize: 20.0, fontWeight: FontWeight.bold)),
        Row(mainAxisAlignment: MainAxisAlignment.center, children: <Widget>[
          Spacer(),
          Text("Primary Color"),
          Spacer(),
          new DropdownButton<Color>(
            value: _colorOptions.primaryColor,
            items: COLOR_DROPDOWN_MENU_ITEMS,
            onChanged: (newValue) {
              setState(() {
                _colorOptions.primaryColor = newValue;
              });
            },
          ),
          Spacer(),
        ]),
        Row(mainAxisAlignment: MainAxisAlignment.center, children: <Widget>[
          Spacer(),
          Text("Background Color"),
          Spacer(),
          new DropdownButton<Color>(
            value: _colorOptions.scaffoldBackgroundColor,
            items: COLOR_DROPDOWN_MENU_ITEMS,
            onChanged: (newValue) {
              setState(() {
                _colorOptions.scaffoldBackgroundColor = newValue;
              });
            },
          ),
          Spacer(),
        ]),
        Row(mainAxisAlignment: MainAxisAlignment.center, children: <Widget>[
```

```
      Spacer(),
      Text("Accent Color"),
      Spacer(),
      new DropdownButton<Color>(
       value: _colorOptions.accentColor,
       items: COLOR_DROPDOWN_MENU_ITEMS,
       onChanged: (newValue) {
        setState(() {
         _colorOptions.accentColor = newValue;
        });
       },
      ),
      Spacer(),
     ]),
     FlatButton(
        child: Text("Apply"),
        onPressed: () => Navigator.pop(context, _colorOptions))
    ]));
  }
}

class SaveAsDialogWidget extends StatelessWidget {
  static final _formKey = GlobalKey<FormState>();
  static final TextEditingController _nameTextController =
     new TextEditingController();

  SaveAsDialogWidget() : super();

  @override
  Widget build(BuildContext context) {
   return Container(
      height: 260.0,
      width: 250.0,
      child: Padding(
        padding: EdgeInsets.all(10.0),
        child: Form(
          key: _formKey,
          child: Column(
            mainAxisAlignment: MainAxisAlignment.spaceAround,
            children: [
              Text("Save As",
                style: TextStyle(
                  fontSize: 20.0, fontWeight: FontWeight.bold)),
              TextFormField(
                autofocus: true,
                validator: (value) {
                 if (value.isEmpty) {
                   return 'Please enter the name.';
                  }
                },
                decoration: InputDecoration(
                  icon: const Icon(Icons.location_city),
                  hintText: 'Save As',
                  labelText: 'Enter the name'),
                keyboardType: TextInputType.text,
                inputFormatters: [
                  WhitelistingTextInputFormatter(RegExp(r'[a-z]'))
                ],
```

```
          onSaved: (String value) {},
          controller: _nameTextController),
      FlatButton(
        child: Text("Save"),
        onPressed: () {
         if (_formKey.currentState.validate()) {
           _formKey.currentState.save();
           Navigator.pop(context, _nameTextController.text);
           _nameTextController.text = "";
         }
        })
     ]))));
  }
}
```

Shared Preferences

Introduction

The 'shared_preferences' package is very useful for providing a local persistent store for simple preference data. This data is lost if the user uninstalls the app or clears the app data.

Each preference item requires its own String key to identify it. In my code example, I use the String key 'themeList' to store the semi-colon delimited list of themes and I use a the theme name as the key for each theme stored as a preference.

More info here: https://pub.dartlang.org/packages/shared_preferences

Methods

Getting a List of All Preferences

This gets a set (similar to a list without duplicates) containing all the keys to local shared preferences.

```
Set<String> getKeys()
```

Getting a Preference

The method you use depends on the type of data stored in the preference.

Method	Description
dynamic get(String key)	Returns a preference for a key, could be any of the types below.
bool getBool(String key)	Returns a boolean preference for a key.
int getInt(String key)	Returns an integer preference for a key.
double getDouble(String key)	Returns a double preference for a key.

String getString(String key)	Returns a string preference for a key.
List<String> getStringList(String key)	Returns a string list preference for a key.

Setting a Preference

The method you use depends on the type of data you want stored in the preference.

Method	Description
Future<bool> setBool(String key)	Sets a boolean preference for a key.
Future<bool> setInt(String key)	Sets an integer preference for a key.
Future<bool> setDouble(String key)	Sets a double preference for a key.
Future<bool> setString(String key)	Sets a string preference for a key.
Future<bool> getStringList(String key)	Sets a string list preference for a key.

Removing a Preference

There is only one method call for all types.

Method	Description
Future<bool> remove(String key)	Removes an entry from persistent storage, whatever the type.

Further Reading

https://medium.com/flutter-community/shared-preferences-how-to-save-flutter-application-settings-and-user-preferences-for-later-554d08671ae9

Example 'persistence_shared_preferences'

This app shows the grid of cat pictures as before and it works in the same way. However, this time it uses the 'shared_preferences' package rather than local files.

Dependencies

Add the following dependencies to your 'pubspec.yaml' file. After that you will need to do a 'flutter packages get' on the command line in the root of your project to download the dependencies.

```
dependencies:
  flutter:
    sdk: flutter
  rxdart: 0.18.1
  # The following adds the Cupertino Icons font to your application.
  # Use with the CupertinoIcons class for iOS style icons.
  cupertino_icons: ^0.1.2
  shared_preferences: ^0.5.1+2
```

Source Code:

Most of the code is the same as the previous example but there are several differences in the ThemeBLOC class:

- The ThemeBLOC loads the SharedPreferences object asynchrously in the constructor.
- The preference 'themeList' is used to store the list of available themes in a single string, delimited by semi-colons.
  - Example of this format: 'themeOne;themeTwo'.
  - In retrospect, it would have been better to use the methods 'getStringList' and 'setStringList' rather than 'getString' and 'setString', instead of storing a list in a single string. It would have made the code less complex.
- Then each theme is stored as its own preference in the same Text / JSON format as in the previous example.

```dart
import 'dart:convert';
import 'dart:io';

import 'package:flutter/material.dart';
import 'package:flutter/services.dart';
import 'package:rxdart/rxdart.dart';
import 'package:shared_preferences/shared_preferences.dart';

void main() => runApp(ThemeBLOC(child: new GridViewApp()));

//TODO Fix horrible color choices. :)
const COLOR_COFFEE = Color.fromARGB(0xFF, 112, 80, 80);
const COLOR_DARK_BROWN = Color.fromARGB(0xFF, 59, 20, 18);
const COLOR_GREY = Color.fromARGB(0xFF, 68, 68, 68);
const COLOR_LIGHT_BLUE = Color.fromARGB(0xFF, 122, 207, 221);
const COLOR_MAROON = Color.fromARGB(0xFF, 86, 18, 16);
const COLOR_NAVY_BLUE = Color.fromARGB(0xFF, 15, 32, 67);
const COLOR_ORANGE = Color.fromARGB(0xFF, 240, 146, 34);
const COLOR_SAND = Color.fromARGB(0xFF, 213, 184, 88);
const COLOR_YELLOW = Color.fromARGB(0xFF, 246, 236, 32);

const COLOR_DROPDOWN_MENU_ITEMS = [
  DropdownMenuItem(value: COLOR_COFFEE, child: const Text("Coffee")),
  DropdownMenuItem(value: COLOR_DARK_BROWN, child: const Text("Dark Brown")),
  DropdownMenuItem(value: COLOR_GREY, child: const Text("Grey")),
  DropdownMenuItem(value: COLOR_LIGHT_BLUE, child: const Text("Light Blue")),
  DropdownMenuItem(value: COLOR_MAROON, child: const Text("Maroon")),
  DropdownMenuItem(value: COLOR_NAVY_BLUE, child: const Text("Navy Blue")),
  DropdownMenuItem(value: COLOR_ORANGE, child: const Text("Orange")),
  DropdownMenuItem(value: COLOR_SAND, child: const Text("Sand")),
  DropdownMenuItem(value: COLOR_YELLOW, child: const Text("Yellow")),
];

class ColorOptions {
  Color primaryColor;
  Color scaffoldBackgroundColor;
  Color accentColor;

  ColorOptions(
    {@required this.primaryColor,
```

```
      @required this.scaffoldBackgroundColor,
      @required this.accentColor});

  ColorOptions.copyOf(ColorOptions other) {
    this.primaryColor = other.primaryColor;
    this.scaffoldBackgroundColor = other.scaffoldBackgroundColor;
    this.accentColor = other.accentColor;
  }

  Map<String, dynamic> toJson() {
    Map<String, dynamic> map = {
      'primaryColor': '${colorToJson(primaryColor)}',
      'scaffoldBackgroundColor': '${colorToJson(scaffoldBackgroundColor)}',
      'accentColor': '${colorToJson(accentColor)}'
    };
    return map;
  }

  ColorOptions.fromJson(Map<String, dynamic> json)
      : primaryColor = jsonToColor(json['primaryColor']),
        scaffoldBackgroundColor = jsonToColor(json['scaffoldBackgroundColor']),
        accentColor = jsonToColor(json['accentColor']);

  static String colorToJson(Color color) {
    DropdownMenuItem menuItemForColor =
        COLOR_DROPDOWN_MENU_ITEMS.firstWhere((item) => item.value == color);
    return (menuItemForColor.child as Text).data;
  }

  static Color jsonToColor(String json) {
    DropdownMenuItem menuItemForColor = COLOR_DROPDOWN_MENU_ITEMS
        .firstWhere((item) => (item.child as Text).data == json);
    return menuItemForColor.value;
  }
}

class GridOptions {
  int crossAxisCountPortrait;
  int crossAxisCountLandscape;
  double childAspectRatio;
  double padding;
  double spacing;

  GridOptions(
      {@required this.crossAxisCountPortrait,
      @required this.crossAxisCountLandscape,
      @required this.childAspectRatio,
      @required this.padding,
      @required this.spacing});

  @override
  String toString() {
    return 'GridOptions{_crossAxisCountPortrait: $crossAxisCountPortrait, _crossAxisCountLandscape:
$crossAxisCountLandscape, _childAspectRatio: $childAspectRatio, _padding: $padding, _spacing:
$spacing}';
  }
}
```

```
class ThemeBLOC extends InheritedWidget {
  SharedPreferences _prefs;

  ThemeBLOC({Key key, @required Widget child})
      : assert(child != null),
        super(key: key, child: child) {
    SharedPreferences.getInstance().then((prefs) => _prefs = prefs);
  }

  ColorOptions _colorOptions = ColorOptions(
      primaryColor: COLOR_NAVY_BLUE,
      scaffoldBackgroundColor: COLOR_LIGHT_BLUE,
      accentColor: COLOR_SAND);

  static ThemeBLOC of(BuildContext context) {
    return context.inheritFromWidgetOfExactType(ThemeBLOC) as ThemeBLOC;
  }

  ThemeData get startingThemeData {
    return createThemeDataFromColorOptions();
  }

  ThemeData createThemeDataFromColorOptions() {
    return ThemeData(
        primaryColor: _colorOptions.primaryColor,
        scaffoldBackgroundColor: _colorOptions.scaffoldBackgroundColor,
        accentColor: _colorOptions.accentColor);
  }

  @override
  bool updateShouldNotify(covariant InheritedWidget oldWidget) {
    // We are going to use a stream for updating widget tree (see StreamBuilder).
    return false;
  }

  // Used to update widget tree (see StreamBuilder).
  Stream<ThemeData> get themeStream => _themeSubject.stream;
  final _themeSubject = BehaviorSubject<ThemeData>();

  ColorOptions get colorOptions => _colorOptions;

  set colorOptions(ColorOptions value) {
    _colorOptions = value;
    _themeSubject.add(createThemeDataFromColorOptions()); // update widget tree
  }

  List<String> get themes {
    // Return list of themes.
    String themes = _prefs.getString("themeList");
    return themes == null ? [] : themes.split(";");
  }

  open(String theme) {
    // Open theme preference.
    String themeAsJson = _prefs.getString(theme);
    ColorOptions newColorOptions =
        ColorOptions.fromJson(jsonDecode(themeAsJson));
    this.colorOptions = newColorOptions;
```

```dart
  }

  saveAs(String theme) {
    // Create new theme preference.
    String themeAsJson = jsonEncode(_colorOptions.toJson());
    _prefs.setString(theme, themeAsJson);

    // Add new theme preference to list of themes.
    String themeList = _prefs.getString('themeList');
    if ((themeList == null) || (themeList.isEmpty)) {
      _prefs.setString("themeList", theme);
    } else if (themeList.indexOf(theme) == -1) {
      _prefs.setString("themeList", themeList + ";" + theme);
    }
  }
}

class GridViewApp extends StatelessWidget {
  // This widget is the root of your application.
  @override
  Widget build(BuildContext context) {
    ThemeBLOC bloc = ThemeBLOC.of(context);
    return StreamBuilder<ThemeData>(
      // listens to stream in ThemeBLOC to know when to update
      stream: bloc._themeSubject,
      initialData: bloc.startingThemeData,
      builder: (context, snapshot) {
        ThemeData themeData = snapshot.data;
        return MaterialApp(
          title: 'Flutter Demo',
          theme: themeData,
          home: HomeWidget(title: 'Flutter Demo Home Page'),
        );
      });
  }
}

class HomeWidget extends StatefulWidget {
  HomeWidget({Key key, this.title}) : super(key: key);

  final String title;

  @override
  _HomeWidgetState createState() => new _HomeWidgetState();
}

class _HomeWidgetState extends State<HomeWidget> {
  List<Widget> _kittenTiles = [];
  int _gridOptionsIndex = 0;
  List<GridOptions> _gridOptions = [
    GridOptions(
      crossAxisCountPortrait: 2,
      crossAxisCountLandscape: 3,
      childAspectRatio: 1.0,
      padding: 10.0,
      spacing: 10.0),
    GridOptions(
      crossAxisCountPortrait: 3,
```

```
        crossAxisCountLandscape: 4,
        childAspectRatio: 1.5,
        padding: 10.0,
        spacing: 10.0),
    GridOptions(
        crossAxisCountPortrait: 2,
        crossAxisCountLandscape: 3,
        childAspectRatio: 2.0,
        padding: 10.0,
        spacing: 30.0),
];

_HomeWidgetState() : super() {
  for (int i = 200; i < 1000; i += 100) {
    String imageUrl = "http://placekitten.com/200/${i}";
    _kittenTiles.add(GridTile(
        header: GridTileBar(
            title:
                Text("Cats", style: TextStyle(fontWeight: FontWeight.bold))),
        footer: GridTileBar(
            title: Text("How cute",
                textAlign: TextAlign.right,
                style: TextStyle(fontWeight: FontWeight.bold))),
        child: Image.network(imageUrl, fit: BoxFit.cover)));
  }
}

void _tryMoreGridOptions() {
  setState(() {
    _gridOptionsIndex++;
    if (_gridOptionsIndex >= (_gridOptions.length - 1)) {
      _gridOptionsIndex = 0;
    }
  });
}

@override
Widget build(BuildContext context) {
  GridOptions options = _gridOptions[_gridOptionsIndex];
  return Scaffold(
    appBar: AppBar(title: Text("GridView"), actions: [
      IconButton(
          icon: Icon(Icons.settings),
          tooltip: 'Color Options',
          onPressed: () => _showColorOptionsDialog()),
      IconButton(
          icon: Icon(Icons.folder_open),
          tooltip: 'Open',
          onPressed: () {
            List<String> names = ThemeBLOC.of(context).themes;
            _showOpenDialog(context, names);
          }),
      IconButton(
          icon: Icon(Icons.save),
          tooltip: 'Save',
          onPressed: () => _showSaveAsDialog(context))
    ]),
    body: OrientationBuilder(builder: (context, orientation) {
```

```
      return GridView.count(
        crossAxisCount: (orientation == Orientation.portrait)
          ? options.crossAxisCountPortrait
          : options.crossAxisCountLandscape,
        childAspectRatio: options.childAspectRatio,
        padding: EdgeInsets.all(options.padding),
        mainAxisSpacing: options.spacing,
        crossAxisSpacing: options.spacing,
        children: _kittenTiles);
    }),
    bottomNavigationBar: Container(
      child: Text(options.toString()), padding: EdgeInsets.all(20.0)),
    floatingActionButton: new FloatingActionButton(
      onPressed: _tryMoreGridOptions,
      tooltip: 'Try more grid options',
      child: new Icon(Icons.refresh),
    ), // This trailing comma makes auto-formatting nicer for build methods.
  );
}

void _showColorOptionsDialog() async {
  ColorOptions colorOptions = await showDialog<ColorOptions>(
    context: context,
    builder: (BuildContext context) {
      return Dialog(
        child: ColorDialogWidget(ThemeBLOC.of(context).colorOptions));
    });
  if (colorOptions != null) {
    ThemeBLOC.of(context).colorOptions = colorOptions;
  }
}

void _showOpenDialog(BuildContext context, List<String> names) async {
  List<SimpleDialogOption> children = names.map((s) {
    return SimpleDialogOption(
      onPressed: () {
        Navigator.pop(context, s);
      },
      child: Text(s),
    );
  }).toList(growable: false);

  String name = await showDialog<String>(
    context: context,
    builder: (BuildContext context) {
      return SimpleDialog(title: const Text('Open'), children: children);
    });

  if (name != null) {
    setState(() {
      ThemeBLOC.of(context).open(name);
    });
  }
}

void _showSaveAsDialog(BuildContext context) async {
  String name = await showDialog<String>(
    context: context,
```

```
        builder: (BuildContext context) {
          return Dialog(child: SaveAsDialogWidget());
        });
      if (name != null) {
        ThemeBLOC.of(context).saveAs(name);
      }
    }
  }
}

class ColorDialogWidget extends StatefulWidget {
  ColorOptions _colorOptions;

  ColorDialogWidget(this._colorOptions) : super();

  @override
  _CustomDialogWidgetState createState() =>
      new _CustomDialogWidgetState(ColorOptions.copyOf(this._colorOptions));
}

class _CustomDialogWidgetState extends State<ColorDialogWidget> {
  ColorOptions _colorOptions;

  _CustomDialogWidgetState(this._colorOptions);

  @override
  Widget build(BuildContext context) {
    return Container(
        height: 400.0,
        width: 250.0,
        child:
          Column(mainAxisAlignment: MainAxisAlignment.spaceAround, children: <
              Widget>[
          Text("Colors",
            style: TextStyle(fontSize: 20.0, fontWeight: FontWeight.bold)),
          Row(mainAxisAlignment: MainAxisAlignment.center, children: <Widget>[
            Spacer(),
            Text("Primary Color"),
            Spacer(),
            new DropdownButton<Color>(
              value: _colorOptions.primaryColor,
              items: COLOR_DROPDOWN_MENU_ITEMS,
              onChanged: (newValue) {
                setState(() {
                  _colorOptions.primaryColor = newValue;
                });
              },
            ),
            Spacer(),
          ]),
          Row(mainAxisAlignment: MainAxisAlignment.center, children: <Widget>[
            Spacer(),
            Text("Background Color"),
            Spacer(),
            new DropdownButton<Color>(
              value: _colorOptions.scaffoldBackgroundColor,
              items: COLOR_DROPDOWN_MENU_ITEMS,
              onChanged: (newValue) {
                setState(() {
```

```
            _colorOptions.scaffoldBackgroundColor = newValue;
          });
        },
      ),
      Spacer(),
    ]),
    Row(mainAxisAlignment: MainAxisAlignment.center, children: <Widget>[
      Spacer(),
      Text("Accent Color"),
      Spacer(),
      new DropdownButton<Color>(
        value: _colorOptions.accentColor,
        items: COLOR_DROPDOWN_MENU_ITEMS,
        onChanged: (newValue) {
          setState(() {
            _colorOptions.accentColor = newValue;
          });
        },
      ),
      Spacer(),
    ]),
    FlatButton(
        child: Text("Apply"),
        onPressed: () => Navigator.pop(context, _colorOptions))
  ]));
  }
}

class SaveAsDialogWidget extends StatelessWidget {
  static final _formKey = GlobalKey<FormState>();
  static final TextEditingController _nameTextController =
      new TextEditingController();

  SaveAsDialogWidget() : super();

  @override
  Widget build(BuildContext context) {
    return Container(
        height: 260.0,
        width: 250.0,
        child: Padding(
          padding: EdgeInsets.all(10.0),
          child: Form(
            key: _formKey,
            child: Column(
              mainAxisAlignment: MainAxisAlignment.spaceAround,
              children: [
                Text("Save As",
                    style: TextStyle(
                        fontSize: 20.0, fontWeight: FontWeight.bold)),
                TextFormField(
                    autofocus: true,
                    validator: (value) {
                      if (value.isEmpty) {
                        return 'Please enter the name.';
                      }
                      if (value == "themeList") {
                        return 'You cannot use this name.';
```

```
            }
          },
          decoration: InputDecoration(
            icon: const Icon(Icons.location_city),
            hintText: 'Save As',
            labelText: 'Enter the name'),
          keyboardType: TextInputType.text,
          inputFormatters: [
            WhitelistingTextInputFormatter(RegExp(r'[a-z]'))
          ],
          onSaved: (String value) {},
          controller: _nameTextController),
        FlatButton(
          child: Text("Save"),
          onPressed: () {
            if (_formKey.currentState.validate()) {
              _formKey.currentState.save();
              Navigator.pop(context, _nameTextController.text);
              _nameTextController.text = "";
            }
          })
      ]))));
  }
}
```

34. Mixins

Introduction

As mentioned at the start of this book, a Mixin is a class that contains methods for use by other classes without it having to be the parent class of those other classes.
So, a Mixin is a class you can use code from without having to inherit from.

It enables developers to piecemeal classes together without having to get involved with inheritance, abstract classes etc.

Mixins

Mixins are often used with Explicit animation code, where some animation has been coded into a StatefulWidget. See the Animation chapter for more information.

Mixins & Code Generators

Mixins are often used to merge generated code into your code. The generator creates abstract classes containing code. Your code then uses the 'with' + the abstract class name to include that code in your class as a mixin.

Example

If you use the 'json_serializable' package and you invoke the build_runner to build the serialization / deserialization code, some of that generated code resides in an abstract class. Later on, you combine that code into your classes using a mixin.

See Generating Code for Serializing & Deserializing for more information.

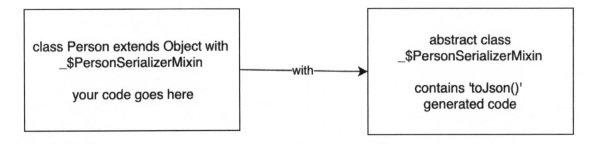

Example – 'mixins'

This app draws circles and squares using a CircleWidget and a SquareWidget. They have corresponding CirclePainter and SquarePainter classes that paint onto the canvas with random colors.

The CirclePainter and SquarePainter use the Colorizer class as a mixin to provide random colors.

Source Code

```
import 'dart:math';

import 'package:flutter/material.dart';

void main() => runApp(new MyApp());

class MyApp extends StatelessWidget {
  // This widget is the root of your application.
  @override
  Widget build(BuildContext context) {
    return new MaterialApp(
      title: 'Flutter Demo',
      theme: new ThemeData(
        primarySwatch: Colors.blue,
      ),
      home: new CircleWidget(),
      routes: <String, WidgetBuilder>{
        '/circle': (context) => CircleWidget(),
        '/square': (context) => SquareWidget(),
      },
    );
  }
}

class Colorizer {
  final _random = new Random();
  int next(int min, int max) => min + _random.nextInt(max - min);

  List<Color> _colors = [];
  _initColors() {
    for (int i = 0; i < 100; i++) {
      _colors.add(Colors.green
```

```dart
          .withRed(next(0, 255))
          .withGreen(next(0, 255))
          .withBlue(next(0, 255)));
    }
  }
}

class CirclePainter extends CustomPainter with Colorizer {
  CirclePainter() {
    _initColors();
  }

  @override
  void paint(Canvas canvas, Size size) {
    for (int i = 0; i < 100; i++) {
      var radius = (i * 10).toDouble();
      canvas.drawCircle(
        new Offset(1000.0, 1000.0),
        radius,
        new Paint()
          ..color = _colors[i]
          ..strokeCap = StrokeCap.round
          ..style = PaintingStyle.stroke
          ..strokeWidth = 15.0);
    }
  }

  @override
  bool shouldRepaint(CirclePainter oldDelegate) {
    return false;
  }
}

class SquarePainter extends CustomPainter with Colorizer {
  SquarePainter() {
    _initColors();
  }

  @override
  void paint(Canvas canvas, Size size) {
    for (int i = 0; i < 100; i++) {
      var inset = (i * 10).toDouble();
      canvas.drawRect(
        new Rect.fromLTRB(inset, inset, 2000.0 - inset, 2000.0 - inset),
        new Paint()
          ..color = _colors[i]
          ..strokeCap = StrokeCap.round
          ..style = PaintingStyle.stroke
          ..strokeWidth = 15.0);
    }
  }

  @override
  bool shouldRepaint(CirclePainter oldDelegate) {
    return false;
  }
}
```

```dart
class CircleWidget extends StatelessWidget {
  CirclePainter _painter = new CirclePainter();
  CircleWidget({Key key}) : super(key: key);

  @override
  Widget build(BuildContext context) {
    return new Scaffold(
      appBar: new AppBar(title: new Text("Circle"), actions: [
        IconButton(
          icon: Icon(Icons.crop_square),
          onPressed: () => Navigator.pushNamed(context, "/square"))
      ]),
      body: new SingleChildScrollView(
        scrollDirection: Axis.horizontal,
        physics: AlwaysScrollableScrollPhysics(),
        child: CustomPaint(
          size: Size(2000.0, 2000.0),
          foregroundPainter: _painter,
        )));
  }
}

class SquareWidget extends StatelessWidget {
  SquarePainter _painter = new SquarePainter();
  SquareWidget({Key key}) : super(key: key);

  @override
  Widget build(BuildContext context) {
    return new Scaffold(
      appBar: new AppBar(
        title: new Text("Square"),
      ),
      body: new SingleChildScrollView(
        scrollDirection: Axis.horizontal,
        physics: AlwaysScrollableScrollPhysics(),
        child: CustomPaint(
          size: Size(2000.0, 2000.0),
          foregroundPainter: _painter,
        )));
  }
}
```

35.Animation

Introduction

Making a really polished app takes more time and effort as the developer has to put more effort into creating an improved user experience, adding animations and effects. However, this time and effort is worth it as these are the things that give an app a 'high quality' feel.

This chapter is about learning how to add these animations to your app as easily as possible.

Animations & State Changes

Animations Are Used to Make UI Changes Look Better

Flutter animations exist to make UI changes (caused by state changes in StatefulWidgets) look better.
It follows that Animations and StatefulWidgets go hand-in-hand.

Examples

- We change the state in our StatefulWidget to show a Dialog box.
- We change state to select a box when the user taps on it.
- We change state to delete an item in a list.

Animations Alter the Way the UI Change Occurs

The same UI changes still occur but the animations apply affects to make the UI change more pleasing to the user.

Many of these animation affects occur by transitioning state (that drives the UI) in a more progressive manner.

Examples

- We change the state in our StatefulWidget to show a Dialog box.
    - The animation could slowly change the visibility of the Dialog box to fade it in.
    - Instead of visibility change straight from 0 to 1, it could be transitioned with 10 intermediate values from 0 to 1 over a second e.g. 0.1, 0.2, 0.3, 0.4 etc.
- We change state to select a box when the user taps on it.
    - The animation could fade in a border color change on the selected box.

- Instead of white to red, it the border color could change from white to red slowly over a second, transitioning through 5 intermediate colors in a second or two.

- We change state to delete an item in a list.
  - The animation could move the deleted item off the screen so it 'slides away'.
  - The animation could change the 'left' position of the item so it transitions from its current 'left' position until it is off-screen, taking a second to do so.

Types of Animations

There are two types of animations available to you in Flutter:
1. Implicit. These are already done for you by Flutter Widgets.
2. Explicit. You have to code these (not too difficult).

Implicit Animations

These are animations in which you change the state of certain Widgets and they handle the animations for you. They are very easy to use but you don't have as much control. Very convenient.

There are many Widgets that are setup to provide animations for you when their property values change. These Widgets are typically prefixed with the word 'Animated':

- AnimatedContainer
- AnimatedList
- AnimatedTextStyle

Example – 'animated_container'

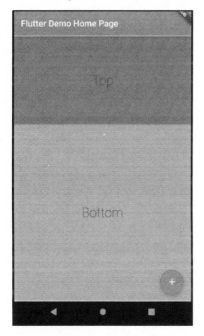 

This app toggles between modes, with the top and bottom panels resizing and changing color in an animated manner.

Source Code

```
import 'package:flutter/material.dart';

void main() => runApp(MyApp());

class MyApp extends StatelessWidget {
  // This widget is the root of your application.
  @override
  Widget build(BuildContext context) {
    return MaterialApp(
      title: 'Flutter Demo',
      theme: ThemeData(
        primarySwatch: Colors.blue,
      ),
      home: MyHomePage(title: 'Flutter Demo Home Page'),
    );
  }
}

class MyHomePage extends StatefulWidget {
  MyHomePage({Key key, this.title}) : super(key: key);
  final String title;

  @override
  _MyHomePageState createState() => _MyHomePageState();
}
```

```
class _MyHomePageState extends State<MyHomePage> {
  bool b = false;

  void _changeMode() {
    setState(() {
      b = !b;
    });
  }

  @override
  Widget build(BuildContext context) {
    return Scaffold(
      appBar: AppBar(
        title: Text(widget.title),
      ),
      body: Center(
        child: Column(
          mainAxisAlignment: MainAxisAlignment.center,
          crossAxisAlignment: CrossAxisAlignment.stretch,
          children: <Widget>[
            AnimatedContainer(
              color: b ? Colors.tealAccent : Colors.blueAccent,
              height: b ? 400.0 : 200.0,
              duration: Duration(seconds: 1),
              child: Center(
                child: Text('Top',
                  style: TextStyle(
                    fontSize: 30.0, fontWeight: FontWeight.w200),
                  textAlign: TextAlign.center))),
            AnimatedContainer(
              color: b ? Colors.redAccent : Colors.orangeAccent,
              height: b ? 200.0 : 400.0,
              duration: Duration(seconds: 1),
              child: Center(
                child: Text('Bottom',
                  style: TextStyle(
                    fontSize: 30.0, fontWeight: FontWeight.w200),
                  textAlign: TextAlign.center))),
          ],
        ),
      ),
      floatingActionButton: FloatingActionButton(
        onPressed: _changeMode,
        tooltip: 'Increment',
        child: Icon(Icons.add),
      ), // This trailing comma makes auto-formatting nicer for build methods.
    );
  }
}
```

Example – 'animated_text'

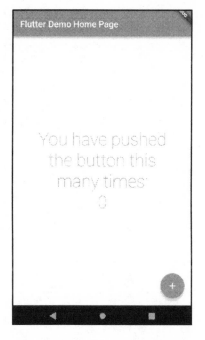
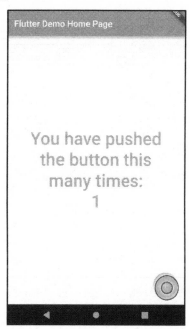

This app is similar to the default Flutter application except that it shows much bigger text. That text is displayed in blue on even numbers, green on odd numbers. There is a one second animation between the text colors.

It's not really much of an animation but it is 'achieved' by wrapping the Text Widgets with a parent AnimatedDefaultTextStyle and setting the duration and style properties of that Widget. The value of the style property changes if the counter is odd or even. The AnimatedDefaultTextStyle simply takes care of the animation when the text style changes.

Source Code

```dart
import 'package:flutter/material.dart';

void main() => runApp(MyApp());

class MyApp extends StatelessWidget {
  // This widget is the root of your application.
  @override
  Widget build(BuildContext context) {
    return MaterialApp(
      title: 'Flutter Demo',
      theme: ThemeData(
        primarySwatch: Colors.blue,
      ),
      home: MyHomePage(title: 'Flutter Demo Home Page'),
    );
  }
}
```

```dart
class MyHomePage extends StatefulWidget {
  MyHomePage({Key key, this.title}) : super(key: key);

  final String title;

  @override
  _MyHomePageState createState() => _MyHomePageState();
}

class _MyHomePageState extends State<MyHomePage> {
  TextStyle textStyle1 = const TextStyle(color: Colors.blue, fontSize: 40.0, fontWeight: FontWeight.w200);
  TextStyle textStyle2 = const TextStyle(color: Colors.green, fontSize: 40.0, fontWeight: FontWeight.w600);
  int _counter = 0;

  void _incrementCounter() {
    setState(() {
      _counter++;
    });
  }

  @override
  Widget build(BuildContext context) {
    TextStyle textStyle = _counter % 2 == 0 ? textStyle1 : textStyle2;
    return Scaffold(
      appBar: AppBar(
        title: Text(widget.title),
      ),
      body: Center(
        child: Column(
          mainAxisAlignment: MainAxisAlignment.center,
          children: <Widget>[
            AnimatedDefaultTextStyle(
              child: Text('You have pushed', textAlign: TextAlign.center,),
                duration: Duration(seconds: 1),style: textStyle),
            AnimatedDefaultTextStyle(
              child: Text('the button this', textAlign: TextAlign.center,),
              duration: Duration(seconds: 1),style: textStyle),
            AnimatedDefaultTextStyle(
              child: Text('many times:', textAlign: TextAlign.center,),
              duration: Duration(seconds: 1),style: textStyle),
            AnimatedDefaultTextStyle(
              child: Text('$_counter', textAlign: TextAlign.center),
              duration: Duration(seconds: 1), style: textStyle),
          ],
        ),
      ),
      floatingActionButton: FloatingActionButton(
        onPressed: _incrementCounter,
        tooltip: 'Increment',
        child: Icon(Icons.add),
      ), // This trailing comma makes auto-formatting nicer for build methods.
    );
  }
}
```

Learn Google Flutter Fast

Example – 'animated_list'

This app shows a list of cats. The user can hit the floating button to add another cat or press down on a cat for a few seconds to delete one. This list is animated, and the cats fade in and fade out.

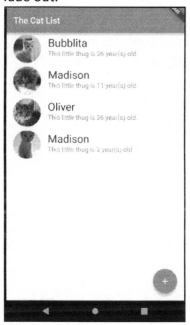

Source Code

```dart
import 'dart:math';

import 'package:flutter/material.dart';

void main() => runApp(MyApp());

class Cat {
  String imageSrc;
  String name;
  int age;
  int votes;

  Cat(this.imageSrc, this.name, this.age, this.votes);

  operator ==(other) => (other is Cat) && (imageSrc == other.imageSrc);

  int get hashCode => imageSrc.hashCode;
}

class MyApp extends StatelessWidget {
  // This widget is the root of your application.
  @override
  Widget build(BuildContext context) {
    return MaterialApp(
      title: 'Cat List',
      theme: ThemeData(
```

Page 417 of 474

```
    primarySwatch: Colors.blue,
  ),
  home: MyHomePage(title: 'The Cat List'),
 );
 }
}

class MyHomePage extends StatefulWidget {
 MyHomePage({Key key, this.title}) : super(key: key);

 final String title;

 @override
 _MyHomePageState createState() => _MyHomePageState();
}

class _MyHomePageState extends State<MyHomePage> {
 final GlobalKey<AnimatedListState> _listKey = GlobalKey();
 List<String> CAT_NAMES = [
  "Tom",
  "Oliver",
  "Ginger",
  "Pontouf",
  "Madison",
  "Bubblita",
  "Bubbles"
 ];

 Random _random = Random();
 List<Cat> _cats = [];

 int next(int min, int max) => min + _random.nextInt(max - min);

 _MyHomePageState() : super() {
  for (int i = 200; i < 250; i += 10) {
   _cats.add(Cat("http://placekitten.com/200/${i}", CAT_NAMES[next(0, 6)],
     next(1, 32), 0));
  }
 }

 _buildItem(Cat cat, {int index = -1}) {
  return ListTile(
   key: Key("ListTile:${cat.hashCode.toString()}"),
   leading: CircleAvatar(
     backgroundImage: NetworkImage(cat.imageSrc), radius: 32.0),
   title: Text(cat.name, style: TextStyle(fontSize: 25.0)),
   subtitle: Text("This little thug is ${cat.age} year(s) old.",
     style: TextStyle(fontSize: 15.0)),
    onLongPress: index != null ? () => _remove(index) : null
  );
 }

 _add() {
  setState(() {
   _cats.add(Cat("http://placekitten.com/200/${next(200, 300)}",
     CAT_NAMES[next(0, 6)], next(1, 32), 0));
   _listKey.currentState
     .insertItem(_cats.length - 1, duration: Duration(seconds: 2));
```

```
      ;
    });
  }

  _remove(int index) {
    setState(() {
      Cat cat = _cats[index];
      _cats.remove(cat);
      _listKey.currentState.removeItem(
        index,
          (BuildContext context, Animation<double> animation) {
          return FadeTransition(
            opacity:
            CurvedAnimation(parent: animation, curve: Interval(0.5, 1.0)),
            child: SizeTransition(
              sizeFactor:
              CurvedAnimation(parent: animation, curve: Interval(0.0, 1.0)),
              axisAlignment: 0.0,
              child: _buildItem(cat),
            ),
          );
        },
        duration: Duration(milliseconds: 600),
      );
    });
  }

  @override
  Widget build(BuildContext context) {
    return Scaffold(
      appBar: AppBar(
        title: Text(widget.title),
      ),
      body: AnimatedList(
        key: _listKey,
        initialItemCount: _cats.length,
        itemBuilder:
          (BuildContext context, int index, Animation<double> animation) {
          return FadeTransition(
            opacity: animation,
            child: _buildItem(_cats[index], index: index), //Change
          );
        },
      ),
      floatingActionButton: FloatingActionButton(
        onPressed: _add,
        tooltip: 'Increment',
        child: Icon(Icons.add),
      ),
    );
  }
}
```

Explicit Animations

These are animations that you code with Animation objects. They are more difficult to use but aren't really that difficult to master. They also give you a lot of control.

Animation

The Animation object holds the current state of the animation and nothing else. It is purely about the state, not what appears on the screen.

State:

- Status
    - Current status of animation
        - dismissed
        - forward
        - reverse
        - completed
- Value
    - Whatever value we want to control with the animation.
    - This is a generic so can be of whatever type you want.

Listeners

You can add the following listeners to this class:

- addListener / removeListener
    - This listener is called every time the value changes.
- addStatusListener / removeStatusListener
    - This listener is called every time the status of the animation changes.
    - This is useful if you want to repeat the validation.
        - Example.
            - You could add code here to reverse the animation once it completes:

```
animation.addStatusListener((AnimationStatus status){
  switch(status){
    ///
    /// At the beginning, play forward
    ///
    case AnimationStatus.dismissed:
      _controller.forward();
      break;

    ///
    /// At the end, play in reverse
    ///
    case AnimationStatus.completed:
      _controller.reverse();
```

```
        break;
    }
});
```

AnimationController

The AnimationController extends the Animation class.

It generates a linear series of values (used to animate something) from the lower bound to the higher bound in in the specified duration of time, calling a ticker callback.

It generates a new value whenever the device is ready to display a new frame (so this happens about 60 values per second).

The AnimationController should be constructed in the 'initState' method of the State class of your StatefulWidget. It should also be destroyed in the 'dispose' method of the State class of your StatefulWidget.

Constructor Arguments

These are the most commonly-used constructor arguments in the AnimationController.

Argument	Description
duration	The duration of the Animation. Optional. However, you need to set the duration before the animation is invoked.
vsync	The ticker provider. Required. Usually set to 'this'.
lowerBound	Value to start with in Animation. Optional. Defaults to 0.
upperBound	Value to end with in Animation. Optional. Defaults to 1.

TickerProvider

When you create the AnimationController, you specify a TickerProvider. This class provides Ticker objects, but it also enables or disables these tickers (and thus animation controllers) in the Widget subtree, based on whether the Widget subtree is visible or not (ie enabled). This is important because Tickers can use a lot of system resources.

Luckily, when you create a class that is a TickerProvider you don't have to write any of this logic. All you do is create a Stateful Widget that has your animation code (more on that in a minute), that uses one of the two mixins available:

1. SingleTickerProviderStateMixin
    - Suitable for when you use only one AnimationController.

2. TickerProviderStateMixin
   - Suitable for when you use more than one AnimationController.

Ticker

A ticker is a class that calls its callback once per animation frame.

When created, a ticker is initially disabled. Call start to enable the ticker.
A Ticker can be silenced by setting muted to true. While silenced, time still elapses, and start and stop can still be called, but no callbacks are called.

Example – 'animated_progress_circle'

When the user clicks on the floating refresh button at the bottom, this app shows an animated progress circle.

It uses an AnimationController in the _HomeWidgetState object that has a value change of 0 to 1 over a duration of 10 seconds. It has a listener that calls a 'setState' to ensure that the HomeWidget is rebuilt everytime the value in the AnimationController changes. The HomeWidget 'build' code draws a progress circle using a CustomPaint object, passing in the percentage.

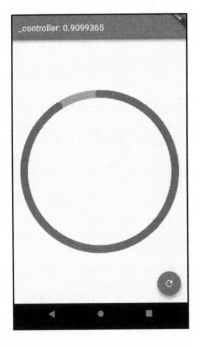
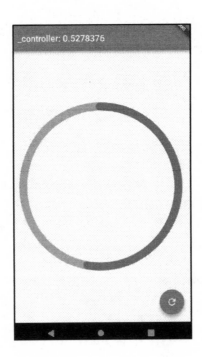

Source Code

```
import 'dart:math';
```

```
import 'package:flutter/material.dart';

void main() => runApp(MyApp());

class MyApp extends StatelessWidget {
 // This widget is the root of your application.
 @override
 Widget build(BuildContext context) {
  return MaterialApp(
   title: 'Flutter Demo',
   theme: ThemeData(
    primarySwatch: Colors.blue,
   ),
   home: HomeWidget(),
  );
 }
}

class HomeWidget extends StatefulWidget {
 HomeWidget({Key key}) : super(key: key);

 @override
 _HomeWidgetState createState() => _HomeWidgetState();
}

class _HomeWidgetState extends State<HomeWidget>
  with SingleTickerProviderStateMixin {
 AnimationController _controller;

 void _performAnimation() {
  setState(() {
   if (_controller.status != AnimationStatus.forward) {
    _controller.forward(from: 0.0);
   }
  });
 }

 @override
 void initState() {
  _controller = AnimationController(
    duration: const Duration(seconds: 10),
    vsync: this)
   ..addListener(() {
    setState(() {
     // Force build.
    });
   });
 }

 @override
 Widget build(BuildContext context) {
  return Scaffold(
   appBar: AppBar(
    title: Text("_controller: ${_controller.value}"),
   ),
   body: Container(child:
     Padding(
      padding: const EdgeInsets.all(20.0),
```

```
        child: CustomPaint(
          foregroundPainter: new ProgressCirclePainter(
            lineColor: Colors.amber,
            completeColor: Colors.blueAccent,
            completePercent: _controller.value * 100,
            width: 18.0)),
      ),
      constraints: BoxConstraints.expand(),
      margin: const EdgeInsets.all(8.0),
    ),
    floatingActionButton: FloatingActionButton(
      onPressed: _performAnimation,
      child: Icon(Icons.refresh),
    ), // This trailing comma makes auto-formatting nicer for build methods.
  );
  }
}

class ProgressCirclePainter extends CustomPainter {
  Color lineColor;
  Color completeColor;
  double completePercent;
  double width;

  ProgressCirclePainter(
    {this.lineColor, this.completeColor, this.completePercent, this.width});

  @override
  void paint(Canvas canvas, Size size) {
    Paint line = new Paint()
      ..color = lineColor
      ..strokeCap = StrokeCap.round
      ..style = PaintingStyle.stroke
      ..strokeWidth = width;
    Paint complete = new Paint()
      ..color = completeColor
      ..strokeCap = StrokeCap.round
      ..style = PaintingStyle.stroke
      ..strokeWidth = width;
    Offset center = new Offset(size.width / 2, size.height / 2);
    double radius = min(size.width / 2, size.height / 2);
    canvas.drawCircle(center, radius, line);
    double arcAngle = 2 * pi * (completePercent / 100);
    canvas.drawArc(new Rect.fromCircle(center: center, radius: radius), -pi / 2,
      arcAngle, false, complete);
  }

  @override
  bool shouldRepaint(CustomPainter oldDelegate) {
    return true;
  }
}
```

Curved Animations

This example above performed a linear, smooth animation. The yellow progress moved smoothly around the circle. However, that is not the only option.

You can use a CurvedAnimation to make the animation transition differently, applying a curve to the animation to modify it. You construct it using the existing AnimationController as its parent, along with the curve. The curve determines the transition. In the exercise below we use a 'bounceInOut' curve to make the progress bar bounce from one side to the other.

Exercise

Step 1 – Open the Example 'animated_progress_circle'.
Open the Example 'animated_progress_circle'.

Step 2 – Add an Instance Variable for the Curved Animation.
See the code in bold below.

```
class _HomeWidgetState extends State<HomeWidget>
  with SingleTickerProviderStateMixin {
  AnimationController _controller;
  CurvedAnimation _curvedAnimation;
```

Step 3 – Set the Instance Variable for the Curved Animation.
See the code in bold below.

```
@override
void initState() {
  _controller =
    AnimationController(duration: const Duration(seconds: 10), vsync: this)
      ..addListener(() {
        setState(() {
          // Force build.
        });
      });
  _curvedAnimation =
    CurvedAnimation(parent: _controller, curve: Curves.bounceInOut);
}
```

Step 4 – Change the Build Method to Use the Curved Animation Value.
See the code in bold below.

```
@override
Widget build(BuildContext context) {
  return Scaffold(
    appBar: AppBar(
      title: Text("_controller: ${_controller.value}"),
    ),
    body: Container(
      child: Padding(
        padding: const EdgeInsets.all(20.0),
        child: CustomPaint(
          foregroundPainter: new ProgressCirclePainter(
            lineColor: Colors.amber,
            completeColor: Colors.blueAccent,
            completePercent: _curvedAnimation.value * 100,
            width: 18.0)),
      ),
```

```
    constraints: BoxConstraints.expand(),
    margin: const EdgeInsets.all(8.0),
  ),
  floatingActionButton: FloatingActionButton(
    onPressed: _performAnimation,
    child: Icon(Icons.refresh),
  ), // This trailing comma makes auto-formatting nicer for build methods.
  );
}
```

Tweens

Introduction

Like Controllers, Tweens generate a linear series of values (used to animate something) from the lower bound to a higher bound.

You can attach one or more Tweens to a parent Animation Controller so that multiple tweens can generate values at the same time, controlled by the same animation. Refer to the example below for this.

Tweens can generate values of different types. For example, Colors. A ColorTween can linearly move from one color to another. Refer to the example below for this.

Types of Tweens:

- AlignmentGeometryTween
- AlignmentTween
- BorderRadiusTween
- BorderTween
- BoxConstraintsTween
- ColorTween
- ConstantTween
- DecorationTween
- EdgeInsetsGeometryTween
- EdgeInsetsTween
- FractionalOffsetTween
- IntTween
- MaterialPointArcTween
- Matrix4Tween
- RectTween
- RelativeRectTween
- ReverseTween
- ShapeBorderTween
- SizeTween

- StepTween
- TextStyleTween
- ThemeDataTween

Example 'yes_no'

This app enables the user to select between a yes and no. It uses Tweens to perform animation for the circle background color and the text foreground color.

Source Code

```
import 'package:flutter/material.dart';

void main() => runApp(MyApp());

class MyApp extends StatelessWidget {
  // This widget is the root of your application.
  @override
  Widget build(BuildContext context) {
    return MaterialApp(
      title: 'Flutter Demo',
      theme: ThemeData(
          primarySwatch: Colors.blue,
          scaffoldBackgroundColor: Colors.teal),
      home: MyHomePage(title: 'Flutter Demo Home Page'),
    );
  }
}

class MyHomePage extends StatefulWidget {
  MyHomePage({Key key, this.title}) : super(key: key);
```

```dart
  final String title;

  @override
  _MyHomePageState createState() => _MyHomePageState();
}

class _MyHomePageState extends State<MyHomePage> {

  _yesOnTap() {
    print('yes');
  }

  _noOnTap() {
    print('no');
  }

  @override
  Widget build(BuildContext context) {
    return Scaffold(
      appBar: AppBar(
        title: Text(widget.title),
      ),
      body: Column(
          mainAxisAlignment: MainAxisAlignment.spaceEvenly,
          crossAxisAlignment: CrossAxisAlignment.center,
          children: <Widget>[
            Text("Do you want to\nbuy this item?",
                textAlign: TextAlign.center,
                style: TextStyle(
                    color: Colors.white,
                    fontSize: 40.0,
                    fontWeight: FontWeight.w200)),
            Row(
              mainAxisAlignment: MainAxisAlignment.center,
              children: <Widget>[
                Spacer(flex: 2),
                SelectButton(text: "YES", onTap: _yesOnTap),
                Spacer(),
                SelectButton(text: "NO", onTap: _noOnTap),
                Spacer(flex: 2),
              ],
            )
          ]),
    );
  }
}

class SelectButton extends StatefulWidget {
  final String text;
  final VoidCallback onTap;

  SelectButton({@required this.text, @required this.onTap});

  @override
  _SelectButtonState createState() => _SelectButtonState();
}

class _SelectButtonState extends State<SelectButton>
```

```
    with SingleTickerProviderStateMixin {
AnimationController _controller;
Animation<Color> _circleTween;
Animation<Color> _textTween;

@override
void initState() {
  // Create animation controller.
  _controller =
    AnimationController(duration: const Duration(seconds: 1), vsync: this)
      ..addListener(() {
        setState(() {
          // Force build.
        });
      })
      ..addStatusListener((AnimationStatus status) {
        if (status == AnimationStatus.completed) {
          waitThenReset();
        }
      });

  // Create tweens.
  _circleTween = new ColorTween(
    begin: Colors.teal,
    end: Colors.white,
  ).animate(_controller);

  _textTween = new ColorTween(
    begin: Colors.white,
    end: Colors.teal,
  ).animate(_controller);
}

Future waitThenReset() async {
  await new Future.delayed(new Duration(milliseconds: 1000), () {
    _controller.reverse(from: 0.9);
    widget.onTap();
  });
}

_onTap() {
  _controller.forward(from: 0.0);
}

@override
Widget build(BuildContext context) {
  double leftPos = widget.text.length == 3 ? 22.0 : 27.0;
  return GestureDetector(
    onTap: _onTap,
    child: Material(
      type: MaterialType.transparency,
      child: Ink(
        decoration: BoxDecoration(
          border: Border.all(color: Colors.white, width: 1),
          color: _circleTween.value,
          shape: BoxShape.circle,
        ),
        width: 100.0,
```

```
              height: 100.0,
              child: Padding(
                  padding: EdgeInsets.only(left: leftPos, top: 32.0),
                  child: Text(widget.text,
                      style: TextStyle(
                          color: _textTween.value,
                          fontSize: 28.0,
                          fontWeight:
                              _controller.status == AnimationStatus.completed
                                  ? FontWeight.w500
                                  : FontWeight.w200))))),
    );
  }
}
```

Custom Behavior

You can add a status listener to the AnimationController to implement custom behavior.

Back & Forth

In the code below, we apply the following logic to make the animation go back and forth endlessly:

- When the animation completes, you can make it reverse.
- When it finishes, you can make it go forward again.

```
_controller =
    AnimationController(duration: const Duration(seconds: 2), vsync: this)
      ..addListener(() {
      setState(() {
        // Force build.
      });
    })
      ..addStatusListener((AnimationStatus status) {
      if (status == AnimationStatus.dismissed) {
        _controller.forward();
      } else if (status == AnimationStatus.completed) {
        _controller.reverse();
      }
    });
```

Doing Something Once the Animation Completes

You can also add code to the status listeners of AnimationControllers to do something once an animation has completed.

Example of Use

- The user buys something on the shopping cart.
- You perform a 'thank you' animation.
- You navigate away after the animation completes.

Example

If you look at the Tween example it waits a second, then resets the button.
See the code in bold below.

```
_controller =
    AnimationController(duration: const Duration(seconds: 1), vsync: this)
      ..addListener(() {
       setState(() {
         // Force build.
       });
      })
      ..addStatusListener((AnimationStatus status) {
       if (status == AnimationStatus.completed) {
         waitThenReset();
       }
      });
```

Transforms

You can use a Transform Widget with an AnimationController to apply transformations to child
Widgets:

- Rotate
- Scale
- Move
- Skew

Example 'transform_rotate'

This app shows the planet earth rotating.

Source Code

```
import 'dart:math' as math;
import 'package:flutter/material.dart';

void main() => runApp(MyApp());

class MyApp extends StatelessWidget {
  // This widget is the root of your application.
  @override
  Widget build(BuildContext context) {
    return MaterialApp(
      title: 'Earth',
      theme: ThemeData(
        primarySwatch: Colors.blue, scaffoldBackgroundColor: Colors.white),
      home: MyHomePage(title: 'Earth'),
    );
  }
}

class MyHomePage extends StatefulWidget {
  MyHomePage({Key key, this.title}) : super(key: key);

  final String title;

  @override
  _MyHomePageState createState() => _MyHomePageState();
}

class _MyHomePageState extends State<MyHomePage>
    with SingleTickerProviderStateMixin {
  AnimationController _controller;

  @override
  void initState() {
    // Create animation controller.
    _controller =
      AnimationController(duration: const Duration(seconds: 10), vsync: this)
        ..addListener(() {
          setState(() {
            // Force build.
          });
        })
        ..addStatusListener((AnimationStatus status) {
          if (status == AnimationStatus.dismissed) {
            _controller.forward();
          } else if (status == AnimationStatus.completed) {
            _controller.reverse();
          }
        });

    // Start animation automatically.
    _controller.forward(from: 0.0);
  }

  @override
  Widget build(BuildContext context) {
    return Scaffold(
```

```
appBar: AppBar(
  title: Text(widget.title),
  ),
  body: Center(
    child: Transform.scale(
      scale: 1.6,
      child: Transform.rotate(
        angle: math.pi * _controller.value, // rotate animation
        child: Image.network(
          "https://ak7.picdn.net/shutterstock/videos/3010597/thumb/1.jpg")))),
  );
}
}
```

Further Reading

https://www.youtube.com/watch?v=dNSteCm-cEY
https://flutter.dev/docs/development/ui/animations/tutorial
https://www.didierboelens.com/2018/06/animations-in-flutter---easy-guide---tutorial/
https://medium.com/flutter-community/a-deep-dive-into-transform-widgets-in-flutter-4dc32cd575a9
https://iirokrankka.com/2018/03/14/orchestrating-multiple-animations-into-visual-enter-animation/

36.Debugging & Performance Profiling

> *"Suddenly, the world I had scrutinised for so long was all around me, as if I had leaned forward and climbed into the television like Alice through the looking-glass. I had no idea just how deep the rabbit hole would go."*
>
> *Simon Pegg*

Introduction

This purpose of this chapter is to help you debug, diagnose issues with and profile your Flutter app. Flutter gives us amazing tools for this purpose, which can provide you with any information you should require. In fact, almost too much information! This is a very deep subject and the most this chapter can do is 'dip your toe in the water'. Flutter Debugging & Profiling is quite a rabbit-hole!

Debugging

You should be running Flutter in checked mode.

Performance Profiling

When you are profiling, you should ensure the following:

- You are connected to a real device.
  - An emulator can 'emulate' the real thing but under the covers it's not the same thing.

- You are running Flutter in profile mode.
  - This mode was written especially for this task, with enough performance to simulate release mode but enough information to help you profile the app.

Programmatical Options

When you write code, it has a purpose – to perform a certain task.
However, you can augment that code with additional code that helps you diagnose issues and performance profile your Flutter app:

- Debugger Statements.

- When you are debugging and attempting to reproduce a condition, you can add temporary code to detect that condition and launch the debugger.

- Print to the Console.
  - You can output to the console to provide runtime information about what is happening in the program, what are variable values set to.
  - You can add output the time taken to perform certain tasks, so that you can change your code to improve that time.

- Assertions.
  - You can add assertions to enable programs to detect their own defects.

Add Debugger Statements

With this statement, Flutter enables the developer to invoke your IDE's debugger from your code. This is similar to the 'JavaScript' debugger statement. This statement has an optional 'when' argument which you can specify to only break when a certain condition is true. Remember to import 'dart:developer' at the top!

Exercise – 'debugging'

This exercise involves the default Flutter app modified to do into debug mode when the counter reaches 5.

Step 1 – Create Default Flutter App
Follow the instructions in <u>Generate Your First App</u>
Leave project open.

Step 2 – Replace Application Code
Replace contents of file 'main.dart' in folder 'lib' with the following:

```
import 'package:flutter/material.dart';
import 'dart:developer';

void main() => runApp(new MyApp());

class MyApp extends StatelessWidget {
  // This widget is the root of your application.
  @override
  Widget build(BuildContext context) {
    return new MaterialApp(
      title: 'Flutter Demo',
      theme: new ThemeData(
        primarySwatch: Colors.blue,
      ),
      home: new MyHomePage(title: 'Flutter Demo Home Page'),
    );
  }
}
```

```
class MyHomePage extends StatefulWidget {
  MyHomePage({Key key, this.title}) : super(key: key);
  final String title;

  @override
  _MyHomePageState createState() => new _MyHomePageState();
}

class _MyHomePageState extends State<MyHomePage> {
  int _counter = 0;

  void _incrementCounter() {
    debugger(when: _counter > 5);
    setState(() {
      _counter++;
    });
  }

  @override
  Widget build(BuildContext context) {
    return new Scaffold(
      appBar: new AppBar(
        title: new Text(widget.title),
      ),
      body: new Center(
        child: new Column(
          mainAxisAlignment: MainAxisAlignment.center,
          children: <Widget>[
            new Text(
              'You have pushed the button this many times:',
            ),
            new Text(
              '$_counter',
              style: Theme.of(context).textTheme.display1,
            ),
          ],
        ),
      ),
      floatingActionButton: new FloatingActionButton(
        onPressed: _incrementCounter,
        tooltip: 'Increment',
        child: new Icon(Icons.add),
      ), // This trailing comma makes auto-formatting nicer for build methods.
    );
  }
}
```

Step 3 – Open Emulator & Run
Follow the instructions in Open Android Emulator & Run Your First App
Run the app in debug mode and hit the '+' floating button until your IDE goes into debug mode and highlights the line containing 'debugger'.

Add Print & DebugPrint Statements

- Both of these print to the system console.

- The print statement comes from Dart, it is a part of dart.core.
  - According to the official documentation: "If you output too much at once, then Android sometimes discards some log lines".
- The debugPrint statement comes from Flutter, it is part of the Flutter foundation library.
  - The Flutter Foundation library contains the core Flutter framework primitives, which are used by other parts of the Flutter framework.
  - According to the official documentation, this does not discard log lines.

Interpolation

Both enable string interpolation, for example:

Example:

```
int a = 123;
String b = "abc";
print('a:${a}, b:${b}');
```

Outputs:

```
I/flutter ( 4397): a:123, b:abc
```

Outputting Object Values

When outputting objects, these statements will attempt to perform a 'toString' on the object.

Example:

```
void main() {
  Employee employee = new Employee("Mark", "Smith", "925 Langford Avenue",
    "Appt 2", "Atlanta", "GA", "303250", "232-323-1232");
  print('employee:${employee}');
  runApp(MyApp());
}

class Employee {
  String firstName;
  String lastName;
  String addr1;
  String addr2;
  String city;
  String state;
  String zip;
  String ssn;

  Employee(this.firstName, this.lastName, this.addr1, this.addr2, this.city,
    this.state, this.zip, this.ssn);

  @override
  String toString() {
    return 'Employee{firstName: $firstName, lastName: $lastName, addr1: $addr1, addr2: $addr2, city:
$city, state: $state, zip: $zip, ssn: $ssn}';
  }
}
```

Outputs:

```
I/flutter ( 4397): employee:Employee{firstName: Mark, lastName: Smith, addr1: 925 Langford Avenue,
addr2: Appt 2, city: Atlanta, state: GA, zip: 303250, ssn: 232-323-1232}
```

Add Assertions

As mentioned above, you can add assertions to your own code to defensively check for unexpected conditions or values, just in case they occur. There is more on the subject of defensive programming here: http://wiki.c2.com/?DefensiveProgramming .

You can develop your Flutter code in Checked (or Debug) Mode, which checks things these assertions. Later on, you can deploy the compiled code that runs in Release mode, skipping them as they are no longer necessary.

Exercise

Step 1 – Create Default Flutter App
Follow the instructions in Generate Your First App
Leave project open.

Step 2 – Amend Method
Replace the existing method '_incrementCounter' in '_MyHomePageState' with the following:

```
void _incrementCounter() {
  setState(() {
    _counter++;
    assert(_counter < 5);
  });
}
```

Step 3 – Open Emulator & Run
Follow the instructions in Open Android Emulator & Run Your First App
The app should run as normal.

Step 4 – Cause Assertion to Occur
Click on the floating '+' button 5 times until the assertion occurs.
You should see the following exception in the console, as you can see the assertion caused an exception:

```
I/flutter ( 4397): ════╡ EXCEPTION CAUGHT BY GESTURE
╞══════════════════════════════════════════════════════════════════
════
I/flutter ( 4397): The following assertion was thrown while handling a gesture:
I/flutter ( 4397): 'package:flutter_app2/main.dart': Failed assertion: line 36 pos 14: '_counter < 5': is not
true.
I/flutter ( 4397):
I/flutter ( 4397): Either the assertion indicates an error in the framework itself, or we should provide
substantially
I/flutter ( 4397): more information in this error message to help you determine and fix the underlying
cause.
I/flutter ( 4397): In either case, please report this assertion by filing a bug on GitHub:
```

```
I/flutter ( 4397):   https://github.com/flutter/flutter/issues/new?template=BUG.md
I/flutter ( 4397):
I/flutter ( 4397): When the exception was thrown, this was the stack:
I/flutter ( 4397): #2    _MyHomePageState._incrementCounter.<anonymous closure>
(package:flutter_app2/main.dart:36:14)
I/flutter ( 4397): #3    State.setState (package:flutter/src/widgets/framework.dart:1122:30)
I/flutter ( 4397): #4    _MyHomePageState._incrementCounter (package:flutter_app2/main.dart:34:5)
I/flutter ( 4397): #5    _InkResponseState._handleTap (package:flutter/src/material/ink_well.dart:513:14)
I/flutter ( 4397): #6    _InkResponseState.build.<anonymous closure>
(package:flutter/src/material/ink_well.dart:568:30)
I/flutter ( 4397): #7    GestureRecognizer.invokeCallback
(package:flutter/src/gestures/recognizer.dart:120:24)
I/flutter ( 4397): #8    TapGestureRecognizer._checkUp (package:flutter/src/gestures/tap.dart:242:9)
I/flutter ( 4397): #9    TapGestureRecognizer.acceptGesture
(package:flutter/src/gestures/tap.dart:204:7)
I/flutter ( 4397): #10    GestureArenaManager.sweep (package:flutter/src/gestures/arena.dart:156:27)
I/flutter ( 4397): #11    _WidgetsFlutterBinding&BindingBase&GestureBinding.handleEvent
(package:flutter/src/gestures/binding.dart:218:20)
I/flutter ( 4397): #12    _WidgetsFlutterBinding&BindingBase&GestureBinding.dispatchEvent
(package:flutter/src/gestures/binding.dart:192:22)
I/flutter ( 4397): #13    _WidgetsFlutterBinding&BindingBase&GestureBinding._handlePointerEvent
(package:flutter/src/gestures/binding.dart:149:7)
I/flutter ( 4397): #14    _WidgetsFlutterBinding&BindingBase&GestureBinding._flushPointerEventQueue
(package:flutter/src/gestures/binding.dart:101:7)
I/flutter ( 4397): #15    _WidgetsFlutterBinding&BindingBase&GestureBinding._handlePointerDataPacket
(package:flutter/src/gestures/binding.dart:85:7)
I/flutter ( 4397): #19    _invoke1 (dart:ui/hooks.dart:223:10)
I/flutter ( 4397): #20    _dispatchPointerDataPacket (dart:ui/hooks.dart:144:5)
I/flutter ( 4397): (elided 5 frames from class _AssertionError and package dart:async)
I/flutter ( 4397):
I/flutter ( 4397): Handler: onTap
I/flutter ( 4397): Recognizer:
I/flutter ( 4397):   TapGestureRecognizer#9510a(debugOwner: GestureDetector, state: ready, won arena,
finalPosition:
I/flutter ( 4397):   Offset(366.4, 647.5), sent tap down)
I/flutter ( 4397):
════════════════════════════════════════════════════════════════════════════════════════════
════════════════════════

I/flutter ( 4397): Another exception was thrown: 'package:flutter_app2/main.dart': Failed assertion: line
36 pos 14: '_counter < 5': is not true.
```

Step 5 – Optional – Run App in Release Mode

Connect your device and add the –release argument to your run configuration in your editor. Or run the following in your project root (I had to specify the device):

```
flutter run --profile
More than one device connected; please specify a device with the '-d <deviceId>' flag, or use '-d all' to act
on all devices.

SM G960U1              • 59334a534c573398 • android-arm64 • Android 9 (API 28)
Android SDK built for x86 • emulator-5554   • android-x86   • Android 9 (API 28) (emulator)
marcuss-mbp:flutter_app2 marcusclow$ flutter run --profile -d 59334a534c573398
```

The app should now come up on your phone. However, the assertion should no longer affect the app, you should be able to hit the '+' button as many times as you want to, without an exception.

Service Extensions

Introduction

Flutter has service extensions that you can turn on and off either as the app is running, or programatically. Service extensions unwrap special Flutter functionality to help you debug & diagnose issues with your app.

We are not going to cover all of them but let's cover some of the more important ones.

Performance Overlay

Flutter apps should run at 60 frames per second, with a smoothly-rendered user interface. Each Flutter UI frame is processed by two threads – first by the UI thread, then by the GPU thread. Each of these threads has a bar chart in the Performance Overlay. The GPU thread frame performance is the first bar chart, the UI thread frame performance is the second bar chart.

The purpose of the Performance Overlay is to be able to use the app while at the same time viewing the frame performance in these bar-charts. This enables the user to see where performance issues occur, as they will appear as tall bars in the charts.

Note that the Performance Overlay displays Max Frame Time and Average Frame Time.

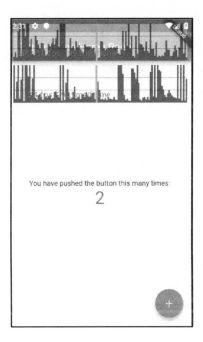

GPU Thread

GPU stands for 'Graphics Processing Unit'.
Flutter comes with its own rendering engine, which runs on this thread. It executes Flutter graphics code, working with a rendering engine underneath, be it hardware or software.

UI Thread

The UI thread executes Dart UI code.

Frames

Each frame has to run through both the UI thread and the GPU thread.
To achieve 60 frames per second, each frame should take no longer than 8 milliseconds to prepare.
Flutter achieves this amazing feat by using extremely efficient change detection (see next chapter) and by using parallelism, the UI thread preparing one frame while the GPU thread prepares the other.

Janky Frames

In the Flutter documentation, it states that any frame that takes longer than that extremely short period is called a 'Janky' frame.

Graphs

The Performance Overlay shows you two bar graphs overlaid on top of the app.
- The GPU thread is shown at the top.
- The UI thread is shown at the bottom.

X Axis

That shows the last 300 frames in a rotating buffer. The last thread is shown in green or red.

Y Axis

Each graph shows the performance of each frame on the 'y' axis. A tall 'y' axis bar means a slow frame.

Detecting Janky Threads

Start your your app in profile mode with the Performance Overlay turned on and try out your code. Watch these graphs for Janky Threads with really high bars and try to figure out the offending code by reproducing the problem.

Further Reading

https://flutter.dev/docs/testing/debugging#performanceoverlay

Show Paint Baselines (debugPaintSizeEnabled)

This shows you the paint size of each widget, adding borders so you can see where they begin and end. Useful when you are writing the UI.

Show Material Grid

This shows you a grid so you can ensure that your UI elements line up as expected. Useful when you are writing the UI.

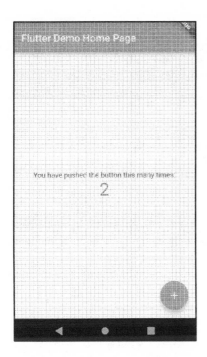

Turn Service Extensions On/Off from Android Studio

- Open Flutter Inspector.
- Hit the white cog to view options.
- Select mode option.

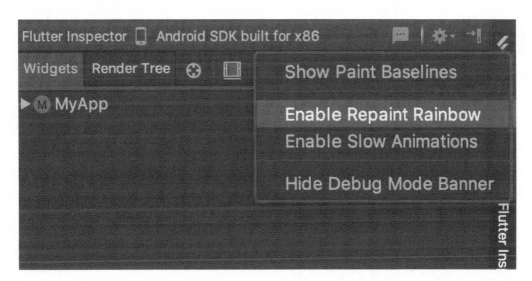

Turn Service Extensions On/Off from Visual Studio Code

- Open Command Palette.
- Type Flutter to view list of available Flutter-related commands.
- Select command for desired mode from the list.

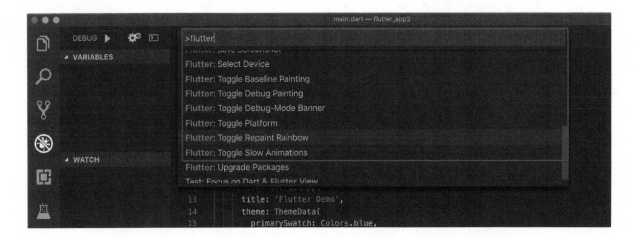

Turn Service Extensions On/Off from Command Line

Run the Flutter app from the command line in the usual manner with the Flutter 'run' command. When you run the Flutter app in this mode, there are various hotkeys available, including one for service extensions:

- p – turns on Show Paint Baselines

```
flutter run
```

Turn Service Extensions On/Off Programmatically

There are two ways that you can turn these extensions from your code.

Modify the Entry Point 'main' to Turn on Extensions

You can add code to the entry point of your app to turn on some extensions.
More info here: https://flutter.dev/docs/testing/ui-performance - debug-flags

Example

```
import 'package:flutter/material.dart';
import 'package:flutter/rendering.dart';

void main() {
  debugPaintSizeEnabled = true;
  runApp(MyApp());
}
```

This turns on a mode to show you the paint size of your widget, adding a border around them so you can see where they begin and end.

Change MaterialApp Constructor Arguments

You may remember that this object builds the foundation for your app. However, it also allows you to turn on some extensions using constructor arguments.

- debugShowMaterialGrid
  - o Defaults to false if not specified.
  - o Shows a UI grid to help you line Widgets up.
- showPerformanceOverlay
  - o Defaults to false if not specified.
  - o Shows a performance graph on top of the app.
- checkerboardRasterCacheImages
  - o Defaults to false if not specified.
  - o Optional rendering performance optimization.
- checkerboardOffscreenLayers
  - o Defaults to false if not specified.
  - o Useful for debugging rendering performance.
- showSemanticsDebugger
  - o Defaults to false if not specified.
  - o Turns on an overlay that shows the accessibility information reported by the framework.
- debugShowCheckedModeBanner
  - o Defaults to true if not specified.
  - o Hides or shows the debug triangle in the corner that indicates that the app is running in slow (checked) mode.

Dart Observatory

Introduction

The official Dart document states:

Observatory allows you to peek inside a running Dart virtual machine (VM) on demand and provides live, immediate reporting of data. You can use it to browse most aspects of an application. Some of Observatory's features allow you to:

- Determine where an app is spending its time.
- Examine allocated memory.
- See which lines of code have executed.
- Debug memory leaks.
- Debug memory fragmentation.

Part of the Dart SDK

You get Observatory, for free, when you download the Dart SDK.

Starting the Observatory

Android Studio

- Open Flutter Inspector.
- Click on Stopwatch.

Visual Studio Code

- Open Command Palette.
- Type Flutter to view Flutter commands.
- Select 'Open Observatory Timeline'.

Command Line

When you run Flutter using the command line below:

```
flutter run
```

it displays the following:

Using hardware rendering with device Android SDK built for x86. If you get graphics artifacts, consider enabling software rendering with "--enable-software-rendering". Launching lib/main.dart on Android SDK built for x86 in debug mode...   Initializing
gradle...   1.5s
Resolving dependencies...   2.5s
Running Gradle task 'assembleDebug'...
Running Gradle task 'assembleDebug'... Done   2.2s
Built build/app/outputs/apk/debug/app-debug.apk.
I/OpenGLRenderer(9459): Davey! duration=3464ms; Flags=1, IntendedVsync=12988638795805, Vsync=12991838795677, OldestInputEvent=9223372036854775807, NewestInputEvent=0, HandleInputStart=12991850107554, AnimationStart=12991850220554, PerformTraversalsStart=12991850649554, DrawStart=12991999356554, SyncQueued=12992001846554, SyncStart=12992012298554, IssueDrawCommandsStart=12992012538554, SwapBuffers=12992066585554, FrameCompleted=12992113932554, DequeueBufferDuration=17154000, QueueBufferDuration=3342000, D/   (9459): HostConnection::get() New Host Connection established 0xe8d9db00, tid 9481   3,018ms
(!)
🔥 To hot reload changes while running, press "r". To hot restart (and rebuild state), press "R".
An Observatory debugger and profiler on Android SDK built for x86 is available at: http://127.0.0.1:60013/
For a more detailed help message, press "h". To detach, press "d"; to quit, press "q".

Notice how it says:

An Observatory debugger and profiler on Android SDK built for x86 is available at: http://127.0.0.1:60013/

If we go to this website http://127.0.0.1:60013 then we see:

Observatory > vm@ws://127.0.0.1:60013/ws	Refresh

VM

name	vm@ws://127.0.0.1:60013/ws
version	2.1.2-dev.0.0.flutter-0a7dcf17eb (Tue Feb 12 01:59:15 2019 +0000) on "android_ia32"
embedder	Flutter
started at	2019-03-28 11:43:42.157
uptime	0:03:34.375000
refreshed at	2019-03-28 11:47:16.536
pid	9459
peak memory	169.9MB
current memory	169.9MB
native zone memory	0B
native heap memory	unavailable
native heap allocation count	unavailable

see flags   view timeline
view native memory profile

Isolates (1)

This website gives you so much information about your Flutter app.
Further information: https://dart-lang.github.io/observatory/

Timeline

The Flutter VM records Flutter events and the timeline can read these events and present them against a horizontal timeline, allowing you to drill in and view the data in more and more detail. There is so much information to wade through that learning how to use the timeline is a skill in itself.

Further information:https://medium.com/flutter-io/profiling-flutter-applications-using-the-timeline-a1a434964af3

Profile Mode

Note that this mode does not work on your emulator. To run in this mode, you are going to have to connect a device.

- Some debugging ability is maintained—enough to profile your app's performance.
- Tracing is enabled, and Dart Observatory can connect to the process.
- Assertions are disabled.
- Some service extensions are left enabled, such as the performance overlay (which is useful when profiling the app).

Further Reading

https://dartcode.org/docs/running-flutter-apps-in-profile-or-release-modes/

Android Studio

- Select 'Edit Run/Debug Configurations' on toolbar, next to the play button.
- Add the '—profile' argument to the additional arguments in the run configuration:

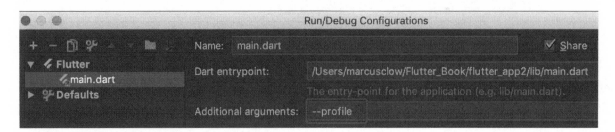

Visual Studio Code

- Select Menu 'Debug'
- Select Menu Option 'Open Configurations'.
- This will open the 'launch.json' file for you to modify as per below:

```json
{} launch.json  ✕
  1   {
  2       // Use IntelliSense to learn about possible attributes.
  3       // Hover to view descriptions of existing attributes.
  4       // For more information, visit: https://go.microsoft.com/fwlink/?linkid=830387
  5       "version": "0.2.0",
  6       "configurations": [
  7           {
  8               "name": "Flutter",
  9               "request": "launch",
 10               "type": "dart",
 11               "flutterMode": "profile",
 12           },
 13       ]
 14   }
```

Command-Line

- Run the following command:

```
flutter run --profile
```

Further Reading

https://flutter.dev/docs/testing/debugging

37.Change Detection, Keys & Rendering

Introduction

As we start to delve deeper into Flutter, we need to start introducing the subject of change detection - how Flutter gets the UI rebuilt when something changes. Efficient change detection is the key to Flutter achieving a 60 frames per second refresh rate.

The purpose of this chapter is to introduce how Flutter performs change detection, how it uses keys and how it renders the UI.

Remember that most of this chapter is an over-simplification of what is really going on. It is my interpretation based on the limited information available at the time of writing the book. Most of the information used for this chapter was taken from the Google Developers channel on YouTube, so I am pretty sure it is correct.

Change Detection

Change detection is when Flutter figures out <u>what needs to be redrawn in the UI</u>, redrawing as <u>little as possible</u> to keep it fast. Optimizing Change Detection, giving Flutter the information that it needs to redraw (quickly calculating the minimal redraw) is the trick to Flutter performance.

Widgets

So, at this point we know that we compose the UI out of many Widget objects, which build a tree of Widgets that represents the desired state of the UI.

Elements

- Unknown to you, the Widgets you create in your Widget 'build' methods each have a corresponding Element object built by the Flutter framework to track <u>where</u> the Widget is in the structure of the UI.
- Elements are expensive to create and <u>if it's possible, they should be reused</u>.
- Elements store as little information as possible:
  - A reference to the Widget they were created from.
  - A reference to the Render object that renders the representation of the Widget/Element.
  - A reference to the State attached to that element (Stateful Widgets).

- - The type of Widget they represent.
  - The children they will have.
  - A key to the Widget (for StatefulWidgets).
- The first time when a widget is created, it is inflated to an Element and then the Element gets inserted it into the Element Tree.

Element Trees

- The Element Tree stores information about the structure of the Widgets to be rendered.
- It is built from the Widget Tree.
- The Rendering Tree is rendered from the Element Tree.

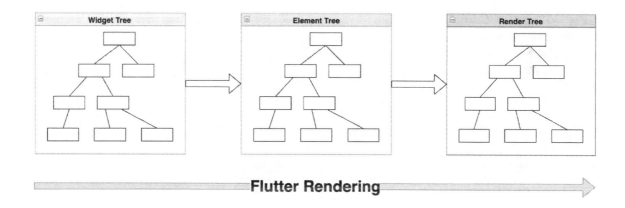

Widgets, Elements, Render Objects

In the trees, Widgets correspond to Elements, which correspond to Render Objects.
The diagram below was taken from a screenshot from a video created by Ian Hickson, one of the founders of Flutter. It represents a Rectangle Widget which has a child Circle Widget.
The Widgets are on the left, the Elements in the middle, the Render Objects on the right.

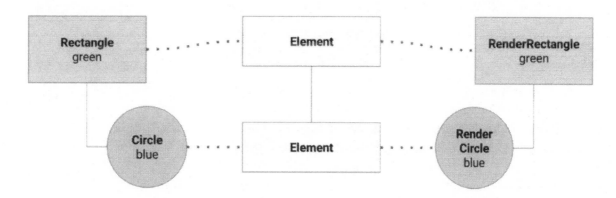

Change Detection & Updates

When performing change detection, Flutter walks the Element Tree and compares it to the Widget tree, matching the two to see what changed structurally.

Detecting Structural Changes

Flutter matches each Element to its corresponding Widget <u>in the same position in the tree</u>.

Examples:

- If there is a Widget in the Widget Tree but there isn't a matching one in the same position in the Element Tree, we know it is either new, or a Widget moved there from somewhere else.
- If there is a Widget in the Element Tree but there isn't a matching one in the same position in the Widget Tree, we know it is either removed or moved somewhere else.

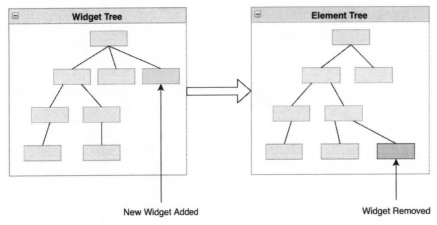

Change Detection

Widget Tree After Changes is Compared with Element Tree Before Changes

New Widget Added   Widget Removed

Matching Elements to Widgets

- The Flutter framework attempts to match each Element to its corresponding Widget <u>in the same position in the tree</u> using a <u>Key (if there is one)</u>.
- If there is no Key to match the two then it uses the <u>Widget Type</u> (along with position) to match. This can cause some issues, which we will cover later in the Key section.
- It <u>doesn't</u> use the Widget reference because Widgets are immutable (even Stateful Widgets have separate State objects) so the Widget may be replaced with another if one of its properties changes.

If there is a Match

- If the Element and Widget match, then the Element & Rendering Object are updated with any changes to the Widget, including a reference to the new Widget if it changed.
- Example:
    - If there is a Text Widget used in the building a parent Widget and that text changes, resulting in a different Text Widget, then the Widget is still matched and the changes to the text are copied over to the Rendering object.

If there is no Match

- If there is an Element at that position in the tree (but no Widget) then the Element & the Render Object are deactivated & removed.
- If there is a Widget at that position in the tree (but no Element & Render Object), then a new Element and Render Object are added to match the Widget.
- Example.
    - Taken from the Mohogany Staircase video. If the Widget Tree was a Rectangle and it had a Circle Widget child that is now replaced by a Triangle Widget child, then the following occurs:
        - The child Widget no longer matches by Type (Triangle != Circle).
            - The Element that corresponded to the Circle is now deactivated and removed from the Element Tree.
            - The Rendering Object that corresponded to the Circle is now deactivated and removed from the Render Tree.
            - A new Child Element is created and attached to the Element Tree.
            - A new Rendering Object is created and attached to the Render Tree.

Optimizations

As mentioned earlier, the logic above is oversimplified and ignores many Optimizations. For example, when Elements, Widgets and RenderObjects are 'deactivated' or 'removed', they are not always thrown away immediately. For example, if a Widget is moved then its Element may be thrown into an 'Element pool' (or similar) so that it may be picked up later if the corresponding Widget is found in another part of the Widget tree.

Render Tree

Render Objects

These are complex objects are used in the rendering later.

They carry more information than the Element objects, including detailed information required to render the object onscreen: position, scaling etc.

They are mutable – i.e. their data can change without them being destroyed and recreated.

Keys

Introduction

You don't need to use Keys often, but you need to know about them incase strange things start to happen. It's to do with Change Detection and Elements!

Example:

A commonly seen example of this is when you have a list of Widgets of the same type that you want to re-order in a UI. You write the code to re-order the list, but nothing happens! You will see this in an example soon.

Elements May or May Not Store a Reference to State

We mentioned earlier that Elements store as little information as is possible to do their job. Elements for StatelessWidgets do not, because there is no State Object for the widget. Elements for StatefulWidgets hold a reference to the State Object for the widget.

Elements for Stateless Widgets Have No Reference to any State

The example below shows the trees for three Stateless Widgets.

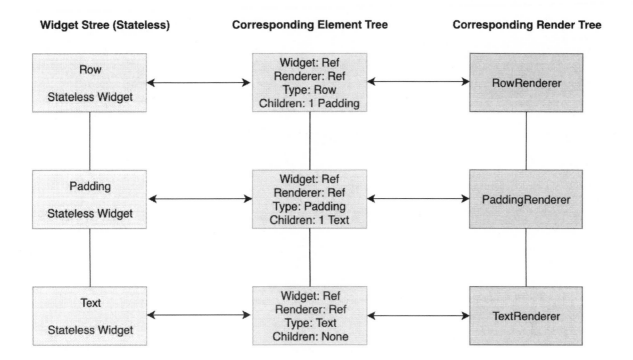

Widget Stree (Stateless)   **Corresponding Element Tree**   **Corresponding Render Tree**

Elements for Stateful Widgets Have A Reference to the State

The example below shows the trees for two Stateless Widgets and one Stateful Widget (the Image Widget at the bottom). Notice how the Element corresponding to the Image Widget has a reference to a State Object.

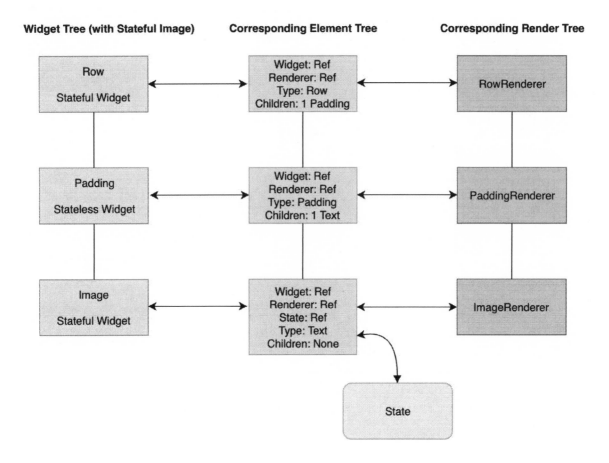

| Widget Tree (with Stateful Image) | Corresponding Element Tree | Corresponding Render Tree |

The 'Losing State' Problem

Stateful Widgets have more baggage in their Element, a State Reference. Sometimes this State can get lost.

Sometimes Stateful Widgets Lose State if They Don't Have Keys

This often happens when you have a list of children (say a list of articles) and you add animations to items in the list and the animations don't work until you add keys to the items in the list. That is because the animations use State and the State gets lost.

How Does State Get Lost?

When you add, remove or reorder Stateful Widgets of the <u>same type</u> you invoke Change Detection. Remember the following:

- To perform Change Detection, Flutter matches each Element to its corresponding Widget <u>in the same position in the tree</u>.
- In the absence of a Key Flutter uses the <u>Widget Type</u> to match the two. This works well in most scenarios but not when you have > 1 children of the <u>same Widget Type</u>.

Matching the Element to the Widget does not work because <u>all of the Widgets are of the same type</u>. There is no way for the Change Detection to differentiate between the Widgets. <u>It always thinks there is a match</u>.

So, Flutter thinks that there was no structural change. The Element and Widget match and the Element reference to the Widget is updated but Flutter doesn't think it has to update the State because nothing changed.

So, nothing changes in the UI.

Adding a Local Key Fixes this Issue

When you add a Local Key to each Widget of the same type, that fixes the issue. That is because Flutter can match the Element to the Widget using the Key rather than the Widget Type. It can figure out something changed and update the Element and Rendering Objects accordingly.

Local Keys

When using local keys, it uses them when checking items in the Element Tree at the same level, not across the whole Tree.

ValueKey
Local key. Useful when you can use a string as the key. This is what we use in the example below.

ObjectKey
Local key. Useful when you use more complex objects as the key.

UniqueKey
Local key. Generates a unique key for a widget.

Example – 'local_keys_cat_voting'

This is an app designed to show how adding Keys fixes the Element matching issue.

It lets you vote for the cutest cat. Click on a cat to vote on one. If you click on the floating button at the bottom, it should shuffle the Cats, preserving the vote counts.

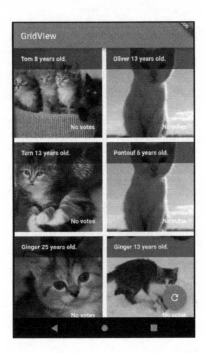

No Key

If you leave the CatTile constructor like this then the shuffle doesn't work:

```
CatTile(this._cat);
```

Add Key to Constructor

If you change the CatTile constructor to set the Key then the matching issue is fixed and the shuffle works fine.

```
CatTile(this._cat): super(key: ValueKey(_cat.imageSrc));
```

Source Code

```dart
import 'dart:math';

import 'package:flutter/material.dart';

void main() {
  runApp(new GridViewApp());
}

class Cat {
  String imageSrc;
  String name;
  int age;
  int votes;

  Cat(this.imageSrc, this.name, this.age, this.votes);

  operator ==(other) => (other is Cat) && (imageSrc == other.imageSrc);

  int get hashCode => imageSrc.hashCode;
}
```

```dart
class GridViewApp extends StatelessWidget {
  // This widget is the root of your application.
  @override
  Widget build(BuildContext context) {
    return new MaterialApp(
      title: 'Cat Voting',
      theme: new ThemeData(
        primarySwatch: Colors.blue,
      ),
      home: new HomeWidget(title: 'Cat Voting Home Page'),
    );
  }
}

class HomeWidget extends StatefulWidget {
  HomeWidget({Key key, this.title}) : super(key: key);

  final String title;

  @override
  _HomeWidgetState createState() => new _HomeWidgetState();
}

class _HomeWidgetState extends State<HomeWidget> {
  List<String> CAT_NAMES = [
    "Tom",
    "Oliver",
    "Ginger",
    "Pontouf",
    "Madison",
    "Bubblita",
    "Bubbles"
  ];
  Random _random = Random();
  List<Cat> _cats = [];
  int next(int min, int max) => min + _random.nextInt(max - min);

  _HomeWidgetState() : super() {
    // Generate list of Cat objects once.
    for (int i = 200; i < 300; i += 10) {
      _cats.add(Cat("http://placekitten.com/200/${i}", CAT_NAMES[next(0, 6)],
        next(1, 32), 0));
    }
  }

  void _shuffle() {
    // Shuffle the list of Cat objects.
    setState(() {
      _cats.shuffle(_random);
    });
  }

  @override
  Widget build(BuildContext context) {
    return Scaffold(
      appBar: AppBar(
        title: Text("GridView"),
      ),
```

```
      body: OrientationBuilder(builder: (context, orientation) {
        return new GridView.builder(
            itemCount: _cats.length,
            gridDelegate: SliverGridDelegateWithFixedCrossAxisCount(
                crossAxisCount: (orientation == Orientation.portrait) ? 2 : 3,
                mainAxisSpacing: 10.0,
                crossAxisSpacing: 10.0),
            itemBuilder: (BuildContext context, int index) {
              return CatTile(_cats[index]);
            });
      }),
      floatingActionButton: new FloatingActionButton(
        onPressed: _shuffle,
        tooltip: 'Try more grid options',
        child: new Icon(Icons.refresh),
      ), // This trailing comma makes auto-formatting nicer for build methods.
    );
  }
}

class CatTile extends StatefulWidget {
  Cat _cat;
  CatTile(this._cat); // Shuffle doesnt work.
  //CatTile(this._cat): super(key: ValueKey(_cat.imageSrc)); // Shuffle works.

  @override
  _CatTileState createState() => new _CatTileState(_cat);
}

class _CatTileState extends State<CatTile> {
  Cat _cat;

  _CatTileState(this._cat);

  @override
  Widget build(BuildContext context) {
    return GestureDetector(
        child: GridTile(
          header: GridTileBar(
            title: Text("${_cat.name} ${_cat.age} years old.",
                style: TextStyle(fontWeight: FontWeight.bold)),
            backgroundColor: Color.fromRGBO(0, 0, 0, 0.5),
          ),
          footer: GridTileBar(
            title: Text(
                _cat.votes == 0 ? "No votes" : "${_cat.votes} votes.",
                textAlign: TextAlign.right,
                style: TextStyle(fontWeight: FontWeight.bold))),
          child: Image.network(_cat.imageSrc, fit: BoxFit.cover)),
        onTap: () => _vote());
  }

  _vote() {
    setState(() => _cat.votes++);
  }
}
```

Global Keys

You can use GlobalKeys to uniquely identify Widgets across the whole Widget Tree. That means you can access Widgets and their State from anywhere.
You should not rely on GlobalKeys too much as it is better to use something like InheritedWidget, a BLoC or some other mechanism to share state data.

Example – 'global_key_shared_widget'

Introduction
This app shows how you can use a global key to share a Widget (including its state) from multiple parent Widgets. For example, you open the app, hit the '+' button to increment the Counter. Then you click on the toolbar and you will see the Counter again with the same number.

Source Code

```
import 'package:flutter/material.dart';
import 'package:flutter/rendering.dart';

void main(){
 runApp(MyApp());
}

class MyApp extends StatefulWidget {
 MyApp();
 @override
 _MyAppState createState() => _MyAppState();
}
```

```
class _MyAppState extends State<MyApp> {
 GlobalKey _counterWidgetGlobalKey = GlobalKey();
 bool _widget1 = true;

 _selectPage() {
  setState(() => _widget1 = !_widget1);
 }

 // This widget is the root of your application.
 @override
 Widget build(BuildContext context) {
  return MaterialApp(
     title: 'Flutter Demo',
     theme: ThemeData(
      primarySwatch: Colors.blue,
     ),
     home: _widget1
         ? Widget1(_counterWidgetGlobalKey, _selectPage)
         : Widget2(_counterWidgetGlobalKey, _selectPage));
 }
}

class Widget1 extends StatelessWidget {
 final GlobalKey _counterWidgetGlobalKey;
 final VoidCallback _selectPageCallback;

 Widget1(this._counterWidgetGlobalKey, this._selectPageCallback);

 @override
 Widget build(BuildContext context) {
  return Scaffold(
     appBar: AppBar(
      title: Text("Widget 1"),
      actions: <Widget>[
       IconButton(
          icon: new Icon(Icons.refresh),
          onPressed: () => _selectPageCallback()
      ],
     ),
     body: Column(
    crossAxisAlignment: CrossAxisAlignment.stretch,
      children: [
       Text("Widget 1", textAlign: TextAlign.center, style: Theme.of(context).textTheme.display2),
       CounterWidget(_counterWidgetGlobalKey)
      ],
      mainAxisAlignment: MainAxisAlignment.spaceAround,
     ));
 }
}

class Widget2 extends StatelessWidget {
 final GlobalKey _counterWidgetGlobalKey;
 final VoidCallback _selectPageCallback;

 Widget2(this._counterWidgetGlobalKey, this._selectPageCallback);

 @override
 Widget build(BuildContext context) {
```

```
    return Scaffold(
      appBar: AppBar(
        actions: [
          new IconButton(
            icon: new Icon(Icons.refresh),
            onPressed: () => _selectPageCallback())
        ],
        title: Text("Widget 2"),
      ),
      body: Column(
        crossAxisAlignment: CrossAxisAlignment.stretch,
        children: [
          Text("Widget 2", textAlign: TextAlign.center, style: Theme.of(context).textTheme.display2),
          CounterWidget(_counterWidgetGlobalKey)
        ],
        mainAxisAlignment: MainAxisAlignment.spaceAround,
      ),
    );
  }
}

class CounterWidget extends StatefulWidget {
  CounterWidget(Key key) : super(key: key);
  @override
  _CounterWidgetState createState() => _CounterWidgetState();
}

class _CounterWidgetState extends State<CounterWidget> {
  int _counter = 0;

  void _incrementCounter() {
    setState(() {
      _counter++;
    });
  }

  @override
  Widget build(BuildContext context) {
    return Column(
      mainAxisAlignment: MainAxisAlignment.center,
      children: <Widget>[
        Text(
          'CounterWidget',
          style: Theme.of(context).textTheme.display2,
        ),
        Text('You have:', style: Theme.of(context).textTheme.display1),
        Text(
          '$_counter',
          style: Theme.of(context).textTheme.display1,
        ),
        IconButton(
          iconSize: 36.0,
          icon: new Icon(Icons.add), onPressed: () => _incrementCounter()),
      ]);
  }
}
```

Example – 'global_key_shared_state'

Introduction

This app shows how you can use a global key to get Widget state out of another Widget. Widget1 is the green one at the top and it has state. Widget2 is the blue one at the bottom.

Widget2 has a button you can press that gets the state out of Widget1. Then it displays that state at the bottom.

Source Code

```
import 'package:flutter/material.dart';

void main() {
  runApp(new MyApp());
}

final key = new GlobalKey<_Widget1State>();

class MyApp extends StatelessWidget {
  @override
  Widget build(BuildContext context) {
    return new MaterialApp(
      theme: ThemeData(
        primarySwatch: Colors.blue,
      ),
      home: new Scaffold(
        body: new Column(
          mainAxisAlignment: MainAxisAlignment.spaceAround,
          children: <Widget>[
            Container(
```

```
              child: Widget1(key: key),
              color: Colors.greenAccent,
            ),
            Container(
              child: Widget2(),
              color: Colors.blueAccent,
            ),
          ],
        ),
      ),
    );
  }
}

class Widget1 extends StatefulWidget {
  Widget1({Key key}) : super(key: key);
  State createState() => new _Widget1State();
}

class _Widget1State extends State<Widget1> {
  String _state = "some state";
  String get state => _state;

  @override
  Widget build(BuildContext context) {
    return Padding(
      padding: EdgeInsets.all(20.0),
      child: Column(
        children: [
          Text("Widget1",
            textAlign: TextAlign.center,
            style: Theme.of(context).textTheme.display1),
          new Text("State: ${_state}",
            textAlign: TextAlign.center,
            style: Theme.of(context).textTheme.display2)
        ],
        crossAxisAlignment: CrossAxisAlignment.stretch,
      ));
  }
}

class Widget2 extends StatefulWidget {
  State createState() => new Widget2State();
}

class Widget2State extends State<Widget2> {
  String _text = '';

  @override
  Widget build(BuildContext context) {
    return Padding(
      padding: EdgeInsets.all(20.0),
      child: Column(
        children: [
          Text("Widget2",
            textAlign: TextAlign.center,
            style: Theme.of(context).textTheme.display2),
          Padding(
```

```
      padding: EdgeInsets.all(20.0),
      child: RaisedButton(
        child: new Text("Get state from Widget1"),
        onPressed: () {
          setState(() {
            _text = key.currentState.state;
          });
        },
      )),
    Text("State: ${_text}",
        textAlign: TextAlign.center,
        style: Theme.of(context).textTheme.display1),
    ],
    crossAxisAlignment: CrossAxisAlignment.stretch,
  ));
}
}
```

Further Reading

https://www.youtube.com/watch?v=kn0EOS-Zilc
https://coder-coacher.github.io/GoogleTechTalks/The-Mahogany-Staircase-Flutters-Layered-Design-dkyY9WCGMi0.html

38.Other Performance Considerations

Introduction

The purpose of this chapter is to be a 'catch-all' for anything else you should consider when building the most performant app possible.

Http Communication

Before we get into more Flutter performance topics, we should mention that most Flutter apps will be communicating with other computers. Such communication over a network is typically much slower than the highly-efficient Flutter user interface, so looking how your app communicates with other computers is a good place to start and can yield significant gains.

- What data are you getting from the server, do you really need all of it?
    - Do you need each element of the data?
    - Are some of the data items not used?
- Is there any way to make this data smaller?
    - Are you using a JSON format? If so, what about making the JSON field names smaller to save on data size.
        - Further reading: https://www.ribice.ba/reduce-json-size/
- Do you really need to return full lists of data or can you implement paging or endless scrolling?
- Can you cache some of the data and only reload it once in a while?
- Can you make any requests to the server parallel and have them execute asynchronously at the same time?
    - For example, when you open a list Widget and you need to load the values of multiple dropdowns?

Single Threaded

- Dart code runs in a single "thread" of execution.
- Code that blocks the thread of execution can make your program freeze.
- Do you have any synchronous code?
- Can you replace it with asynchronous code or code that runs in another thread?

Use Constants When Possible

Avoid Rebuilding Widgets

When using stateless widgets, avoid possible instantiation/rebuilds by using the const keyword (for example the Texts in the example below)

```
@override
 Widget build(BuildContext context) {
  return new Scaffold(
    appBar: new AppBar(title: new Text("Rows")),
    body: new Column(
     mainAxisAlignment: MainAxisAlignment.center,
     children: <Widget>[
       Row(
        mainAxisAlignment: MainAxisAlignment.spaceEvenly,
        children: <Widget>[
          const Text("the quick brown wolf"),
          const Text("the quick brown wolf"),
          const Text("the quick brown wolf")
        ],
       )
     ],
    ));
 }
```

Using Constants Saves Memory

For any given const value, a single const object will be created and re-used no matter how many times the const expression(s) are evaluated.

```
getConst() => const [1, 2];
main() {
 var a = getConst();
 var b = getConst();
 print(a === b); // true
}
```

39. Publishing Your App

Introduction

The purpose of this chapter is to a 'catch-all' for anything related to publishing your app.

Platform

This is a class used to provide you with information about the Platform that the app is running on:

- Number of processors.
- Path separator.
- Operating System.
- Operating System version.
- Local hostname.
- Version.

When developing you need to ensure that you take the Platform into consideration.

Example

If you are developing an App with files, you need to use the path separator from the Platform class rather than hardcoding the one that works in your development environment.

Release Mode

Note that this mode does not work on your emulator. To run in this mode, you are going to have to connect a device.

- Assertions are disabled.
- Debugging information is stripped out.
- Debugging is disabled.
- Compilation is optimized for fast startup, fast execution, and small package sizes.
- Service extensions are disabled.

Further Reading

https://dartcode.org/docs/running-flutter-apps-in-profile-or-release-modes/

Android Studio

- Select 'Edit Run/Debug Configurations' on toolbar, next to the play button.
- Add the '—release' argument to the additional arguments in the run configuration:

Visual Studio Code

- Select Menu 'Debug'
- Select Menu Option 'Open Configurations'.
- This will open the 'launch.json' file for you to modify as per below:

```json
{
    // Use IntelliSense to learn about possible attributes.
    // Hover to view descriptions of existing attributes.
    // For more information, visit: https://go.microsoft.com/fwlink/?linkid=830387
    "version": "0.2.0",
    "configurations": [
        {
            "name": "Flutter",
            "request": "launch",
            "type": "dart",
            "flutterMode": "release",
        },
    ]
}
```

Command-Line

- Run the following command:

```
flutter run --release
```

Android-Specific Files

This is where Android-specific code resides in the 'Android' folder.

Dependency Management

When building for Android, Flutter uses Gradle as the dependency manager.

iOS-Specific Files

This is where iOS-specific code resides in the 'ios' folder.

Dependency Management

Flutter uses Cocoapods as the dependency manager.

Application Package Files

APK Files

An .apk (Android Package Kit) file is an Android application archive file that stores an Android app. You can use such a file to install an Android app to your phone or a emulator.
For example, you can open your Android emulator and drag-and-drop a .apk file onto the open program to install it.

Mac IPA Files

An .ipa (iOS App Store Package) file is an iOS application archive file which stores an iOS app.

How Does Deployment Work?

Android

Android-specific settings and code resides in the 'android' folder.
When building for Android, Flutter uses Gradle as the dependency manager.

ios

iOS-specific settings and code resides in the 'ios' folder.
When building for iO, flutter uses Cocoapods as the dependency manager.

When JIT compiling in debug mode:
- Flutter compiles the project's Dart code into the folder 'App.framework', in the snapshot_blob.bin file. This file include source code for debugging.
- Flutter compiles the Flutter Framework into the folder 'Flutter.framework'.

When AOT compiling in release mode:
- Flutter compiles the project's Dart code into the folder 'App.framework'.
- Flutter compiles the Flutter Framework into the folder 'Flutter.framework'.

Further Reading

https://hackernoon.com/making-the-most-of-flutter-from-basics-to-customization-433171581d01

40.Flutter Resources

Introduction

I could not have done even 10% of this book without information from the resources below. I am very grateful those who contributed to those resources listed below.

Official Resources

- Google Flutter website.
https://flutter.io/

    o In case you want an offline copy, the source code is here: https://github.com/flutter/website. You can clone the repository and build/run the website locally quite easily. This is great if you sometimes have to work without an internet connection.

    o Some great flutter example code here: https://flutter.dev/docs/cookbook

- Google developers' channel on YouTube. https://www.youtube.com/channel/UC_x5XG1OV2P6uZZ5FSM9Ttw

Other Resources

- Those contributing to the Flutter Dev group on Reddit: https://www.reddit.com/r/FlutterDev/

- Those contributing to the Flutter Dev group on Google: https://groups.google.com/forum/ - !forum/flutter-dev

- Those contributing to the Medium flutter community: https://medium.com/flutter-community

- Tutorials point: https://www.tutorialspoint.com/dart_programming

- Flutter by example: https://flutterbyexample.com

- Awesome Flutter talks:
https://github.com/Rahiche/awesome-flutter-talks

- This is a nice article where a developer lists out his favorite Flutter resources:
https://medium.com/coding-with-flutter/my-favourite-list-of-flutter-resources-523adc611cbe